Orthodontic Applications of Osseointegrated Implants

Orthodontic Applications of

OSSEOINTEGRATED IMPLANTS

Edited by
Kenji W. Higuchi, DDS, MS

Foreword by
Per-Ingvar Brånemark, MD, PhD

Contributors
Michael S. Block, DMD
John B. Brunski, MS, PhD
Kenji W. Higuchi, DDS, MS
Vincent G. Kokich, DDS, MSD
Larry J. Oesterle, DDS, MS
W. Eugene Roberts, DDS, PhD
James M. Slack, DDS, MS
Ward M. Smalley, DDS, MSD
Frank M. Spear, DDS, MSD
Birgit Thilander, LDS, Odont Dr
Minoru Ueda, DDS, PhD

Quintessence Publishing Co, Inc
Chicago, Berlin, London, Tokyo, Paris, Barcelona, São Paulo, Moscow, Prague, and Warsaw

To my family, for their love and support—my wife, Mary, and
my children, Chris, Dan, Lauren, and Kyle.

Library of Congress Cataloging-in-Publication Data

Orthodontic applications of osseointegrated implants / edited by Kenji W. Higuchi.
    p. cm.
  Includes bibliographical references and index.
  ISBN 0-86715-356-3
  1. Osseointegrated dental implants. 2. Orthodontics. I. Higuchi, Kenji, 1944–
  [DNLM: 1. Dental Implantation, Endosseous. 2. Orthodontics.]
  RK667.I45 O78 2000
  617.6'43—dc21

                              99-056574

quintessence books

© 2000 Quintessence Publishing Co, Inc

Quintessence Publishing Co, Inc
551 Kimberly Drive
Carol Stream, Illinois 60188

Editor: Lisa C. Bywaters
Design: Michael Shanahan
Production: Libertine C. Venzuela

Printed in Hong Kong

Contents

Contributors

Michael S. Block, DMD
Professor
Department of Oral and Maxillofacial Surgery
Assistant Dean for Research
Louisiana State University School of Dentistry
New Orleans, Louisiana

John B. Brunski, MS, PhD
Professor
Department of Biomedical Engineering
Rensselaer Polytechnic Institute
Troy, New York

Kenji W. Higuchi, DDS, MS
Diplomate, American Board of Oral and Maxillofacial Surgery
Private Practice
Spokane, Washington

Vincent G. Kokich, DDS, MSD
Professor
Department of Orthodontics
School of Dentistry
University of Washington
Seattle, Washington

Larry J. Oesterle, DDS, MS
Chair
Department of Growth and Development
School of Dentistry
University of Colorado Health Sciences Center
Denver, Colorado

W. Eugene Roberts, DDS, PhD
Professor and Head
Department of Orthodontics
Indiana University School of Dentistry
Indianapolis, Indiana

Department of Physiology and Biophysics
Indiana University School of Medicine
Indianapolis, Indiana

James M. Slack, DDS, MS
Diplomate, American Board of Orthodontics
Private Practice
Spokane, Washington

Ward M. Smalley, DDS, MSD
Diplomate, American Board of Orthodontics
Private Practice
Seattle, Washington

Frank M. Spear, DDS, MSD
Specialist in Fixed Prosthodontics
Private Practice
Seattle, Washington

Birgit Thilander, LDS, Odont Dr
Professor of Orthodontics
Faculty of Odontology
University of Göteborg
Göteborg, Sweden

Minoru Ueda, DDS, PhD
Professor and Chairman
Department of Oral Surgery
Nagoya University School of Medicine
Nagoya, Japan

Foreword

According to the osseointegration principle, lack of relative motion between tissue and titanium is a basic engineering imperative for establishing and maintaining bone-anchored prostheses. A large number of long-term multicenter clinical studies have documented reliable predictability in the transfer of masticatory load to a bone-anchored prosthetic replacement in edentulous patients.

Biological and mechanical tests have provided some insight into the character of the interface between bone and titanium. Application of lateral load does not seem to disturb long-term clinical function, whereas early undue torque during the healing phase is likely to cause loss of integration and formation of a nonmineralized interface.

Early experimental studies by Adell indicate a remarkable resistance of single implants to lateral load, much higher than those experienced in orthodontic appliances. The pioneering work by Higuchi and Slack, followed by other explorers of osseointegration in orthodontics, suggested the possibility of using osseointegrated implants as topographical reference points for controlled movement of teeth in their natural habitat. The basic difference between a titanium implant in jaw bone without and teeth with an intermediate soft tissue capsule seems to represent an important addition to the technical procedures applied in orthodontics.

This book provides a bioengineering background, experiments, clinical trials, and suggestions for clinical application, as well as some long-term results in clinical orthodontics. The wide coverage of the topic and the challenging opportunities to add a controllable, topographical stability reference to the orthodontic armament means that the information contained in this book opens up a new and exciting modality in the field of controlled reorientation and repositioning of teeth.

Per-Ingvar Brånemark, MD, PhD

Preface

Of the significant advances in dentistry during the twentieth century, arguably none has extended the treatment horizons more than the successful use of osseointegrated implants. Applying the principles of osseointegration, clinicians are able to predictably replace missing teeth with excellent long-term esthetic and functional results. It is the premise of this text that the specialty of orthodontics plays a major role in the interdisciplinary management of patients treated with implants. Using a team approach, the restorative dentist, orthodontist, and surgeon are able to develop a treatment plan relying on the unique skills of each discipline. The following chapters review the synergistic relationship of osseointegrated implant therapy in orthodontics including treatment planning, presurgical orthodontic preparation, tooth replacement, and implant-orthodontic anchorage.

Although designed to benefit any restorative dentist, prosthodontist, or surgeon involved with implant treatment, this book focuses on the specific interests of orthodontists, a subject that has been inadequately addressed. It is hoped that this material will encourage the use of osseointegrated implant therapy in orthodontic patients and that this will lead to superior clinical results. I extend my sincere thanks to each of the contributors, without whose dedication and effort this project would not have been possible. To close, I would like to express my sincere gratitude to Professor P-I Brånemark, who has encouraged my activities in diverse areas of osseointegration, but more important, has taught me always to keep the patient's welfare foremost.

Kenji W. Higuchi, DDS, MS

1 | Ortho-Integration: The Alliance Between Orthodontics and Osseointegration

Kenji W. Higuchi, DDS, MS

In 1969, Brånemark[1] introduced the possibility of direct bone anchorage of a dental prosthesis for permanent tooth replacement. This therapy has since become well accepted in oral rehabilitation and has changed treatment-planning standards throughout dentistry. The influence of osseointegrated implant treatment has extended into routine management of orthodontic patients. It is the premise of this text that the relationship between clinical orthodontics and certain areas of implant dentistry is symbiotic, combining the treatment goals and benefits of tooth replacement and tooth movement. Contemporary orthodontic practice may involve implant treatment in the following areas:

- Facilitation of the treatment-planning process for the orthodontic patient
- Prosthetic replacement of missing teeth
- Presurgical orthodontic alignment to optimize implant use
- Use of intraoral implants as stationary anchorage

This book addresses selected clinical, biological, and biomechanical considerations related to these implant applications in orthodontics. Although it has been almost 20 years since the principles of osseointegration were accepted on an international basis, many orthodontists still have limited understanding of the process. As the intended readership of this text includes orthodontists in clinical practice, it will include a review of the basic factors affecting successful osseointegration, with a summary of current applications and expected results.

Osseointegration: Definitions and Applications

The rehabilitative benefits of osseointegration rely upon the creation and maintenance of a rigid alloplastic retentive element in remodeling bone. The end product of osseointegration is implant-bone anchorage, making possible a permanently fixed prosthesis. Osseointegration has been defined by several authors since Brånemark[2] coined the term in 1977: "A direct, on the light microscopic level, contact between living bone and an implant" (Albrektsson et al, 1981)[3]; "A structural and functional connection between ordered, living bone and the surface of a low-carrying implant" (Brånemark et al, 1985)[4]; "A bony attachment with resistance to shear and tensile forces" (Steineman et al, 1986)[5]; "A continuing structural and functional co-existence, possibly in a symbiotic manner, between differentiated, adequately remodeling, biologic tissues and strictly defined and controlled synthetic components providing lasting specific clinical functions without initiating rejection mechanisms" (Brånemark, 1990)[6]; "A process whereby clinically asymptomatic rigid fixation of alloplastic materials is achieved and maintained in bone during functional loading" (Albrektsson and Zarb, 1991)[7]; "An implant is said to be biomechanically osseointegrated if there is no progressive relative motion of living bone and implant under functional levels and types of loading for the entire life of the patient" (Skalak et al, 1991)[6]; "Direct bone apposition onto the surface of an implant; no interposed fibrous connective tissue between the implant and supporting bone; ring on percussion due to direct conduction to bone; absence of physiologic drift; no movement when used for orthodontic anchorage; functional equivalent of dental 'ankylosis'" (Roberts, 1994).[8]

A common feature of these proposed definitions is the clinical expectation of long-term implant fixation under functional loading. However, predictable osseointegration is not a chance event and is influenced by a number of factors. Albrektsson et al[3] have recognized the following six critical variables in osseointegration:

1. Implant material
2. Implant design (macrostructure)
3. Implant finish (microstructure)
4. Status of the bone
5. Surgical technique
6. Implant-loading conditions

Currently, a wide variety of implant systems with differing materials, geometries, and surface finishes is available for clinical use. A recent meta-analysis of the literature between 1986 and 1996 by Lindh et al[9] revealed a cumulative survival rate for threaded cylindrical implants placed in partially edentulous arches supporting fixed partial dentures (including single teeth) of over 90% for the 19 qualifying studies using this statistical approach. On the other hand, a number of reports[10–13] have documented unacceptable implant failure rates involving certain implant systems. Many authors[7,14,15] have emphasized that the literature is replete with poorly designed clinical trials documenting implant performance. Van Steenberghe[14] has emphasized the importance of well-designed multicenter clinical trials with precisely identified success-failure criteria to substantiate the suitability of an oral implant system.

Esposito and colleagues[16] have summarized factors associated with increased implant failure rates, such as medical status of the patient, patient smoking, irradiation therapy, bone quality, grafting procedures, parafunctions, operator experience, degree of surgical trauma, bacterial contamination, immediate loading, submerged procedure, number of implants supporting a prosthesis, surface properties, and implant design. At present there is incomplete understanding of the effects of these factors.

Scope of Application

Implant therapy in orthodontics involves tooth replacement or intraoral rigid anchorage assistance in the movement of teeth. The breadth of clinical applications for the osseointegration process in medicine and dentistry is impressive. Patients suffering from missing body parts may seek surgical-prosthetic treatment ranging from the replacement of a single tooth (Fig 1-1) to an entire extremity (Fig 1-2), or from the functional and esthetic reconstruction of a cleft palate (Fig 1-3) to the restoration of a face deformed by tumor resection (Fig 1-4). Osseointegration makes it possible to rebuild an entire dentition congenitally forgotten (Fig 1-5) or to fasten a bone-anchored hearing aid to improve conduction hearing loss and replace a missing external ear (Fig 1-6). The unifying theme of these anatomically diverse procedures is the osseointegration process, which transfers the bone-to-implant fixation to a connecting prosthesis, providing a restoration of function and appearance. In the remainder of this chapter, we will examine the relationship between orthodontics and osseointegration in the context of treatment planning, tooth replacement, and implant anchorage for tooth movement.

Facilitating Orthodontic Treatment Planning

The option of replacing missing or compromised teeth with an implant-supported crown or fixed partial denture may help the orthodontist and restorative dentist solve a dilemma in treatment planning with predictably favorable results. For example, a unilateral congenitally absent tooth, such as a maxillary lateral incisor or mandibular second premolar in an otherwise Class I nonextraction occlusion, may be more successfully managed with orthodontic space opening and implant replacement than with space closure, conventional crown and bridge prosthetics, or less appropriately, with additional extractions. Figure 1-7 demonstrates the effectiveness of combined orthodontic-implant therapy in achieving excellent esthetic, occlusal, and biological results.

Treatment planning is further facilitated in combined restorative-orthodontic management when anticipated anchorage problems are resolved using implants as points of anchorage and later as prosthetic abutments for tooth replacement. The ability to obtain orthodontic anchorage in situations where anchorage is limited extends the treatment

possibilities for patients and the biomechanical possibilities for clinicians. Examples of how implants are used to solve anchorage problems appear later in this text. The clinical application of implants for orthodontic anchorage requires that the desired orthodontic and restorative objectives for each patient be precisely defined before initiating treatment. The use of osseointegrated implants for tooth replacement and orthodontic anchorage in a collaborative treatment-planning process can offer alternative solutions for problematic patients.

Prerestorative Orthodontic Alignment to Optimize Implant Use

Although the number of adult patients is increasing, most of those seeking orthodontic treatment are teenagers.[17] It is not uncommon for both young and adult orthodontic patients to present with missing teeth requiring replacement. Later in this chapter, specific conditions such as hypodontia, traumatic tooth loss, impacted and ankylosed teeth, and tooth loss due to pathology will be reviewed separately.

Conditions associated with hypodontia, and to a lesser extent with tooth loss from other causes, are seldom optimal for implant treatment inasmuch as adjacent teeth may drift, rotate, tip, or supraerupt, causing reduced vertical dimension and poorly spaced and unesthetically positioned teeth (Figs 1-8 and 1-9). Preliminary orthodontics is frequently necessary to achieve restorative and occlusal goals. Chapters 2 and 3 present two different approaches in treatment planning for implant sites associated with full-treatment orthodontics compatible with a predetermined restorative plan. For those partially edentulous patients not needing implant anchorage, presurgical orthodontic management is fairly straightforward. However, a patient whose problem is more involved will require detailed orthodontic and restorative diagnostic waxups and good communication among implant team members. The following questions and comments address issues pertinent to routine prerestorative orthodontic-implant considerations:

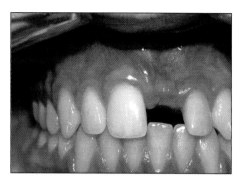

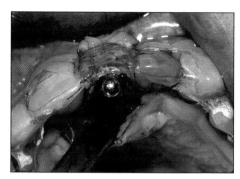

Fig 1-1a Traumatic loss of maxillary central incisor with uneven gingival level.

Fig 1-1b Surgical placement guide for use in implant positioning.

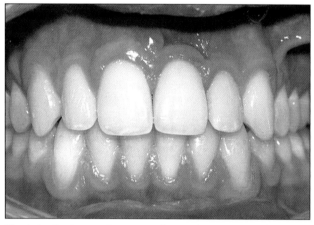

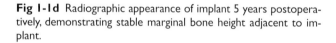

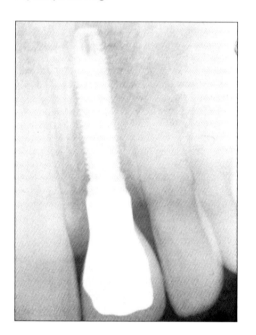

Fig 1-1c Implant replacement of central incisor with soft tissue correction.

Fig 1-1d Radiographic appearance of implant 5 years postoperatively, demonstrating stable marginal bone height adjacent to implant.

Has there been adequate evaluation and treatment planning for implant placement by the restorative dentist, surgeon, and orthodontist?

In addition to patient preference, the implant team must confirm that implant treatment is indicated and that any conditions limiting optimal results are addressed. The restorative dentist should identify clinical problems that may interfere with obtaining favorable esthetic and functional restorative results. Anatomic proportion and symmetry of the anterior dentition, and its relationship to esthetic references, such as the interpupillary line, facial midline, and lips, are important.[18] The status of any deficient crowns, restorations, or endodontically treated teeth should be assessed along with the nature of the occlusion. In general, the overall restorative and prosthetic plan must be formulated in view of orthodontic and surgical objectives. The surgeon has the responsibility of evaluating the implant site(s) and the soft tissue, bony, and dental environment relative to the proposed implant treatment. Ridge shape, contour, and bone volume, as well as the proposed space available to accommodate implant and restorative components, are criti-

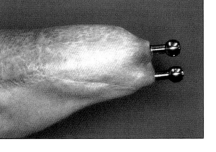

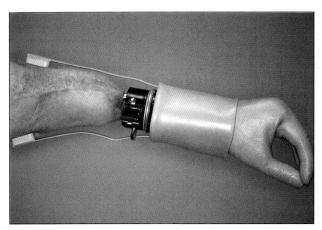

Fig 1-2a Forearm amputation reconstructed with osseointegrated implants and skin-penetrating abutments.

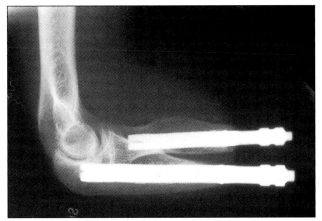

Fig 1-2b Osseointegrated implants in residual radius and ulna.

Fig 1-2c Hand prosthesis with electronic myocutaneous attachment to improve functional performance.

cal in determining the surgical placement of an implant and ultimately the quality of the prosthetic outcome. Soft tissue or bone-grafting procedures should be acknowledged before treatment, not as an afterthought. Problems with root angulation of adjacent teeth should be identified by both surgeon and orthodontist and each should have a clear understanding of the factors influencing the number and location of implants placed.

Is there any growth potential remaining for the patient?

Chapter 8, "Implant Considerations in the Growing Child," reviews the effect of potential growth on implant treatment. Briefly, except in rare cases of anodontia or ectodermal dysplasia, it is usually advisable to wait until growth has been completed before placing implants. Maintenance of space and root alignment is important if orthodontic treatment is to be completed before implant placement.

What are the space requirements for implants?

Within the dental arch, the orthodontist is requested to create the appropriate mesiodistal and vertical space at both crown and root levels to accommodate fixture, abutment, and restorative components. Each implant system has slightly different dimensions, so the attending surgeon or restorative dentist should advise the orthodontist of specific space requirements. As a general guideline, at least 1 mm of bone support is needed on each side of an implant. For narrow-diameter implants (3.25 mm to 3.3 mm), a minimum of 5.5 mm is advisable, while implants of 3.75-mm diameter should have 6.5 mm to 7.0 mm of space. It is also important to

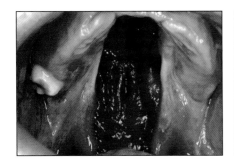

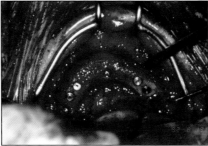

Fig 1-3a Large, unrepaired cleft palate in adult.

Fig 1-3b Onlay-inlay bone graft from hip to cleft defect and simultaneous implant placement.

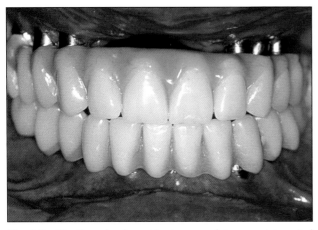

Fig 1-3c Maxillary fixed prosthesis secured to osseointegrated implants in grafted cleft palate.

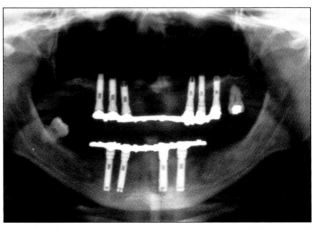

Fig 1-3d Panoramic view of implant anchorage of fixed partial dentures in an edentulous repaired cleft palate.

recognize the dimensions of connecting abutments. These are usually wider than fixture diameters and may interfere with the minimal biological width necessary for healthy interproximal soft tissue. To avoid injury to the adjacent teeth, slight orthodontic divergence of the roots is desirable. Because of space limitations, single mandibular central incisors and, in most cases, mandibular lateral incisors are usually not replaced with implants.

How should the occlusion be managed with implants?

As with all prosthetic replacements, axial forces are preferable to lateral forces and group function is usually recommended in order to lessen moment forces on implant components and reduce mechanical problems. More detailed recommendations

concerning restorative issues are addressed in Chapter 7, "Restorative Considerations in Combined Orthodontic-Implant Therapy."

Orthodontic-Implant Considerations for Specific Types of Tooth Loss

Multiple causes of tooth loss are seen in the clinical practice of orthodontics. Table 1-1 is a summary of these causes.

Traumatic tooth loss

Injury to the oral region may be associated with the immediate or delayed loss of teeth and alveolar bone. Based on a survey of 7,707 patients aged 6 to 50 years, Kaste and colleagues[19] reported that

Table I-I Tooth loss in orthodontic patients

Growing patients	Adult patients
Hypodontia and oligodontia	Restorative failures
Traumatic tooth loss	Endodontic problems
Impacted teeth	Periodontal disease
Impacted teeth nonresponsive to uncovering procedures	Severely malposed, tipped, and supraerupted teeth
Ankylosed teeth	
Root resorption	
Dental pathology	

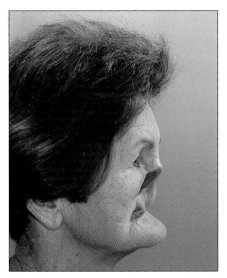

Fig I-4a Anterior maxillectomy and facial resection in a patient with squamous cell carcinoma.

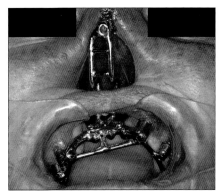

Fig I-4b Prosthetic framework stabilized by osseointegrated implants in the nasal, zygomatic, and bone-grafted maxillary regions. This superstructure supports a clip-on maxillary overdenture-obturator and a silicone nasal and midfacial prosthesis.

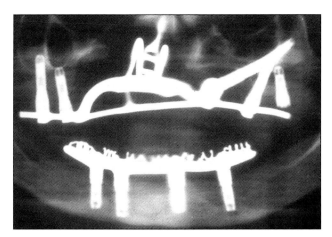

Fig I-4c Panoramic view of implant-anchored prostheses. Note the longer implant extending into the left zygoma.

Fig I-4d Final appearance of the patient with implant-retained facial prosthesis.

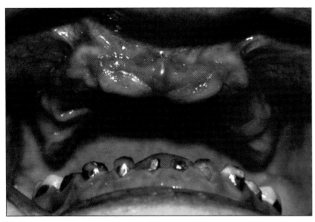

Fig 1-5a Intraoral view of 17-year-old female with anhydrotic ectodermal dysplasia and congenital absence of the permanent dentition.

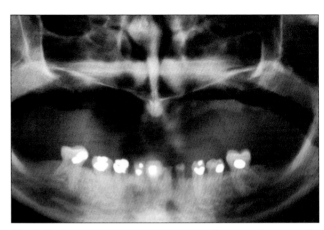

Fig 1-5b Preoperative panoramic view of patient shown in Fig 1-5a.

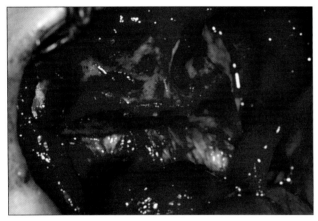

Fig 1-5c Surgical exposure of atrophic edentulous maxilla prior to bone-graft augmentation.

Fig 1-5d Onlay iliac bone graft with simultaneous implant placement. Note relationship of the implant fixture mounts to the mandibular arch.

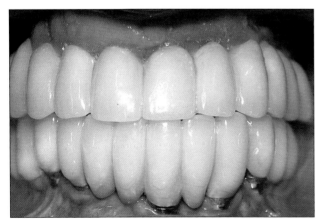

Fig 1-5e Ceramometal maxillary and mandibular fixed partial dentures following implant rehabilitation.

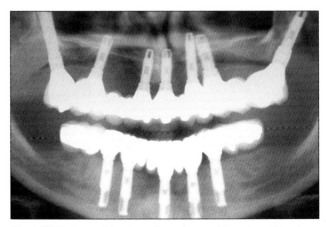

Fig 1-5f Radiographic view of number and location of implants supporting the prosthesis. Note the posterior cantilever of the mandibular fixed partial denture.

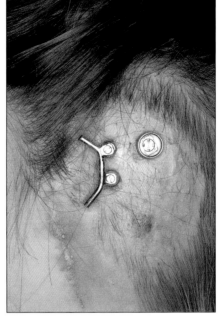

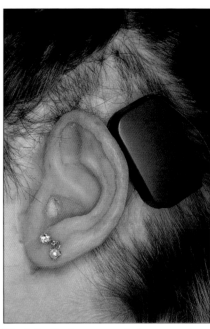

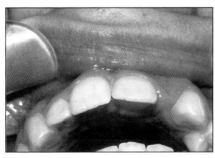

Fig 1-6a Craniofacial fixtures placed in the temporal bone to support an ear prosthesis and bone-anchored hearing aid.

Fig 1-6b Skin-penetrating abutments with supporting bar and hearing aid attachment.

Fig 1-6c Final position of clip-retained ear prosthesis and bone-anchored hearing aid.

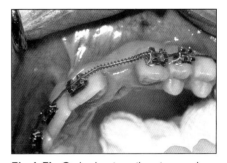

Fig 1-7a Congenitally missing maxillary left lateral incisor with inadequate mesiodistal space for implant replacement.

Fig 1-7b Orthodontic coil spring mechanics to increase space for implant placement.

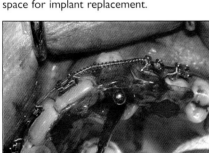

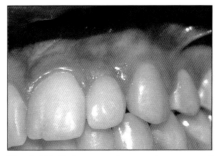

Fig 1-7c Use of surgical placement guide for implant positioning.

Fig 1-7d Esthetic implant replacement of lateral incisor following orthodontic alignment. Note the healthy and natural gingival appearance associated with the implant crown.

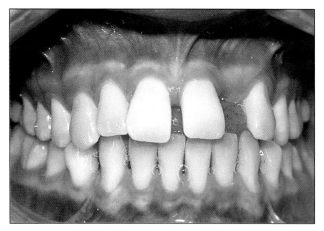

Fig 1-8 Unsightly drifting of anterior maxillary teeth into edentulous site of a congenitally missing lateral incisor.

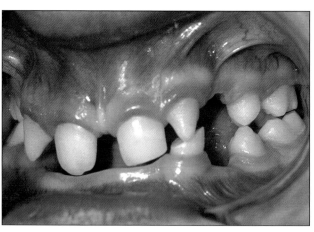

Fig 1-9 Supraeruption and tipping of the dentition associated with oligodontia.

25% of the population of the United States has evidence of anterior tooth trauma and that 0.6% of the population has experienced tooth loss from trauma. The maxillary central incisors suffered the highest incidence of trauma; males were more likely to be involved than females. During the active preadolescent and teenage years, the prominent position of the incisors exposes them to injury; it is not uncommon for orthodontists to assist in the management of these injuries. For functional and esthetic reasons, the maxillary central incisors are best replaced with prosthetic alternatives. Implant rehabilitation of traumatic tooth loss is influenced by the extent of immediate alveolar bone loss, long-term bony resorption in the edentulous site, and the patient's growth potential. Deficiencies involving alveolar contour and volume affect successful osseointegration and the long-term anchorage function of an implant. Reduced amounts of keratinized tissue may result in an unbalanced soft tissue appearance. The use of augmentation bone grafting and adjunctive soft tissue procedures should be considered with such alveolar defects. Figure 1-10 illustrates an alveolar defect, subsequent bone-graft reconstruction, and delayed implant placement. The timing of graft and implant placement is based upon the growth status of the patient and factors affecting optimal incorporation of the bone graft. Partial dentures or orthodontic retainers replacing teeth usually require modifica-

tion over a bone graft site to avoid loading pressure on the region. Patients who lose teeth before or during the course of active orthodontic therapy should have appropriate consultation so that if implant replacement is an option, orthodontic alignment of adjacent teeth can be included in the overall treatment program.

Impacted teeth unresponsive to surgical-orthodontic uncovering

Impacted teeth that do not respond to surgical-orthodontic uncovering procedures may have to be removed. Impaction of maxillary permanent canines occurs in 1.5% to 2% of the population[20,21] and are usually observed palatally and unilaterally. Buccal impactions are found in 7% to 16% of cases and are generally considered to be more difficult to align than those that are palatal. In most patients, surgical-orthodontic uncovering and alignment is successful. McSherry[21] has suggested that the following factors affect the prognosis of orthodontic alignment of impacted canines: patient age, arch length, root morphology, and canine location. The more apically, horizontally, and distally positioned the canine is, the poorer the prognosis. Under unfavorable clinical conditions, surgical-orthodontic uncovering and alignment of the canine may be neither possible nor advisable.

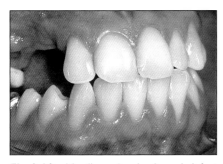

Fig 1-10a Maxillary alveolar buccal defect associated with missing premolar and canine.

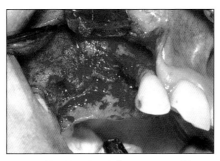

Fig 1-10b Alveolar defect at time of bone-graft reconstruction.

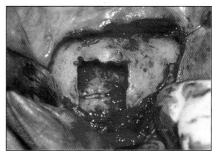

Fig 1-10c Donor site from symphysis region of mandible.

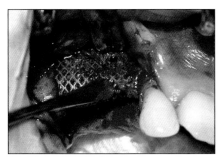

Fig 1-10d Particulate autogenous bone graft placed over alveolar defect with titanium mesh coverage.

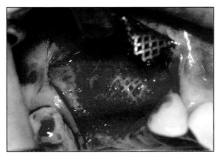

Fig 1-10e Augmented alveolar defect 6 months after autogenous grafting.

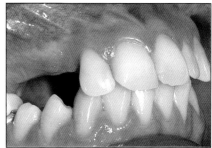

Fig 1-10f Pre-implant clinical appearance of reconstructed alveolus.

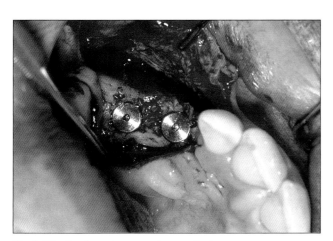

Fig 1-10g Implant placement into grafted area.

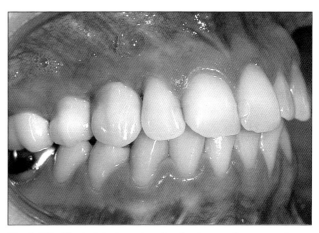

Fig 1-10h Final clinical results after implant replacement of premolar and canine.

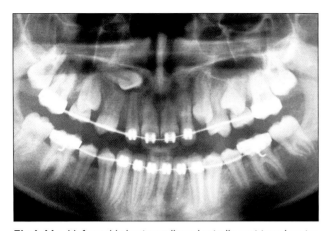

Fig 1-11a Unfavorable horizontally and apically positioned canine with poor prognosis for surgical-orthodontic repositioning.

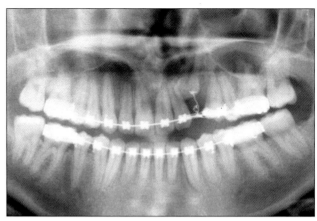

Fig 1-11b Ankylosed canine resistant to orthodontic traction causing intrusion of adjacent teeth and lateral open bite.

An ankylosed, unerupted canine in an adult may have to be removed (Fig 1-11). During orthodontic repositioning of an impacted canine, or during the natural eruption process itself, adjacent incisor roots may be damaged, possibly creating the need for prosthetic replacement. In the management of a missing maxillary canine, the clinician must determine whether prosthetic replacement or orthodontic space closure is most appropriate. Other causes of tooth loss are localized oral pathology, root resorption, periodontal bone loss, and endodontic and restorative failures.

The absence of single or multiple teeth in orthodontic patients is therefore not uncommon and the combined orthodontic-restorative management of those patients requires an interdisciplinary approach.

Congenitally missing teeth

Rehabilitation of patients experiencing hypodontia is an example of collaborative planning and clinical execution involving the orthodontist, restorative dentist, and surgeon. This process will now be reviewed. Hypodontia (missing one to five teeth) has been reported to vary with gender, ethnicity, family history, and certain syndromes.[22–25] The incidence of hypodontia (excluding third molars) has

been observed to range from 2% to 10%,[21] while oligodontia (missing six or more teeth) has been reported to vary between 0.07% and 0.2%.[23] Bergendal and colleagues[24] have pointed out a number of possible orthodontic and prosthodontic problems in patients having oligodontia:

- Decreased vertical and transverse growth in alveolar processes
- Deep bite
- Low anterior facial height
- Attrition of retained primary mandibular incisors
- Overeruption of maxillary incisors
- Generally smaller permanent teeth
- Root resorption of primary teeth even when permanent successor is missing
- Risk of large spaces when primary teeth are lost
- Wrong position of permanent abutment teeth
- Possible ankylosis and infraocclusion of persistent primary molars
- Overeruption of permanent molars
- Difficult positioning of the remaining permanent teeth
- Possible anchorage problems during orthodontic treatment

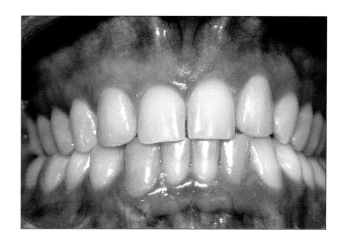

Fig 1-12 Favorable clinical result with canine substitution of congenitally missing lateral incisors.

Maxillary lateral incisors

The reported incidence of agenesis of maxillary lateral incisors varies from 0.95% to 2.5% in the general population[24,26,27]; thus it is a frequent problem in orthodontic and restorative practices. It can be treated either through canine substitution and reshaping with orthodontic space closure or prosthetic replacement of the missing lateral incisor. Each has advantages and disadvantages; the best choice will depend upon specific clinical conditions and patient preference. Before implants were available, many authors[28–33] emphasized favorable results with orthodontic canine substitution, which has been reported to be more sound periodontally than conventional fixed partial dentures.[32] Nor does the reshaping of canines to resemble lateral incisors appear to create long-term clinical or radiographic reactions when performed properly.[33] An example of a good outcome using canine substitution is seen in Fig 1-12. In 1973, McNeil and Joondeph[30] recommended orthodontic space closure in major malocclusions requiring the extraction of permanent mandibular teeth and orthodontic space opening of the lateral incisor site in Class I buccal occlusions not requiring mandibular extractions. These and other considerations, such as tooth size, lip length, and color and position of the canine, can influence the decision to orthodontically open or close the lateral incisor space.

The alternative to orthodontic space closure with canine substitution is prosthetic replacement. Considerations such as patient age, restorative status of the adjacent teeth, existing soft tissue and bony conditions, esthetics, financial limitations, and patient preference all affect the selection of the best treatment approach. The following alternatives are available for lateral incisor replacement:

• Orthodontic retainer or treatment partial denture
• Conventional removable or fixed partial denture
• Resin-bonded fixed partial denture
• Osseointegrated implant replacement

In the growing patient, it is necessary to use a relatively noninvasive interim option before providing a more definitive replacement such as a conventional fixed partial denture or a single-tooth implant after growth has ceased. Detailed considerations for the growing patient and timing of implant placement are discussed later in this text. The reader is referred to other sources[18,34] for additional discussion of the merits and indications for resin-bonded prostheses and conventional fixed and removable partial dentures. The factors previously acknowledged must be considered for each patient before selecting the best prosthetic replacement.

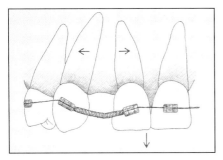

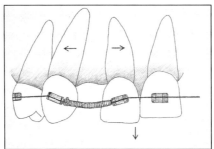

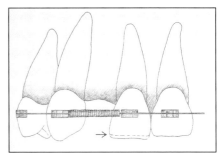

Fig 1-13a Bracket positioning and coiled spring mechanics to facilitate root divergence. (Modified from Orthod Dialog.[52] Used with permission.)

Fig 1-13b Progressive orthodontic root separation to increase apical space for implant replacement. Note slight extrusion of mesioincisal angle of central incisor. (Modified from Orthod Dialog.[52] Used with permission.)

Fig 1-13c Incisal edge equilibration to compensate for mesioincisal tipping. (Modified from Orthod Dialog.[52] Used with permission.)

Implant Replacement of Missing Teeth

Single and multiple implant replacement of missing teeth has become well accepted because of excellent clinical results, high patient satisfaction, and the avoidance of preparing healthy, unrestored teeth. Several centers have reported 5- to 10-year success rates as high as 97% for single-tooth implant replacements.[35,36] Lekholm et al[37] have documented 10-year multicenter prospective results in partially edentulous patients, following 461 implants in 89 patients, with implant survival rates of 90.2% in the maxilla, 93.7% in the mandible, and 94% prosthesis stability. In this longer-term study, shorter implants were lost more often than longer implants, and the majority of failures occurred before loading or within the first 1 to 2 years of function. Only four implants were lost during the last 5-year period of observation. Average marginal bone loss associated with the implants over a 10-year period was only 0.7 mm. Hence, the benefits of implant replacement of a single tooth or groups of teeth have been recognized by dentists and patients alike.[38] The advantages of using osseointegrated implants compared with removable or crown and bridge prosthetics have been summarized by Engelman[39] and include avoidance of ad-

jacent tooth preparation, accessibility of proximal contacts, absence of caries, bone maintenance, and retrievability. Disadvantages attributed to implant treatment include implant failure, loosening of the screw, inability to place missing interdental papilla, visibility of metal through tissues, length of treatment time, and need for surgery.

Congenitally missing lateral incisors

In the case of congenitally missing maxillary lateral incisors, if implant rehabilitation is planned, the orthodontist, restorative dentist, and surgeon must assess the needs of their respective areas of expertise and make recommendations compatible with agreed-upon restorative goals. In the orthodontic patient, certain guidelines for implant planning may prove useful:

1. In younger patients, eruption of the canine into the lateral incisor site should be encouraged so as to stimulate alveolar development. Primary lateral incisors and canines should be extracted to facilitate this process.
2. At the appropriate age, orthodontic retraction of canine into Class I position should be performed, with correct spacing between canine and central incisor at crown and root levels.

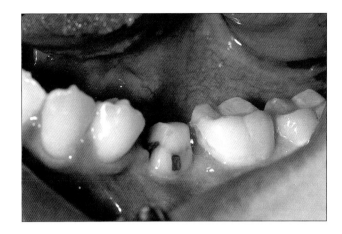

Fig 1-14 Retained left primary mandibular second molar with reduced mesiodistal width and occlusal buildup to prevent supraeruption of opposing tooth. The mandibular second premolar is congenitally missing.

3. Optimal spacing of the lateral incisor site depends upon esthetic and functional requirements of the ideal crown width, size of the contralateral incisor, and implant and abutment dimensions. Most often this requires a minimum of 5.5 mm for narrow implants and 6.5 mm for standard implant diameters at both crown and apical levels.
4. Roots of the canine and central incisors should be slightly divergent. This can be achieved with bracket angulation changes. Figure 1-13a illustrates positioning of the brackets.
5. Changes in central incisor root angulation may open the contact point, which can be overcome by slight gingival interproximal stripping.
6. Angulating brackets to open space may extrude the mesioincisal edge of the central incisor, which may then require slight equilibration (Figs 1-13b and 1-13c).
7. The periodontium of the adjacent teeth must be evaluated for acceptable bone support, mucogingival health, and esthetics.

Congenitally missing second premolars

Several studies[39,40] have suggested that, excluding third molars, the second premolar is the most commonly congenitally absent tooth and is frequently associated with infraocclusion of the retained primary molar. The presence of primary and secondary teeth is recognized to be important for the growth and maintenance of alveolar bone height. Impaired development of transverse and vertical alveolar bone dimensions is frequently present in hypodontia.[42] Kurol and Thilander[40] have observed that ankylosis and infraocclusion of primary molars are often associated with congenitally missing second premolars. Possible clinical sequelae associated with infraoccluded mandibular primary second molars include reduced alveolar height, supraeruption of opposing teeth, tipping of the first molar, delayed root resorption of the primary molars, and ankylosis. If implant replacement of congenitally missing mandibular premolars is a possibility, then timely management of this region is important. The following guidelines may prove useful:

1. Allow the primary second molars to remain in place (if not ankylosed) to preserve alveolar height and width. Reduce the mesiodistal width to approximately 7.0 mm and (if infraoccluded) build up occlusally to prevent supraeruption of opposing tooth (Fig 1-14).

2. Remove ankylosed primary second molars as soon as diagnosed (infraocclusion, sharp sound on percussion, decreased marginal bone height sloping to cementoenamel junction of infraoccluded primary molar).
3. Encourage eruption of the first premolar into the second premolar site to stimulate alveolar ridge development. If possible, orthodontically retract the first premolar into the second premolar site and place the implant in the first premolar location, possibly anterior to the mental foramen.

Surgical Considerations for the Implant Patient

Prior to placement of an implant, the surgical and restorative factors affecting a successful outcome should be carefully analyzed. A well-thought-out treatment objective should be determined preoperatively based on the optimal restorative result and patient concerns. The roles of the orthodontist and surgeon are to optimize the functional and esthetic characteristics of the implant prosthesis for the restorative dentist and the patient. The task of the orthodontist is, while considering the esthetic and occlusal characteristics of the existing dentition, to manage the vertical and mesiodistal tooth position with respect to crown length and width and provide proper root alignment so as to permit implant placement.[18] Equally important, the orthodontist and restorative dentist should understand the surgical issues that influence successful implant anchorage and the final bony and soft tissue anatomy surrounding the implant-restored dentition. This text focuses primarily on the orthodontic and restorative aspects of implant treatment and on surgical considerations as they affect the orthodontic and restorative treatment. For a broader review of surgical principles and techniques, the reader is referred to other sources.[43]

Implant treatment should be preceded by a thorough clinical examination, appropriate imaging studies, informed patient consent, and treatment planning with the restorative dentist and orthodontist. Existing alveolar ridge shape and bone volume, soft tissue conditions, edentulous space dimensions (vertical and mesiodistal), adjacent crown and root alignment, health and prognosis of nearby teeth, occlusion, and special esthetic concerns must be assessed. If existing clinical conditions restrict implant placement or obstruct final restorative goals, then these factors are corrected with orthodontics or surgery, or the treatment plan is modified. Appropriate presurgical orthodontics is performed to achieve suitable spacing to accommodate implant and prosthetic components. When the alveolar ridge contour or existing bone volume is deficient, preliminary augmentation, using a variety of bone- and soft tissue–grafting procedures, is available. In certain situations, a staged approach, where the grafting is accomplished prior to implant placement, is preferred. In other circumstances, it is done at the time of implant placement. Once the clinical conditions are acceptable for implant placement, some form of surgical placement guide is recommended, which will vary according to arch location and the surgeon's preference.

Implant Surgery

The surgery is performed under standard operating room conditions with a gentle surgical technique, emphasizing low-speed drilling and minimal tissue trauma.[4] Primary stability of the implant, which is critical to achieving osseointegration, is influenced by bone quality, surgical technique, and implant geometry. At present, most implants are placed in a two-step protocol where implant placement and soft tissue coverage are followed by an unloaded healing period of 3 to 6 months before the abutments are placed. Recently, several authors have reported favorable results under specific conditions using a one-step method that minimizes the extent of loading[44,45]; however, specific indications for the partially edentulous patient have not yet been established. Directional implant placement by means of a surgical guide must accommodate the recipient site with respect to ridge morphology, bone volume, and adjacent anatomic structures. The incisive foramen, nasal and maxillary sinuses, and inferior alveolar and mental nerves will affect implant length and positioning.

Implant-Orthodontic Anchorage: Surgical Considerations

A variety of anatomic sites have been recommended for implant anchorage to facilitate orthodontic tooth movement. Table 1-2 summarizes potential implant locations.

Implants located within the dentoalveolus can serve two purposes: first as orthodontic anchorage and later as abutments for prosthetic tooth replacement. Implants located outside the standard dental arch can provide intraoral anchorage during orthodontic treatment and then be removed or buried. When possible, it is advantageous to select a site in an edentulous region of the arch so that the added benefits of prosthetic support can be realized. The surgical placement of implants in anchorage locations follows the standard protocol except in the retromolar and ramal regions of the mandible, where access is restricted. In general, implants placed in the palate or retromolar region will be limited in length by the amount of available bone. Wehrbein and colleagues[46-48] have characterized the favorable bone response to orthodontic loading forces in dogs and human subjects, as well as the efficacy of using the palate as an anchorage site for one-stage implant placement. In patients who are not missing teeth within the arch, conventional implant anchorage may not be cost-effective because of its additional treatment time, cost, surgery, and compromised sites for implant placement. To avoid or reduce these concerns, recent attention has been focused on using smaller, nonosseointegrated anchorage devices and biodegradable implants as orthodontic anchorage elements.[49-51] Future laboratory and clinical research is certain to explore these possibilities, which may improve the cost-effectiveness of implant anchorage in the orthodontic patient.

Fortunately, the magnitude of forces associated with orthodontic anchorage is relatively low and usually does not exceed the capacity of the bone-implant interface. A thorough review of clinical, biomechanical, and biological events associated with orthodontic anchorage is provided in chapters 4, 5, 6, and 9.

Table 1-2 Implant anchorage sites

Maxilla	Mandible
Edentulous space in dental alveolus	Edentulous space in dental alveolus
Palate	Retromolar region
Zygomatic process	Ramus

Summary

Although the effectiveness and predictability of implant therapy has expanded treatment options in dentistry, it must be emphasized that this alternative should be used appropriately with respect to timing and to evidence-based indications. Clinically verified concepts such as restorative and periodontal preservation of teeth, traditional forms of prosthetics, and canine substitution for lateral incisors should be considered along with implant rehabilitation when formulating a treatment plan. The authors of this text recognize that there is often more than one acceptable clinical pathway in the treatment of a condition. While acknowledging other alternatives, this text focuses on the unique benefits of osseointegrated implant use in orthodontic patients, though the opinions expressed by each author are not necessarily a consensus view or those of the editor. Future applications of osseointegration in the orthodontic patient will undoubtedly occur, and chapters 6 and 10 provide some insight into these possibilities.

References

1. Brånemark P-I, Adell R, Breine U, et al. Intra-osseous anchorage of dental prostheses. I. Experimental studies. Scand J Plast Reconstr Surg 1969;3:81.

2. Brånemark P-I, Hansson B, Adell R, et al. Osseointegrated Implants in the Treatment of the Edentulous Jaw. Experience from a 10-Year Period. Stockholm: Almquist and Wiksell 1977.

3. Albrektsson T, Brånemark P-I, Hansson HA, et al. Osseointegrated titanium implants. Requirements for ensuring a long-lasting, direct bone-to-implant anchorage in man. Acta Orthop Scan 1981;52:155.

4. Brånemark P-I, Zarb G, Albrektsson T. Tissue-Integrated Prostheses. Osseointegration in Clinical Dentistry. Chicago: Quintessence, 1985.

5. Steineman SG, Eulenberger J, Maeusli PA, et al. Adhesion of bone to titanium. In: Christel P. Meunier A, Lee AJC (eds). Biological and Biomechanical Performance of Biomaterials. Amsterdam: Elsevier, 1986:409–414.

6. Rydevik B, Brånemark P-I, Skalak R (eds). International Workshop on Osseointegration in Skeletal Reconstruction and Joint Replacement. Göteborg: The Institute for Applied Biotechnology, 1991.

7. Albrektsson T, Sennerby L. State of the art in oral implants. J Clin Periodontol 1991;18:474–481.

8. Roberts WE. The use of dental implants in orthodontic therapy. In: Davidovitch Z (ed). The Biological Mechanisms of Tooth Eruption, Resorption and Replacement by Implants. Boston: Harvard Society for the Advancement of Orthodontics, 1994:631–642.

9. Lindh T, Gunne J, Tillberg A, Molin M. A meta-analysis of implants in partial edentulism. Clin Oral Implants Res 1998;9:80–90.

10. De Bruyn H, Collaert B, Lindén U, et al. Clinical outcome of screw vent implants. A 7-year prospective follow-up study. Clin Oral Implants Res 1999;10:139–148.

11. Rosenberg ES, Totosian JP, Slots J. Microbiological differences in two clinically distinct types of failures of osseointegrated implants. Clin Oral Implants Res 1991;2:134–144.

12. Malmquist JP, Sennerby L. Clinical report on the success of 47 consecutively placed core-vent implants followed from 3 months to 4 years. Int J Oral Maxillofac Implants 1991;5:53–60.

13. Block MS, Gardiner D, Kent JN, et al. Hydroxylapatite-coated cylindrical implants in the posterior mandible: 10-year observations. Int J Oral Maxillofac Implants 1996;11:626–633.

14. Van Steenberghe D. Outcomes and their measurement in clinical trials of endosseous oral implants. Ann Periodontol 1997;2:291–298.

15. Roos T, Sennerby L, Albrektsson T. An update on the clinical documentation on currently used bone anchored endosseous oral implants. Dent Update 1997;24: 194–200.

16. Esposito M, Hirsch J-M, Lekholm U, et al. Biological factors contributing to failures of osseointegrated implants. (I) Success criteria and epidemiology. Eur J Oral Sci 1998;106:527–551.

17. Gottlieb EL, Nelson AH, Vogels DS III. 1997 JCO orthodontic practice study. Part I: Trends. J Clin Orthod 1997; 31:675–684.

18. Chiche GJ, Pinault A. Esthetics of Anterior Fixed Prosthodontics. Chicago: Quintessence, 1994.

19. Kaste L, Gift H, Bhat M, Swango P. Prevalence of incisor trauma in persons 6 to 50 years of age: United States, 1988-1991. J Dent Res 1996 (Special issue):696–705.

20. Ericson S, Kurol J. Radiographic assessment of maxillary canine eruption in children with clinical signs of eruption disturbance. Eur J Orthod 1986;8:133–140.

21. McSherry PF. The assessment of and treatment options for the buried maxillary canine. Dental Update 1996; Jan-Feb: 7-10.

22. Schalk-van der Weide Y. Oligiodontia. A Clinical Radiographic and Genetic Evaluation [thesis]. Utrecht, The Netherlands: Univ of Utrecht, 1992.

23. Montague MFA. The significance of the variability of the upper lateral incisor teeth in man. Hum Biol 1940; 12:323–350.

24. Bergendal B, Bergendal T, Hallonsten A-L, et al. A multidisciplinary approach to oral rehabilitation with osseointegrated implants in children and adolescents with multiple aplasia. Eur J Orthod 1996;18:119–129.

25. Stewart R. The dentition and anomalies of tooth size, form, structure, and eruption. In: Stewart R, Barber T, Troutman K (eds). Pediatric Dentistry. St. Louis: Mosby, 1982:91.

26. Silverman NE, Ackerman JL. Oligiodontia: A study of its prevalence and variation in 4032 children. J Dent Child 1979;46:470–477.

27. Meskin LH, Gorlin RJ. Agenesis and peg-shaped permanent maxillary lateral incisors. J Dent Res 1963;42: 1476–1479.

28. Carlson H. Suggested treatment for missing lateral incisors. Angle Orthod 1952;22:205–216.

29. Tuverson DL. Orthodontic treatment using canines in place of missing maxillary lateral incisors. Am J Orthod 1970;59(2):109–127.

30. McNeil RW, Joondeph DR. Congenitally absent maxillary lateral incisors: Treatment planning considerations. Angle Orthod 1973;43:24–29.

31. Sabri R. Management of missing maxillary lateral incisors. JADA 1999;130:80–84.

32. Nordquist GG, McNeil RW. Orthodontic vs. restorative treatment of the congenitally absent lateral incisor: Long term periodontal and occlusal evaluation. J Periodontol 1975;46(13):139–143.

33. Thordarson A, Zachrisson BU, Mjör IA. Remodeling of canines to the shape of lateral incisors by grinding: A long-term clinical and radiographic evaluation. Am J Orthod Dentofac Orthop 1991;100:123–132.

34. Simon J, Gartrell R, Grogono A. Improved retention of acid-etched fixed partial dentures: A longitudinal study. J Prosthet Dent 1992;68:611–615.

35. Henry P, Laney W, Jemt T, et al. Osseointegrated implants for single-tooth replacement: A prospective 5-year multi-center study. Int J Oral Maxillofac Implants 1996; 11:450–455.

36. Priest G. Single-tooth implants and their role in preserving remaining teeth: A 10-year survival study. Int J Oral Maxillofac Implants 1999;14:181–188.

37. Lekholm U, Gunne J, Henry P, et al. Survival of the Brånemark implant in the partially edentulous jaw. A 10 year prospective multicenter study. Int J Oral Maxillofac Implants (accepted for publication August 1999).

38. Meffert RM. Issues related to single-tooth implants. JADA 1997;128:1383–1390.

39. Engelman MJ. Clinical Decision Making and Treatment Planning in Osseointegration. Chicago: Quintessence, 1996.

40. Kurol J, Thilander B. Infraocclusion of primary molars with aplasia of the permanent successor. A longitudinal study. Angle Orthod 1984;54:283–294.

41. Thilander B, Myrberg N. The prevalence of malocclusion in Swedish school children. Scand J Dental Res 1973; 81:12–21.

42. Higuchi K, Worthington P, Brånemark P-I. Hypodontia and oligiodontia. In: Worthington P, Brånemark P-I (eds). Advanced Osseointegration Surgery: Applications in the Maxillofacial Region. Chicago: Quintessence, 1992: 248–252.

43. Worthington P, Brånemark P-I (eds). Advanced Osseointegration Surgery: Applications in the Maxillofacial Region. Chicago: Quintessence, 1992.

44. Buser D, Merickse-Stern R, Bernard J, et al. Long-term evaluation of non-submerged ITI implants. Part 1: 8-year life table analysis of a prospective multi-center study with 2359 implants. Clin Oral Implants Res 1997;8:161–172.

45. Becker W, Becker B, Israelson H, et al. One-step surgical placement of Brånemark implant: A prospective multi-center clinical study. Int J Oral Maxillofac Implants 1997;12:454–462.

46. Wehrbein H, Diedrich P. Endosseous titanium implants during and after orthodontic load—An experimental study in dog. Clin Oral Implants Res 1993;4:76–82.

47. Wehrbein H, Merz B, Diedrich P, et al. The use of palatal implants for orthodontic anchorage. Design and clinical applications of the ortho system. Clin Oral Implants Res 1996;7:410–416.

48. Wehrbein H, Merz B, Hämmerle C, et al. Bone to implant contact of orthodontic implants in humans subjected to horizontal loading. Clin Oral Implants Res 1998; 9:348–353.

49. Bousquet F, Bosquet P, Mauran G, et al. Use of an impacted post for anchorage. J Clin Orthod 1996; 30:261–265.

50. Kanomi R. Mini-implant for orthodontic anchorage. J Clin Orthod 1997;31:763-767.

51. Glatzmaier J, Wehrbein H, Diedrich P. Biodegradable implants for orthodontic anchorage. A preliminary biomechanical study. Eur J Orthod 1996;18:465–469.

52. American Association of Orthodontists. The role of the orthodontist on the maxillary anterior implant team. Orthod Dialog 1998;10(2):3–5.

2 | Comprehensive Management of Implant Anchorage in the Multidisciplinary Patient

Vincent G. Kokich, DDS, MSD

In recent years, dental implants have become an accepted method of replacing missing teeth. Today millions of implants are placed annually to rehabilitate and reestablish patients' occlusions. However, in many of these individuals, the teeth may be in less than ideal position to accept the integration of single implants or groups of implants with the remaining teeth. Many of these patients could benefit from orthodontics to reposition malposed teeth to enhance the overall occlusal scheme. However, if significant numbers of teeth are missing, the orthodontist is at a disadvantage because of a lack of anchorage to effect the desired tooth movement. Past studies have shown that implants can be used as anchors for both orthopedic and orthodontic movement.[1-5] However, some studies describing the use of implants for orthodontic anchorage do not recommend utilizing the implant as a restorative abutment after the orthodontic movement.[6] Although nonroot-form onplants and implants can be placed in nonalveolar bone, used for anchorage,[7,8] and then removed, this type of implant anchorage is not useful in patients having many missing teeth and multiple edentulous spaces. In this type of dental patient, an interdisciplinary approach of placing the implant prior to orthodontics, using it as an orthodontic anchor, and then using the same implant as a restorative abutment may be a more appropriate and cost-effective solution. This chapter will discuss the interdisciplinary management of implants that are used for orthodontic anchorage and as restorative abutments. The chapter will also describe the indications for implant anchorage, methods of locating the appropriate implant position, timing of orthodontic loading, types of provisional restorations appropriate for attaching orthodontic brackets, and the effects of orthodontic loading on the integrity of osseointegration and final restoration.

Indications for Implant Anchorage

Although several situations can be found where implants can be used for both orthodontic and restorative anchorage, this section will identify four generic possibilities that include many different situations. One possibility would be to use the implant as an anchor to facilitate intra-arch intrusion of a tooth or teeth that have supraerupted. This situation is often seen in patients with missing teeth in one arch, leaving teeth in the opposing arch without an occlusal counterpart (Figs 2-1a and 2-1b). In these situations, teeth tend to supraerupt beyond the plane of occlusion and encroach into the restorative space of the opposite dental arch. If a single tooth erupts 1 to 2 mm beyond the occlusal plane, and teeth are present adjacent to the overerupted tooth, the adjacent teeth will usually provide sufficient anchorage to orthodontically intrude the overerupted tooth. However, if two or more teeth have erupted beyond the occlusal plane, or if the adjacent teeth are missing, there may be insufficient anchorage to intrude the overerupted teeth (Figs 2-1a and 2-1b). In the latter situation, if implants are planned to replace the missing teeth, these implants may be used to intrude the overerupted teeth prior to restoration. In such cases, the implants must be positioned accurately prior to the orthodontics so they can be used as restorative abutments following tooth movement.

A second indication for using implants as both orthodontic and restorative anchorage is to facilitate interarch intrusion of teeth. This situation arises when several teeth in the opposing dental arch have been missing for several years and the edentulous space has not been restored (Fig 2-1c). In this case, three or more teeth may supraerupt into the opposing edentulous space. If a segment of teeth has supraerupted, intra-arch intrusion using adjacent teeth in the same arch is generally not possible without causing eruption of the adjacent teeth. In some of these situations, the only possible method for intruding the overerupted teeth is through segmental orthognathic surgery. However, if implants are planned as restorative replacements for the teeth in the opposing arch, the implants may be used as abutments for orthodontic intrusion. In this situation, implants are placed as anchors, and samarium-cobalt magnets are used to provide the intrusive force to the overerupted teeth. After reintrusion of the overerupted segment of teeth, the implants in the opposing arch may be used as restorative abutments to provide occlusal stops and rehabilitate occlusal function.

A third possibility for using an implant as an orthodontic anchor and a restorative abutment is in the patient requiring intra-arch retraction/protraction of adjacent teeth within the same arch. This situation occurs when single or multiple teeth are missing, and the treatment plan requires consolidation of part of the space by moving the teeth in only one direction (Figs 2-1d and 2-1e). Generally, tooth movement is reciprocal. If a tooth is used to provide anchorage for adjacent tooth movement, the anchor will also move—a sometimes undesirable sequela. In addition, there may be no posterior or anterior tooth to provide anchorage for orthodontic movement. In such cases, an implant can provide absolute anchorage for orthodontic movement and later be used as an abutment for a restoration to replace the missing teeth within that dental arch.

The fourth and final indication for the interdisciplinary use of an implant for orthodontic and restorative anchorage is interarch retraction/protraction. This situation occurs when several teeth are missing in both dental arches and the remaining teeth in one or both arches require significant movement. If implants cannot be used for retraction in one arch, they may be placed in the opposite arch, and interarch forces can be used to move teeth in the opposing arch (Fig 2-1f). After the desired tooth movement, the implant may be used as a restorative abutment.

Determining the Appropriate Implant Position

If several permanent teeth are missing but the remaining teeth are appropriately positioned and sufficient space remains for the placement of implants, the surgeon and restorative dentist may construct a placement guide to position the im-

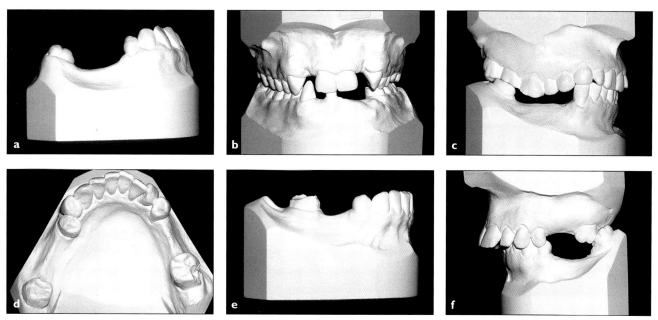

Fig 2-1 The indications for implant anchorage to facilitate orthodontic tooth movement consist of *intra-arch intrusion* (a, b), where implants are used to intrude adjacent teeth within the same arch; *interarch intrusion* (c), where implants placed in one arch are used as abutments to intrude the teeth in the opposite arch; *intra-arch retraction* (d, e), where implants are used to retract (d) or protract (e) adjacent teeth within the same arch; and *interarch retraction* (f), using implants in one arch to retract teeth in the opposite arch.

plants properly. However, if the adjacent teeth are not in their proper positions and the implants are to be used to reposition the teeth, the placement guide must be constructed from a simulation of the final tooth positions. This simulation, or diagnostic wax setup, must be constructed correctly so the implants and teeth will be in their proper positions.[9,10]

Construction of the diagnostic setup varies, depending on the number of teeth to be moved during orthodontic treatment. In some situations, only a few teeth will be moved (Fig 2-2). In other situations, all teeth will undergo some repositioning (Fig 2-3). In either case, a series of four steps should be followed during the implant construction. The first step is to duplicate the base *and* tooth portions of the original dental casts (Figs 2-2a to 2-2d, 2-3a, 2-3b, and 2-3d). The second step is to cut the teeth out of the plaster. However, all teeth cannot be cut out initially or the reference will be lost and the setup will not represent the actual outcome of treatment. Only the teeth to be moved during orthodontics should be cut out (Figs 2-2e to 2-2g). A third important step is to always leave a reference tooth when sectioning the dental casts. If all the teeth are to be repositioned during construction of the setup, then half the maxillary and mandibular arches should be sectioned at the midline on the duplicated casts (Figs 2-3c and 2-3f). The remaining, or contralateral, central incisor will serve as the reference tooth when replacing the plaster teeth in the wax. If only a few teeth are to be moved during the orthodontics, then only those teeth should be sectioned from the duplicated dental casts.

After wax is added to the dental bases, the final step is to reposition the plaster teeth in their bases. It is generally recommended that the nonimplant arch be repositioned first in order to determine how much tooth movement is needed in the arch intended for implants (Figs 2-2h, 2-2i, 2-3d, 2-3g, and 2-3h). After the nonimplant arch is set up, the plaster teeth in the arch containing the implants are positioned in their proper occlusal relationship. The space remaining after simulated orthodontic movement will determine the positions of the implants.

Fig 2-2 Placement of implants for orthodontic anchorage requires precise location of the implant so that it will be appropriate for both the orthodontist and the restorative dentist. If possible, only the teeth that are to be moved during the orthodontic treatment should be sectioned and replaced in the setup. This will allow the remaining teeth to serve as a reference during construction of the placement guide. In this patient, the mandibular right canine and first premolar would be intruded during the orthodontics. However, in order to place implants properly in the mandibular left first premolar and canine and right lateral incisor locations, the anticipated maxillary tooth movement was created in the diagnostic setup. This allowed the placement of plastic teeth in the mandibular incisor region to determine the precise position of the eventual implant abutments for the lower fixed partial denture. A placement guide was fabricated from the plaster cast of the setup and used to locate the implants prior to orthodontic treatment.

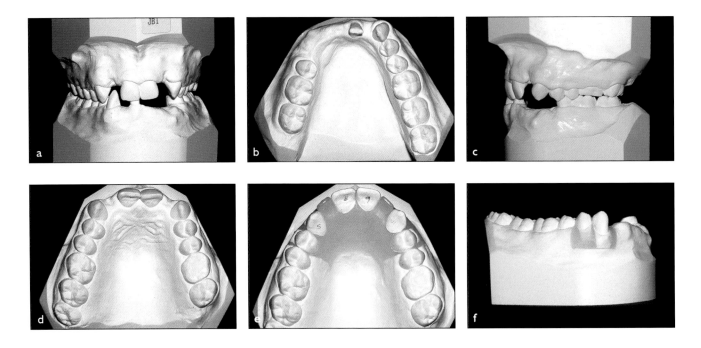

If the implants are to be used eventually as fixed partial denture abutments after orthodontic anchorage, plastic or wax teeth simulating the eventual size of the crowns and pontics must be added to the diagnostic setup (Figs 2-2h, 2-2i, 2-3d, 2-3g, and 2-3h). These prosthetic teeth should be the exact size of the eventual restorations so that they can pinpoint for the surgeon the position of the implants.

The next step is to transfer the information regarding implant position to the original dental cast in order to construct a plastic placement guide. Two different methods can be used to do this. If only a few teeth were repositioned during the setup, then a plaster duplicate of the wax setup can

be made (Fig 2-2j). A plastic stent is then constructed to simulate the positions of the orthodontically moved teeth and the implant teeth (Fig 2-2k). The portion of plastic involving the repositioned teeth can then be removed from the stent so it will fit accurately over the teeth in their original positions (Fig 2-2l). In areas where the eventual pontics or implant crowns create a void, the stent is filled with plastic so the surgeon will have a more accurate guide for precise positioning of the implant in all directions (Figs 2-2m to 2-2o).

If all the plaster teeth were repositioned during the setup process, then the transfer of information back to the original dental cast must be accomplished using a different method. If the dental

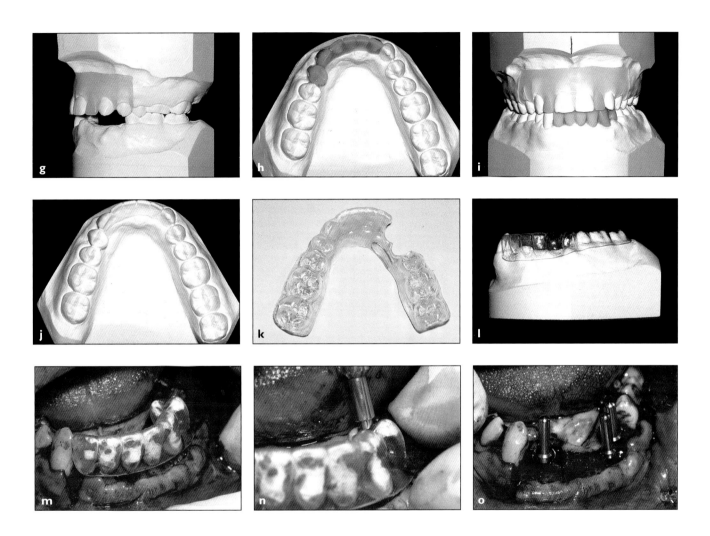

bases were also accurately replicated during the duplication process, the borders of the dental base may be used as a reference for transferring the implant position to the original dental casts. In this situation, a caliper is used to measure the distance from a point on the base of the dental cast to the center of the implant (Fig 2-3i). Then this distance is transferred back to the original plaster cast, using the same reference point on the dental base (Fig 2-3j). A pencil mark is made on the spot where the implant should be positioned (Fig 2-3k). Then the plastic placement guide can be constructed and a hole placed in the guide corresponding to the pencil mark (Fig 2-3l).

The stent is then positioned intraorally to verify its fit over the occlusal surfaces of the teeth. By simulating where the implants will be positioned, it is now possible to determine if sufficient bone is present in those areas (Fig 2-2m). If sufficient bone is not present, then a bone graft can be accomplished prior to implant placement. The setup and stent will help the surgeon identify the exact location and amount of bone grafting necessary to support the implants (Figs 2-2n and 2-2o). The last step is to use the stent to place the implants. It is important to position the stent securely over the occlusal surfaces of the teeth so that the implants will be accurately positioned.

Fig 2-3 If all teeth are to be relocated during the orthodontic treatment, the diagnostic setup to determine the position of the anchorage implants must be constructed in the proper manner. In this situation, the bases of the plaster casts are used as a reference. The setup is constructed one side at a time with the teeth on the opposite side acting as a reference. Generally, the teeth in the arch opposite the implants are set up first. Then the opposing arch is positioned to simulate the desired final tooth position and occlusion. Using the base of the cast as a reference, calipers may be employed to transfer the location of the implants back to the original dental cast. Then the placement guide may be fabricated to position the implant precisely prior to the initiation of orthodontics.

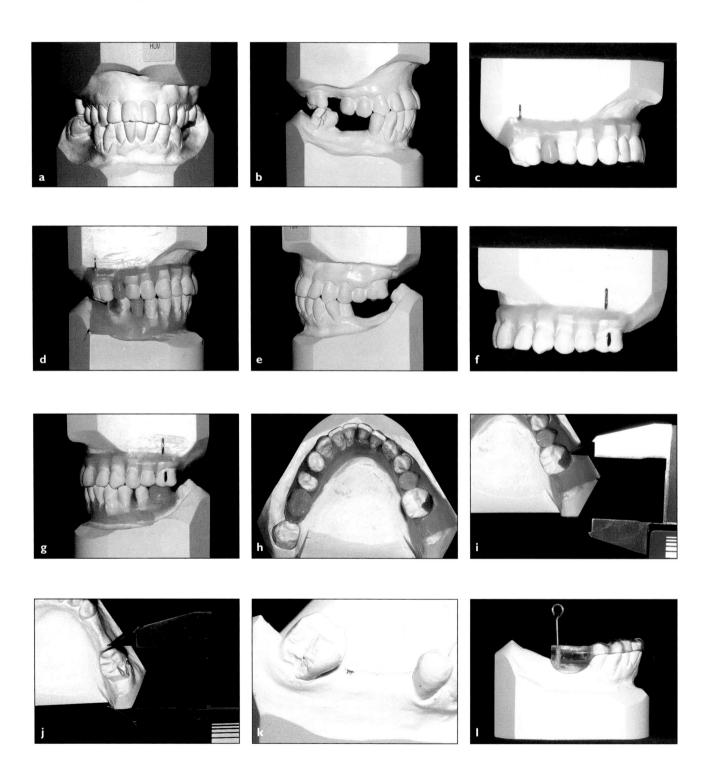

Timing of Orthodontic Loading

Uncovering of the implants and application of orthodontic loading must be timed properly to avoid loss of osseointegration of the implant. The timing of implant loading for single implants is determined by the amount of time required by the bone adjacent to the implant to undergo secondary osteon (remodeling) formation around the implant.[11] If multiple implants are placed at the same time, they are often loaded occlusally immediately after placement, using a provisional prosthesis. Even though the bone around the implant has not completely remodeled, the rigidity supplied by cross-arch splinting has been shown to be sufficient to allow for integration to occur around the functioning implants.

However, if single-tooth implants are placed, it is probably disadvantageous to load them immediately. The healing process around an implant goes through several stages. The first process to occur is necrosis of the bone adjacent to the implant. This is due to the trauma and heat that accompany the drilling and tapping process. After resorption of the necrotic bone, osteoid, the organic precursor of bone, is deposited around the implant. Then this organic matrix calcifies with the deposition of calcium and phosphorus salts. However, before the implant is loaded orthodontically, the woven bone should be allowed to undergo remodeling with the development of secondary osteons. Although the exact timing of secondary osteon formation around implants is not known and may vary between individuals, it is probably between 14 and 18 months. Secondary remodeling probably occurs faster in the mandible than in the maxilla. In summary, the orthodontist should wait about 4 to 6 months before loading the implant orthodontically.

Types of Provisional Restorations

After the implant has been uncovered, a provisional restoration must be placed so the orthodontic force can be attached to the implant. The type of provisional restoration varies, depending on the type of orthodontic mechanics. In some situations, a tooth-shaped plastic restoration is required. However, in other situations, a metal abutment is sufficient to provide the anchorage. In general, if orthodontic brackets are not to be used, a simple metal cap can be placed on top of the implant (Fig 2-4a). This can be used to facilitate attachment of a plastic stage, housing a samarium-cobalt magnet that can be used for interarch intrusion (Fig 2-4b).

In other situations, if the teeth adjacent to the implant are to be moved toward the implant, a provisional plastic restoration is necessary to permit accurate positioning of these teeth during the orthodontic process (Figs 2-4c and 2-4d). In these situations, the size of the provisional crown can be ascertained from the diagnostic setup used to create the placement guide. In some cases, multiple provisional restorations (Figs 2-4e and 2-4f) or a provisional fixed partial denture (Figs 2-4g and 2-4h) may be necessary to provide adequate orthodontic anchorage and ensure proper tooth positioning.

Effect of Implant Loading

The amount of orthodontic force applied to the implant may be considerable. In addition, the direction of force may be different in various situations. If the implant is being used to produce intra-arch intrusion, the force on the implant is to *extrude* it out of the alveolus (Figs 2-5a to 2-5h). If the implant is being used for interarch intrusion using samarium-cobalt magnets, the force on the implant is *intrusive* (Fig 2-6), pushing it farther down into the bone. If the implant is being used for intra-arch retraction/protraction, the force on the implant is *compressive*, pushing it laterally against the alveolus (Fig 2-7). Finally, if the implant is being used to anchor interarch retraction/protraction, the force on the implant will be a *tipping* force (Figs 2-5i to 2-5l). In each of the examples used in this chapter to illustrate the effect of implant anchorage to facilitate orthodontic movement, the radiographic response to implant loading was not destructive to the bone-implant interface. For example, during intra-arch intrusion of overerupted teeth, the force on the implant is extrusive, tending to pull the implant out

Fig 2-4 After the implants have been uncovered, abutments must be placed on them to facilitate attachment of the orthodontic appliances. The abutments could consist of a metal attachment if brackets are not necessary *(a,b)*; single *(c,d)* or multiple *(e,f)* plastic provisional crowns; or a plastic provisional fixed partial denture *(g,h)*.

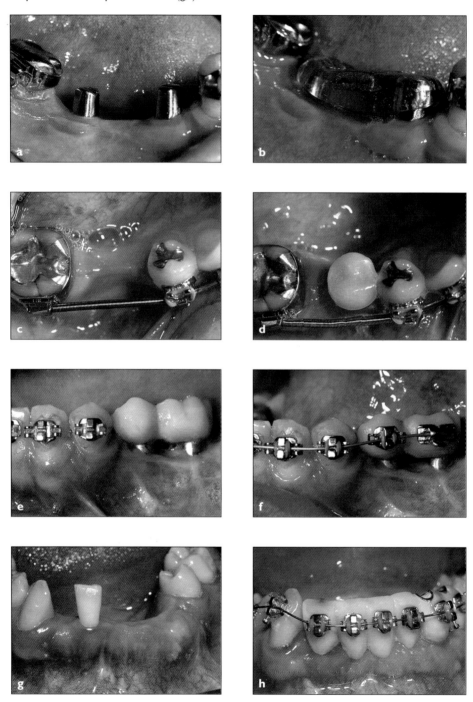

Fig 2-5 When implants are used for *intra-arch intrusion* (a-h) or *interarch retraction* (i-l), they do not move through the bone. The loading of the implants caused no loss of integration.

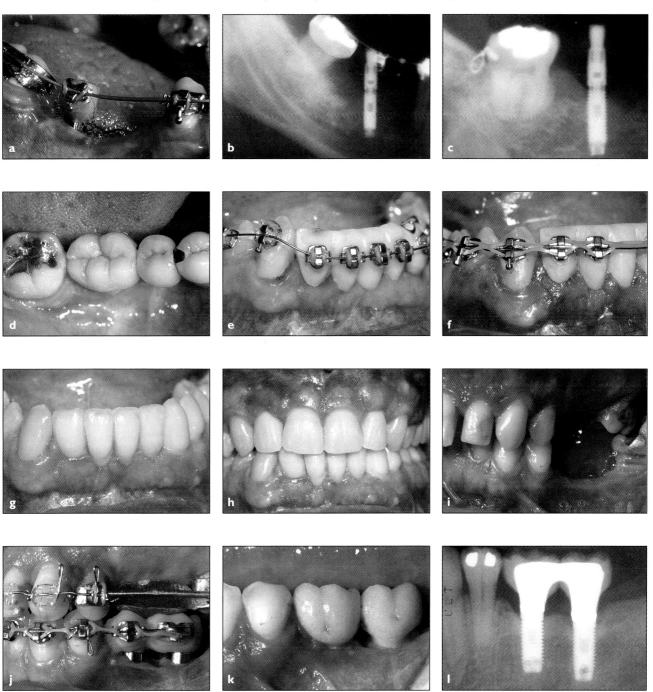

Fig 2-6 When implants are used for *interarch intrusion*, the intrusive force on the implants causes no loss of osseointegration around the implants.

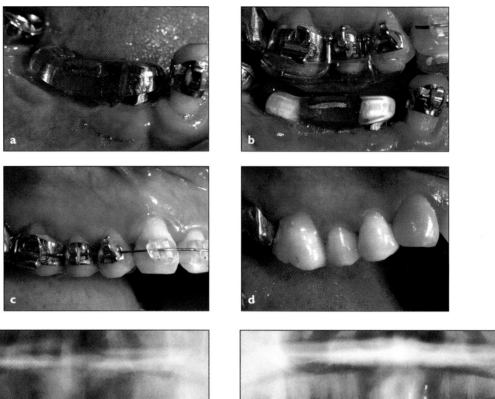

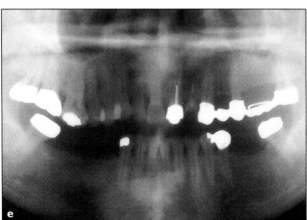
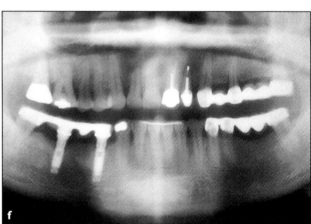

of the bone (Figs 2-5a to 2-5h). However, if the implant has integrated adequately, movement of the implant is nil. A natural tooth has a periodontal membrane that allows for resorption on the pressure side of the alveolus and deposition of new bone on the tension side, resulting in movement of the socket and tooth through the bone. However, when an orthodontic force is placed on an implant, histologic studies have shown that the bone is gen-erally thicker on the pressure side of the implant and thinner on the opposite side. This thickening of bone deposited on the medullary side of the implant-bone interface is called *buttressing* bone. Although this phenomenon has been reported previously, the biologic mechanism for it is not well understood. Therefore, it appears that loading of the implant actually results in thicker bone and not in dissolution of the bone around the implant.

Fig 2-7 When implants are used for *intra-arch retraction* or *protraction*, the loading of the implant does not cause disintegration of the bone around the implant. Since the orthodontic forces are continuous and in one direction, the physiologic response is thickening of the bone on the pressure side of the implant.

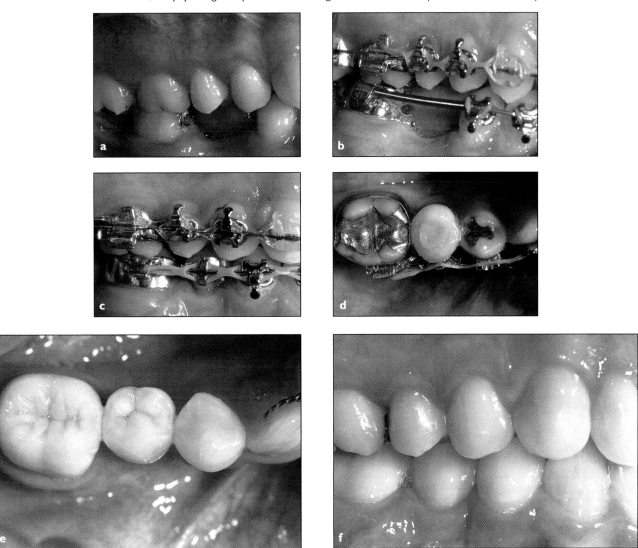

Earlier articles in the literature have suggested that excessive occlusal loading may cause implants to disintegrate. Why would occlusal loads produce a different response than the favorable reaction observed when implants are loaded orthodontically? Although this difference cannot be conclusively determined in the scope of this chapter, it is believed to be due to two fundamental differences between an occlusal load and an orthodontic load. First, orthodontic loads are generally continuous and not intermittent. Occlusal loads, on the other hand, are intermittent. Second, orthodontic loads are usually in one direction, whereas occlusal loads are in different directions. If a load on the implant is intermittent and in different directions, the biomechanical message transmitted to the bone surrounding the implant is not consistent. Therefore, no uniform response in the bone is produced. If, however, the force is continuous and in the same direction, as in an orthodontic force, then the biomechanical message to the bone will produce a uniform response at the bone-implant interface. Therefore, orthodontic loads on an implant could be perceived as more physiological than occlusal loads.

Summary

This chapter has shown how orthodontic tooth movement can be enhanced with implant anchorage. The indications for implant anchorage have been elucidated; the method of locating the proper position for placing the implant has been described and illustrated in detail; the timing of uncovering and loading of the implant has been explained; the types of abutments that may be necessary to attach orthodontic appliances has been summarized; and finally, the effect of implant loading on the integrity of the bone-implant interface has been elucidated. Although implant anchorage is generally needed for routine orthodontic treatment of children and adolescents, it may be critically useful for the adult orthodontic patient with missing teeth. When planning orthodontic treatment for these types of patients, the orthodontist, surgeon, and restorative dentist must collaborate and plan the treatment precisely so the implants will not only be in the proper position for the orthodontist but, more important, so they will also be in the correct position for adequate restoration of the patient's dentition after the orthodontic treatment has been completed.

References

1. Turley P, Shapiro P, Moffett B. The loading of bioglass-coated aluminum oxide implants to produce sutural expansion of the maxillary complex in the pigtail monkey. Arch Oral Biol 1980;25:459–464.

2. Smalley W, Shapiro P, Hohl T, et al. Osseointegrated titanium implants for maxillofacial protraction in monkeys. Am J Orthod Dentofac Orthop 1988;94:285–295.

3. Gray J, Steen M, King G, et al. Studies on the efficacy of implants as orthodontic anchorage. Am J Orthod 1983;83:311–317.

4. Douglas J, Killinay D. Dental implants used as orthodontic anchorage. J Oral Implantol 1988;13:28–38.

5. Kokich V. Managing complex orthodontic problems: The use of implants for anchorage. Semin Orthod 1996;2:153–160.

6. Roberts WE, Helm F, Marshall K, et al. Rigid endosseous implants for orthodontic and orthopedic anchorage. Angle Orthod 1989;59:247–255.

7. Roberts WE, Marshall K, Mozsary P. Rigid endosseous implant used as anchorage to protract molars and close an atrophic extraction site. Angle Orthod 1990;60:135–152.

8. Block M, Hoffman D. A new device for absolute anchorage for orthodontics. Am J Orthod Dentofac Orthop 1995;107:251–258.

9. Smalley W. Implants for orthodontic tooth movement: Determining implant location and orientation. J Esthet Dent 1995;7:62–72.

10. Smalley W, Blanco A. Implants for tooth movement: A fabrication and placement technique for provisional restorations. J Esthet Dent 1995;7:150–154.

11. Roberts WE, Smith R, Zilberman Y, et al. Osseous adaptation to continuous loading of rigid endosseous implants. Am J Orthod 1984;86:95–111.

3 | Clinical and Laboratory Procedures for Implant Anchorage in Partially Edentulous Dentitions

Ward M. Smalley, DDS, MSD

The use of osseointegrated endosseous implants for orthodontic anchorage can be invaluable for correcting malocclusions in adult patients who lack adequate toothborne anchorage. This is especially true in partially edentulous patients with multiple missing teeth. Since most partially edentulous patients need orthodontic correction, they may benefit from the use of implant anchorage. The absence of teeth decreases the amount of anchorage available, often making correction of malocclusions in partially edentulous patients difficult if not impossible. Endosseous implants can supplant toothborne anchorage and provide stable and efficient skeletal anchorage for the movement of teeth[1-22] and facial bones.[3,23] The implants can also provide support for prosthetic replacement of missing teeth during and after the course of orthodontic treatment.

Implants are usually placed prior to the start of orthodontic treatment, which can be difficult because the postorthodontic position of existing teeth needs to be determined beforehand. The location and orientation of the implants depend on the final position of the teeth.[24] Placement of implants without knowing the final position of the teeth will invariably compromise the end result by not allowing the teeth to be optimally positioned for proper correction of the malocclusion. Without proper tooth position, prosthetic replacement of the missing teeth will be compromised as well.

Requirements

An orthodontic setup on dental casts is required to determine the postorthodontic position of the teeth. The maxillary and mandibular casts must be accurately related to one another. Hand-held orthodontic casts may be used in simple cases involving a few missing teeth; however, articulated casts provide a more accurate spatial relationship

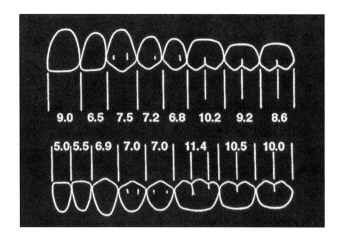

Fig 3-1 Average mesiodistal width of natural teeth. (From Reynolds[25]; reprinted with permission.)

of the teeth. Articulated casts are essential for orthodontic setups when multiple teeth are missing, especially when the number of teeth missing do not allow hand-held casts to relate accurately or when changes in occlusal vertical dimension are anticipated. Reference lines may be drawn on the casts at selected sites prior to sectioning of the teeth to assist in evaluating changes in tooth position.

The orthodontic setup must represent not only tooth movement that is achievable through orthodontic treatment, but also any limitations of tooth movement that may exist. Limitations of tooth movement are usually the result of insufficient toothborne anchorage or inadequate supporting alveolar bone. Most limitations associated with deficiencies in toothborne anchorage are easily overcome using implant anchorage, while those related to inadequacies of supporting bone may indeed restrict tooth movement unless the bony relationships are altered through augmentation procedures or orthognathic surgery. An orthodontist, who is aware of the limitations related to tooth movement, should therefore be the one to complete the orthodontic setup; a laboratory technician or another dental specialist usually has no knowledge of these limitations.

Besides showing the realistic and desired position of the existing teeth, the orthodontic setup should establish spaces for optimal replacement of missing teeth, usually corresponding to the sizes of the natural teeth that are missing (Fig 3-1).[25,26] Spaces that do not represent the sizes of natural teeth compromise the prosthetic replacement of any missing teeth. The orthodontist needs to be aware of the prosthetic requirements of partially edentulous patients. Since most orthodontists have had little if any training in these requirements, management of these patients requires an interdisciplinary approach to treatment. The restorative-prosthetic dentist should confirm the acceptability of spaces established on the orthodontic setup casts.

Sometimes it is more appropriate to replace a missing molar with a premolar, especially if a standard-sized implant will be used to support the prosthetic tooth. A premolar substitution for a missing molar is acceptable and often advantageous for several reasons. Because of resorption, the edentulous ridge in the area of a missing molar is often only wide enough for a standard-sized implant (about 4 mm in diameter). Since a standard-sized implant is about the size of a premolar root (mesiodistally), it is more appropriate to have a premolar-sized rather than a molar-sized replacement tooth on a standard-sized implant. In addition, this establishes a more favorable distribution of forces to the implant and produces a better emergence profile. Replacement of multiple missing posterior teeth in the same quadrant with multiple premolar-sized prosthetic teeth also is acceptable, especially if the available bone is only wide enough for standard-sized implants. The resulting posterior occlusion with a cusp fossa or cusp embrasure relationship is acceptable without compromising the functional, esthetic, and hygienic needs of the patient.

After the orthodontic setup has been completed and acceptable spaces have been established for the missing teeth, the restorative-prosthetic dentist or laboratory technician can wax the planned prosthetic teeth to the exact size and shape of the teeth to be replaced. For posterior tooth replacement, wax teeth are preferred over denture teeth because posterior denture teeth usually are smaller than the natural teeth they replace. Wax teeth also are less expensive and are easier to place on dental casts and modify to the size and shape needed. Use of denture teeth for anterior tooth replacement is acceptable because they correspond to the size and shape of natural teeth. The wax prosthetic teeth will determine the location of the implants and serve to fabricate provisional implant restorations used during orthodontic treatment as well as definitive implant restorations placed after orthodontic treatment has been completed.

The location of the implants needs to be transferred to a set of casts that reflect the existing tooth positions. This process will determine whether any malpositioned teeth exist at desired implant sites, in which case placement of implants at these sites would occur after completion of orthodontic treatment. The wax prosthetic teeth also need to be accurately transferred to casts of the malpositioned teeth to facilitate fabrication of an implant placement guide (stent) and provisional implant restorations after placement and osseointegration of the implants have occurred. The implant placement guide will facilitate the accurate placement of implants.[27–37]

Identical casts are required for the transfer process to be accurate. Without identical casts, it is impossible to transfer the established relationships from one set of casts to another; therefore, the original casts should be accurately duplicated a minimum of three times. If an articulator is being used, two sets of the casts should be cross-mounted on the articulator. The first set should be used for the orthodontic setup of the existing malpositioned teeth and diagnostic waxing of the planned prosthetic teeth, and the second set will provide a baseline representation of the pretreatment tooth position for comparison with the setup casts. One set of unmounted casts is used to produce a set of composite casts representing the position of both the malpositioned natural teeth and the prosthetic teeth that will be placed prior to orthodontic treatment. This set of composite casts will facilitate fabrication of radiographic guides to assess available bone relative to planned implant sites, implant placement guides, and provisional implant restorations used during orthodontic treatment.

Technique

Duplication of casts

The original set of dental casts is usually produced from alginate impressions of the patient's teeth. Before pouring the impression with dental stone, it is helpful to block out the lingual area of the lower impression with additional alginate material so as to establish a smooth surface in this region of the mandibular cast, absent of undercuts that do not represent anatomical structures. This step produces an appropriate reference area on the mandibular cast for use during the transfer process. The palatal region of the maxillary cast will serve as a reference area for this purpose as well. Placement of dimples or bumps in these reference areas prior to duplication of the casts is recommended to increase the accuracy and stability of templates and registrations used during the transfer process. If the mandibular cast has lingual undercuts that may make the transfer process difficult and potentially

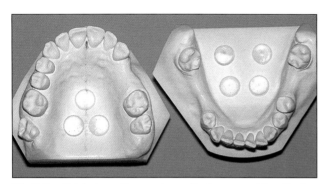

Fig 3-2a Original maxillary and mandibular casts with self-adhesive vinyl pads placed prior to duplication. Missing are maxillary second molars and left premolars and mandibular first and second molars and right second premolar.

Fig 3-2b Biostar pressure-molding machine.

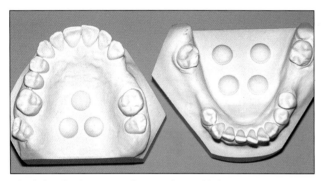

Fig 3-2c Duplicate maxillary and mandibular stone casts with bumps produced from molded forms of original casts.

inaccurate, then the addition of dimples or bumps is essential. Dimples are prepared in the cast using a large round-ended laboratory bur, whereas bumps are created by placing self-adhesive vinyl pads (Shepard Hardware) at desired locations on the reference areas of the casts (Fig 3-2a). Bumps are preferred over dimples because they are easier to place and do not permanently alter the original casts. Two or more bumps or dimples are recommended.

Duplication of the original casts is best accomplished using some type of molding machine. A vacuum-forming machine is acceptable, but a Biostar pressure-molding machine (Great Lakes Orthodontics) is preferred because undesirable undercuts on the dental casts can be blocked out with

metal beads supplied by the manufacturer (Fig 3-2b). Elimination of significant undercuts allows the molded material to be easily removed from the casts. Impression materials also may be used, although alginate impression material is not recommended because it may distort or tear during separation from the casts or when poured more than once. Using the Biostar machine, 3-mm mouthguard material (Great Lakes Orthodontics) is molded around each original cast. The molded forms are poured at least three times to obtain the recommended number of duplicate casts. Regardless of the method of duplication, the duplicated casts should be carefully checked to ensure accuracy of reproduction (Fig 3-2c).

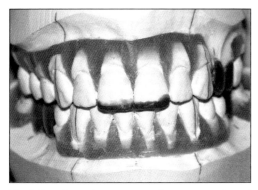

Fig 3-3a Orthodontic setup of existing teeth and diagnostic waxing of prosthetic teeth.

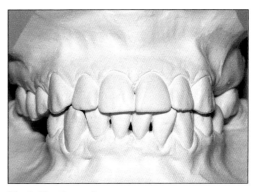

Fig 3-3b Original casts.

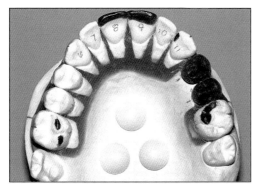

Fig 3-3c Occlusal view of maxillary orthodontic setup and diagnostic waxing of prosthetic teeth. Anterior teeth were retracted to decrease incisor proclination. Red marks indicate occlusal adjustment of teeth.

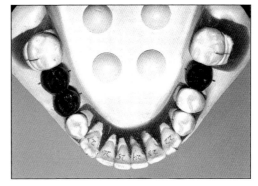

Fig 3-3d Occlusal view of mandibular orthodontic setup and diagnostic waxing of prosthetic teeth with premolar replacement of missing first molars. Anterior teeth were retracted to allow retraction of maxillary anterior teeth. Implant anchorage will be used to retract teeth.

Determination of Implant Locations

Once the orthodontic setup and diagnostic waxing of the prosthetic teeth have been completed, implant location can be determined (Fig 3-3) and then transferred to the unmounted set of duplicate casts. First, an outline of each wax tooth is drawn with a colored pencil on the orthodontic setup–diagnostic waxing casts at the juncture where the wax tooth and stone cast meet (Figs 3-4). Silicone registrations are made of the occlusal/incisal and lingual surfaces of the wax teeth and the palatal and lingual reference areas of the respective casts (Fig 3-5a). The registrations will facilitate the transfer of the wax prosthetic teeth to the unmounted duplicate original casts; polyvinylsiloxane putty impression material (Reprosil, LD Caulk, Dentsply, or Express STD, 3M Dental)

works well for this purpose. After the material has set, the silicone registrations are removed from the casts (Fig 3-5b) and then the wax prosthetic teeth are removed. The center of each implant is marked within the outlines of the prosthetic teeth (Figs 3-6a and 3-6b) to determine the location of each implant on the orthodontic setup casts; any deficiencies of the edentulous ridge at desired implant locations will be apparent at this time. The silicone registrations are then trimmed to fit only over the wax prosthetic teeth and the respective reference areas of each cast; any portion of the silicone registration associated with the orthodontic setup is cut away with a sharp Bard-Parker blade and discarded (Figs 3-6c and 3-6d). This step is easy because the line of demarcation between the stone cast and the waxed area of the orthodontic setup is recorded in the silicone registration. Removal of

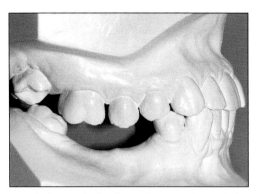 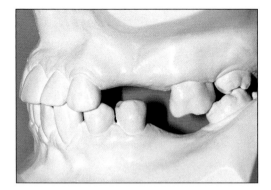

Figs 3-4a and 3-4b Original casts, right and left sides.

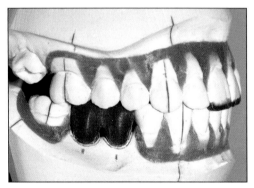 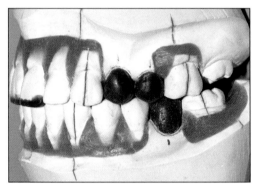

Figs 3-4c and 3-4d Right and left lateral views of orthodontic setup and diagnostic waxing of prosthetic teeth with blue reference lines to assess mesiodistal changes in tooth position (placed on casts prior to sectioning of teeth) and red lines drawn around wax prosthetic teeth at juncture of wax and stone cast. Maxillary third molar was not moved in setup for reference but would be moved into second molar position during orthodontic treatment.

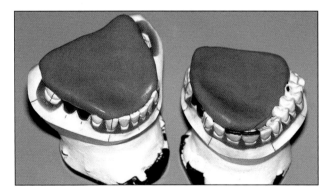 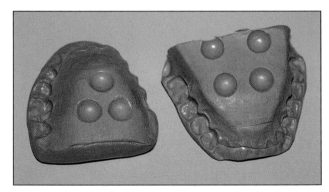

Fig 3-5a Silicone registrations of wax prosthetic teeth and reference areas of orthodontic setup casts.

Fig 3-5b Silicone registrations removed from orthodontic setup casts. Note recording of bumps in registrations for accurate positioning of registrations on duplicate original casts.

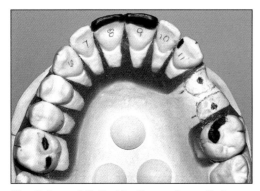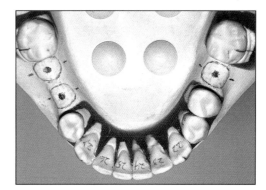

Figs 3-6a and 3-6b Maxillary and mandibular setup casts with wax prosthetic teeth removed and location of implants marked within outline of prosthetic teeth (usually at center).

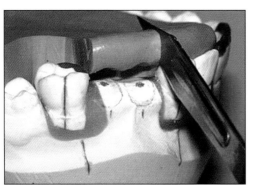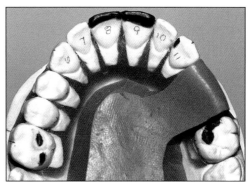

Fig 3-6c Modification of silicone registration to remove portions associated with orthodontic setup of existing teeth.

Fig 3-6d Modified silicone registration accurately placed on maxillary setup cast. Silicone registration no longer contacts any portion of cast associated with orthodontic setup of existing teeth.

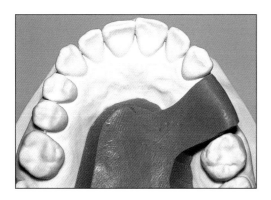

Fig 3-6e Modified silicone registration accurately placed on duplicate original cast. Reference area facilitates accurate positioning of the registration on the cast.

this portion will allow each silicone registration to be accurately placed on the duplicate original casts of the malpositioned teeth because the lingual and palatal reference areas of each respective cast are identical (Fig 3-6e).

The next step is to transfer the location of each implant to the set of unmounted duplicate original casts of the malpositioned teeth. Clear templates are first fabricated on the casts to facilitate transfer of the implant locations. The templates are made

Fig 3-7a Duplicate unmounted maxillary cast positioned in metal beads of Biostar pressure-molding machine for fabrication of transfer template.

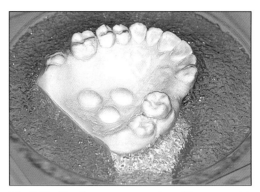

Fig 3-7b Duplicate unmounted maxillary cast with molded 0.5 mm clear Bioacryl II resin material for transfer template.

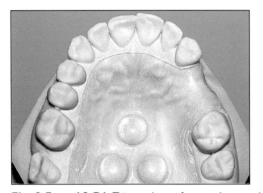

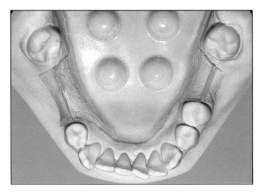

Figs 3-7c and 3-7d Trimmed transfer templates molded on maxillary and mandibular duplicate original casts. Templates contact casts only in palatal and lingual reference areas and over edentulous areas.

by molding 0.5 mm Bioacryl II acrylic material (Great Lakes Orthodontics) onto the casts using the Biostar pressure-molding machine (Figs 3-7a and 3-7b). Each molded template is trimmed with scissors to fit over only the reference and edentulous areas of the respective casts (Figs 3-7c and 3-7d). The templates are trimmed further to fit over the edentulous areas of the orthodontic setup casts by superimposing each one with the corresponding silicone registration (Figs 3-8a to 3-8c). This usu-

ally is required because the edentulous areas on the setup casts may be narrower than on the original casts from tooth movement determined by the setup (Figs 3-9a and 3-9b). With each template positioned on the orthodontic setup casts, implant locations are transferred by marking the template with a permanent-marking pen (Figs 3-9c to 3-9e). The templates are removed from the casts, and holes about 2 mm in diameter are drilled in each template at the sites marked. Afterward, the tem-

Fig 3-8a Superimposition of maxillary template with corresponding silicone registration to facilitate further trimming of template to fit on orthodontic setup cast.

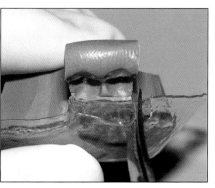

Fig 3-8b Section of transfer template superimposed on silicone registration being trimmed with scissors to fit in area of planned prosthetic teeth.

Fig 3-8c Trimmed maxillary transfer template superimposed on silicone registration.

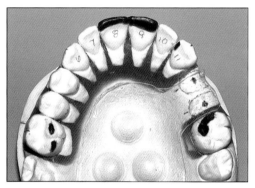

Fig 3-9a Transfer template positioned on maxillary orthodontic setup cast in preparation for transferring location of implants.

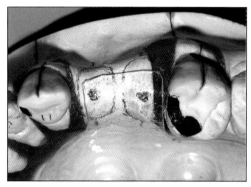

Fig 3-9b Section of transfer template in place on maxillary orthodontic setup cast to transfer location of implants. Note that implant location in area of second premolar may be too close to original position of first molar. Transfer of implant location to duplicate original cast of malpositioned teeth will determine whether desired implant location and position of first molar are too close to permit placement of implant prior to orthodontic treatment.

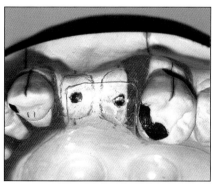

Fig 3-9c Section of transfer template in place on maxillary orthodontic setup cast with black dots marked to transfer the implant locations to the template.

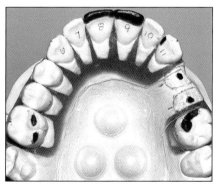

Figs 3-9d and 3-9e Maxillary and mandibular setup casts with implant locations marked on transfer templates.

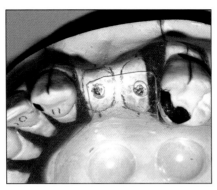

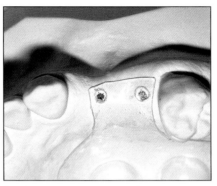

Fig 3-10a Section of transfer template on maxillary setup cast with holes prepared at each implant site to check accuracy of hole preparation.

Fig 3-10b Section of transfer template on duplicate maxillary original cast with implant locations transferred to the initial cast with a colored pencil through the prepared holes in the templates. The bumps in the reference area of the cast facilitate accurate positioning of the transfer template. Note that the transferred implant location in the area of the second premolar appears to be too close to the first molar. A final determination will be made through radiographic assessment of the area.

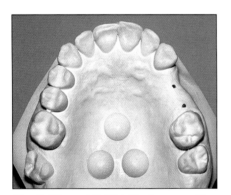

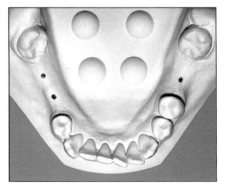

Figs 3-10c and 3-10d Duplicate maxillary and mandibular original casts with transferred implant locations.

plates are placed back on the setup casts to check the accuracy of the prepared holes (Fig 3-10a). The templates are then placed on the duplicate original casts for transferral of the implant locations. A colored pencil is used to mark each location through the holes prepared in the transfer templates (Figs 3-10b to 3-10d). As this technique implies, the im-

plant locations are prosthetically rather than surgically determined. If anatomic limitations exist at implant sites, the sites should be altered or augmented prior to implant placement. Such limitations might include existing teeth in close proximity to implant sites as determined by the orthodontic setup and diagnostic waxing of the

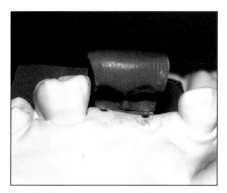
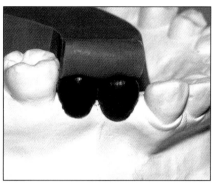
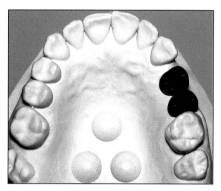

Fig 3-11a Section of duplicate maxillary original cast marked with implant locations with silicone registration in place to transfer wax prosthetic teeth previously removed from orthodontic setup cast.

Fig 3-11b Placement of wax prosthetic teeth on section of duplicate maxillary original cast using silicone registration for accurate orientation.

Fig 3-11c Duplicate maxillary original cast with wax prosthetic teeth attached.

prosthetic teeth. Placement of implants at these locations will have to wait until after the involved teeth have been moved away from the area as dictated by the orthodontic setup. Alternatively, the need for an implant at that site may be eliminated by moving the involved teeth into the site. Implants should not be placed in unacceptable or unplanned sites, as they would interfere with correction of the malocclusion and compromise prosthetic replacement of missing teeth in terms of function, parafunction, esthetics, and oral hygiene.

To complete the transfer process, the wax replacement teeth from the orthodontic setup casts are placed on the unmounted duplicate original casts marked with the implant locations. The silicone registrations made on the setup casts are used for accurate positioning of these teeth (Figs 3-11a to 3-11c). If significant lingual undercuts exist on the mandibular cast, the silicone registration can be cut in half to facilitate placement and removal (Figs 3-12a and 3-12b). The prosthetic teeth are attached by heating the wax at the area of contact with the casts. Additional wax may be needed to fill in any deficient areas. After the wax has cooled, the silicone registrations are removed from the casts. Dimples or bumps placed in the reference area of the original mandibular cast prior to

duplication will ensure accurate placement of the sectioned registrations. In esthetic areas, the facial/buccal outline of each wax tooth is drawn on the casts at the juncture of the wax and stone to mark the anticipated level of marginal gingiva. The lines are similar to those drawn on the orthodontic setup–diagnostic waxing casts to mark the outline of the prosthetic teeth, except that they do not extend lingually around the wax teeth. These reference lines will be used in conjunction with the implant placement guide to establish proper depth of implant placement. The casts are then duplicated by taking an impression using silicone impression material, which is preferred over alginate to allow for accurate multiple pours (Fig 3-13a). The impressions should be poured in dental stone. As stated earlier, the composite casts produced by this method reflect the original position of the patient's natural teeth as well as the position of the planned prosthetic teeth (Figs 3-13b and 3-13c). Composite casts facilitate the fabrication of (1) radiopaque guides for radiographic assessment of planned implant sites, (2) implant placement guides, (3) registration guides for recording the location of each implant during implant-placement surgery, and (4) provisional implant restorations during orthodontic treatment.

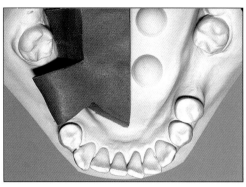

Fig 3-12a Duplicate mandibular cast with silicone registration cut in half to facilitate placement of wax prosthetic teeth and subsequent removal of registration. The bumps allow accurate placement of the sectioned silicone registration.

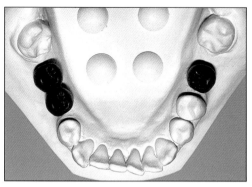

Fig 3-12b Duplicate mandibular original cast with wax prosthetic teeth attached.

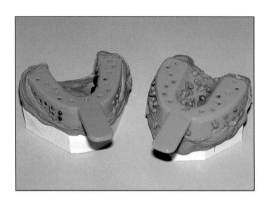

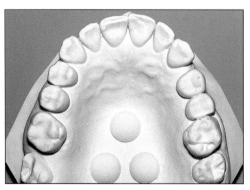

Fig 3-13a Polyvinylsiloxane impressions of duplicate original casts with attached wax prosthetic teeth.

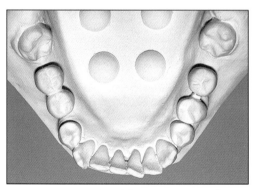

Figs 3-13b and 3-13c Maxillary and mandibular composite stone casts produced from impression of duplicate original casts with wax prosthetic teeth attached.

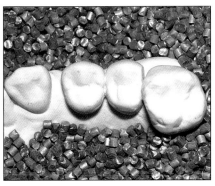

Fig 3-14a Maxillary composite cast positioned in metal beads on Biostar pressure-molding machine for fabrication of preliminary radiographic guide.

Fig 3-14b Section of maxillary composite cast positioned in metal beads on Biostar machine. Metal beads are positioned around cast to block out significant undercuts and allow easy removal of the molded form.

Fig 3-14c Maxillary composite cast with molded 1.0 mm Bioacryl II splint material fabricated on Biostar machine.

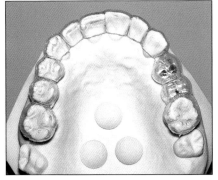

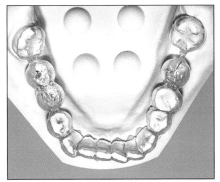

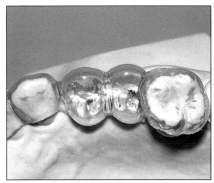

Figs 3-14d and 3-14e Duplicate maxillary and mandibular original casts with marked implant locations and trimmed Bioacryl molded forms (preliminary radiographic guides). The guides have been trimmed to include the molded forms of the prosthetic teeth and the occlusal, incisal, and lingual surfaces (coronal to the height of contour) of the existing teeth.

Fig 3-14f Section of maxillary preliminary radiographic guide on duplicate maxillary original cast with marked implant locations.

Radiographic guides

To fabricate the radiopaque guides, 1.0 mm of clear splint Bioacryl II acrylic material is molded over each composite cast on the Biostar machine. Significant undercuts apical to the teeth are first blocked out with metal beads (Figs 3-14a to 3-14c). The molded Bioacryl forms are trimmed back with a laboratory bur to include only the prosthetic teeth and the occlusal, incisal, and lingual surfaces (coronal to height of contour) of the existing natural teeth. These preliminary guides are then placed on their respective duplicate original casts to confirm proper fit (Figs 3-14d to 3-14f). Once proper fit has been confirmed, the preliminary guides are removed to block out any proximal undercuts on the adjacent natural teeth apical to the proximal contact areas with wax, and a separating medium is applied to the casts.

The preliminary guides are again placed on the duplicate original casts for injection of radiopaque acrylic resin into the molded forms of the prosthetic teeth. Clear orthodontic acrylic resin polymer (LD Caulk) is mixed with diatrizoate sodium powder (Hypaque, Nycomed) in a ratio of about 2:1 by volume. Clear monomer is added to the mixture in a ratio of 1:2 by volume, mixed, and injected into the molded forms using a plastic syringe (Monoject, Sherwood Medical) (Figs 3-15a and 3-15b). Any excess acrylic resin extending beyond the contours

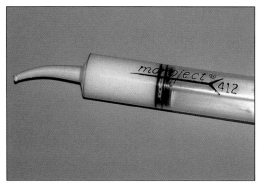

Fig 3-15a Monoject syringe with radiopaque autopolymerizing acrylic resin.

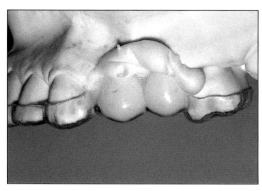

Fig 3-15b Section of maxillary radiographic guide with radiopaque autopolymerizing acrylic resin injected into molded forms of prosthetic teeth.

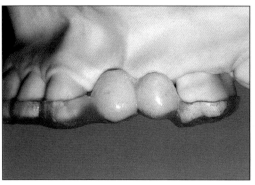

Fig 3-15c Section of maxillary radiographic guide with excess radiopaque acrylic resin removed.

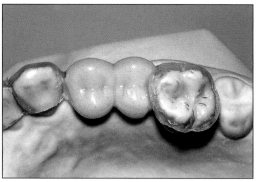

Fig 3-15d Section of maxillary radiographic guide (occlusal view) with excess radiopaque acrylic resin removed prior to reinforcement with clear autopolymerizing acrylic resin.

of the prosthetic teeth may be removed with a sharp instrument. The guides are then placed in a pressure container with warm water until cured. After curing they are removed from the casts, and a laboratory bur is used to remove any remaining excess resin extending beyond the contours of the prosthetic teeth (Figs 3-15c and 3-15d). The guides are reinforced by placing them on their respective casts and adding clear autopolymerizing acrylic resin to the lingual surfaces of the radiopaque prosthetic teeth and to the occlusal, incisal, and lingual surfaces of the guides supported by the existing natural teeth (Figs 3-15e and 3-15f). The guides are again placed in the pressure container for curing of the added resin. After fabrication of the radiopaque guides is complete, they are disinfected and placed in the patient's mouth to confirm proper fit.

The patient is then referred for appropriate radiographic assessment of the planned implant sites. Computed tomography (CT) is preferred, especially for multiple implants (Figs 3-16a to 3-16d)[38–42]; otherwise, linear tomography is acceptable. Ridge mapping may also be used to assess the topography of alveolar bone in cross section at planned implant sites[43,44]; this method of assessment is relatively easy, especially in the maxillary arch, and requires no special equipment. After the appropriate area is anesthetized with a local anesthetic, measurements of the soft tissue thickness buccal/facial and palatal/lingual to the underlying bone at each implant site are obtained by sounding down to bone with a periodontal probe (Fig 3-17). The recorded measurements are transferred to duplicate casts of the patient's teeth that have been

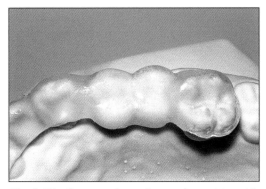

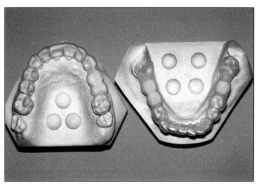

Fig 3-15e Section of maxillary radiographic guide (occlusal view) reinforced with clear autopolymerizing acrylic resin.

Fig 3-15f Maxillary and mandibular radiographic guides on their respective casts.

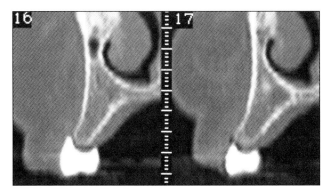

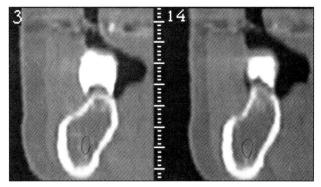

Figs 3-16a and 3-16b Computed tomograph (cross-sectional view) showing morphology of bone and image of radiopaque prosthetic tooth in area of missing maxillary first premolar *(left)* and mandibular left first molar *(right)* (view from posterior).

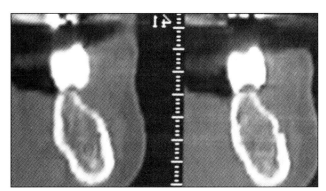

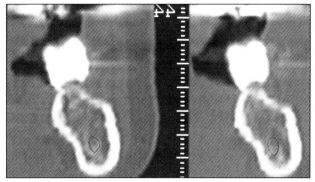

Figs 3-16c and 3-16d Computed tomograph (cross-sectional view) showing morphology of bone and image of radiopaque prosthetic tooth in area of missing mandibular right second premolar *(left)* and mandibular right first molar *(right)* (view from posterior).

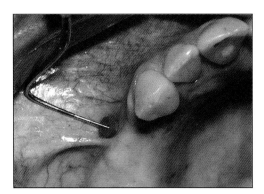 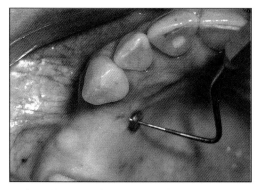

Figs 3-17a and 3-17b Mapping of edentulous ridge in area of maxillary right first premolar. Periodontal probe is used to assess topography of underlying alveolar bone by measuring depth of soft tissue buccal *(left)* and palatal *(right)* to edentulous ridge at site.

trimmed to expose the edentulous ridge in cross section at each planned implant site. A dot is marked on the trimmed surface of the cast for each measurement of soft tissue thickness to bone (Fig 3-18a). A line connecting the marked dots is drawn on the cast to indicate the topography of the bony ridge (Figs 3-18b and 3-18c).

Once acceptable CT scans, tomograms, or ridge maps have been obtained, the radiographic guide is modified for conventional radiographic assessment. The desired mesiodistal angulation of the implants is determined first. This is accomplished by removing the buccal or facial half of each acrylic resin radiopaque prosthetic tooth. Resin is removed parallel to the long axis of the tooth until the reduced surface bisects the mark on the cast that indicates the center of each implant to be placed (Figs 3-19a to 3-19c). A segment of round orthodontic wire (0.036 inch or larger stainless steel wire is preferred) is attached with sticky wax to the reduced surfaces of each prosthetic tooth (Fig 3-20a). The orientation of the wires should correspond to the desired mesiodistal angulation of the implants, which can be assessed based on existing radiographs and the teeth on the cast. To prevent displacement during exposure of radiographs, the wires should not extend beyond the occlusal/incisal surfaces of the guides. The guides, with attached wires, are disinfected and placed in

the patient's mouth on the respective teeth. Periapical and panoramic radiographs of the sites are exposed; the wires indicate the estimated mesiodistal angulation of the implants (Fig 3-20b). If the angulation of any of the wires is inappropriate, the guide is removed from the patient's mouth, and change in the desired angulation of the wires is made by heating the sticky wax. The guide is again placed in the patient's mouth for additional radiographs. This process is repeated until the desired angulation of all implants is confirmed.

An alternative method for establishing proper angulation that may be preferable is to position a metal orientation slot in the guides for each implant to be placed (Fig 3-21a). Metal slots also will be used to direct the surgical drill during implant placement after radiographic assessment of each implant site has been completed and the definitive implant placement guides have been fabricated. They can be custom fabricated from stainless steel needle stock tubing or purchased through a vender. To position the metal slot, a groove larger than the metal slot is prepared in the acrylic resin of the guides at each implant site. Holes are prepared through the lingual surface of each groove to accommodate the lingual lugs used to secure the position of the slot relative to the guide (Figs 3-21b and 3-21c). Care must be taken not to prepare excessively large holes that could lead to fracture of the

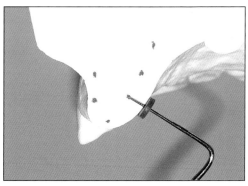

Fig 3-18a Transfer of recorded soft tissue depths to the sectioned duplicate original cast at the planned implant site by marking a dot on the cast with a colored pencil at each measured site.

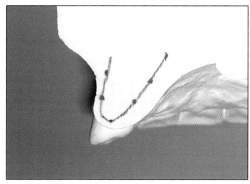

Fig 3-18b Line is drawn on cast by connecting recorded dots. Outline on cast reflects topography of underlying alveolar bone in area.

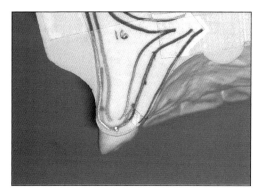

Fig 3-18c Ridge-mapped cast in area of missing maxillary left first premolar with superimposed tracing of cross-sectional CT scan of planned implant site showing accuracy of ridge mapping technique.

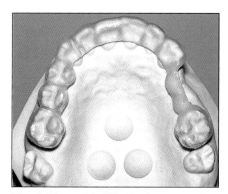

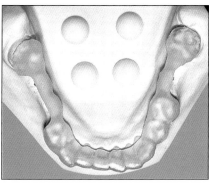

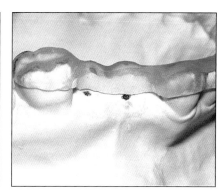

Figs 3-19a and 3-19b Duplicate maxillary and mandibular original casts with preliminary implant placement guides. Buccal half of acrylic resin in area of prosthetic teeth has been removed.

Fig 3-19c Section of maxillary preliminary implant placement guide with buccal half of acrylic resin removed.

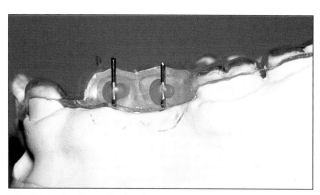

Fig 3-20a Radiographic/preliminary implant placement guide of another patient with segments of round stainless steel wire placed to assess the mesiodistal angulation of planned implant placement.

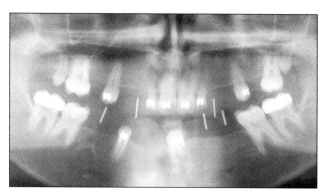

Fig 3-20b Panoramic radiograph of radiographic/preliminary implant placement guide with wire segments attached and placed intraorally. Note planned mesiodistal angulation of implants reflected by images of wire segments.

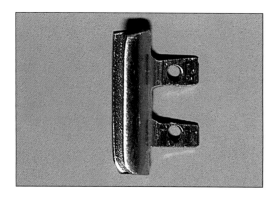

Fig 3-21a Custom-fabricated metal slot to be placed in implant placement guide for each implant to be placed. Metal slot allows radiographic assessment of implant angulation and orientation of surgical drills during placement of implants.

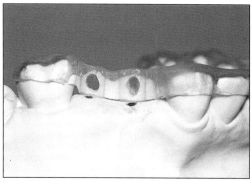

Fig 3-21b Section of maxillary radiographic/preliminary implant placement guide with grooves prepared for placement of metal slots. Holes have been prepared through the lingual surface of each groove for the attachment of the metal slots.

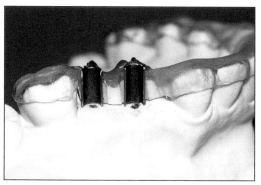

Fig 3-21c Section of maxillary radiographic/preliminary implant placement guide with metal slots placed in the prepared grooves (buccal view).

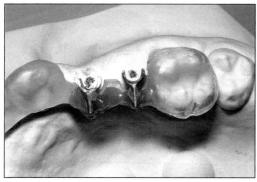

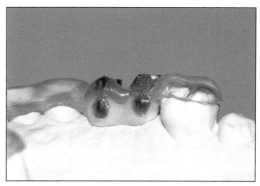

Fig 3-21d Section of maxillary radiographic/preliminary implant placement guide with metal slots placed in the prepared grooves (occlusal view). Sticky wax has been added to temporarily secure the metal slots in place.

Fig 3-21e Section of maxillary radiographic/preliminary implant placement guide with metal slots temporarily secured in place with sticky wax (lingual view).

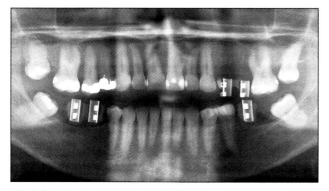

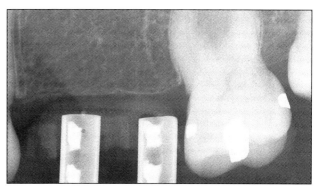

Fig 3-21f Panoramic radiograph of radiographic/preliminary implant placement guide with metal slots attached and placed intraorally. Note planned mesiodistal angulation of implants reflected by images of metal slots.

Fig 3-21g Periapical radiograph of radiographic/preliminary implant placement guide with metal slots attached and placed intraorally. Note planned mesiodistal angulation of implants reflected by images of metal slots. Periapical radiographs can clarify any apparent disparities in angulation of metal slots occasionally seen in panoramic radiographs as a result of distortion.

guides. The lugs are initially attached to the guide with sticky wax in a manner similar to that for attaching orthodontic wires in the previously described method (Figs 3-21d and 3-21e). The guides, with attached metal slots, are then disinfected and placed in the patient's mouth for radiographic assessment of each implant site. Radiographic images of the metal slots should indicate the desired mesiodistal orientation of the implants to be placed (Figs 3-21f and 3-21g). Changes can be made by heating the sticky wax holding the slot, changing the angulation, and taking another radiograph to confirm proper orientation. It should be noted that this is not necessarily the procedure recommended by suppliers of commercially available metal slots or tubes, but it is preferred.

Implant placement guides

After the correct mesiodistal orientation of the implants has been determined, the radiographic guide is converted to an implant placement guide. Orientation grooves for the surgical drills on the buccal/facial side of the implant placement guide give the surgeon good access to the surgical sites and the ability to change the buccolingual angle of the drill, if necessary, to place each implant within the bony alveolus; however, this can be a disadvantage if the drill is angled too much away from the guide. Determination of the buccolingual orientation of the grooves presurgically will eliminate this potential problem. If wires were used to determine the mesiodistal angulation of implant placement,

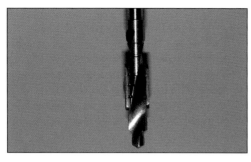

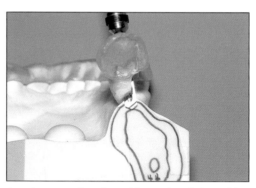

Fig 3-22a Hybrid 3-mm–2-mm drill (Deplaque) seated in custom-fabricated 3-mm metal slot for initial implant site preparation.

Figs 3-22b and 3-22c Maxillary and mandibular casts sectioned across edentulous ridge at site of planned implant with tracing of cross-sectional CT image of bony ridge (and underlying mapping of ridge for demonstration purposes only) attached to cast for determining buccolingual orientation of drill groove or slot. Surgical drill is placed in the guide at the site and angled to direct the drill within the center of the bony ridge.

the position of each wire is recorded. The occlusal/incisal and apical surfaces of each prosthetic tooth are marked with a fine, permanent-marking pen by drawing a line directly lingual to the end of each wire. The wires are then removed, and grooves are prepared in the guides with the same orientation as the wires. The lines aid in maintaining this orientation by being centered in the depth of each groove. The drill grooves may be 2 mm in diameter or greater, depending on the preferences of the surgeon and the implant system being used.

An alternative and preferred method, using prefabricated metal slots previously described, avoids the need to cut grooves for the surgical drills and the potential inaccuracies that can occur during the removal of wires and the cutting of grooves. Since the grooves are cut in acrylic resin, it is relatively easy to make the grooves larger than the drill used for preparing the implant site, which can lead to undesirable implant angulation. Metal slots ensure more accurate placement of implants. A 3-mm slot

is preferred over a 2-mm slot to allow larger drills to be used directly with the implant placement guides. To avoid the problem of centering a 2-mm twist drill in a 3-mm groove or slot, a stepped 3-mm–2-mm twist drill (Deplaque) may be used (Fig 3-22a).

The buccolingual angulation of each implant can be determined prior to implant surgery as well. Ridge-mapped casts or duplicate original casts with tracings of the cross-sectional CT or tomographic images at each implant site (which may require additional casts depending on the number of implants to be placed) are useful for this purpose. Similar to ridge-mapped casts, the casts with tracings provide a view of the bony topography at planned implant sites. The buccolingual angulation of each prepared groove or metal slot can be assessed by placing a surgical drill in the groove or metal slot of the implant placement guide and projecting it apical to the guide onto the traced or mapped alveolar bone (Fig 3-22b and 3-22c). If the angulation of the im-

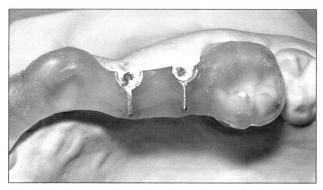

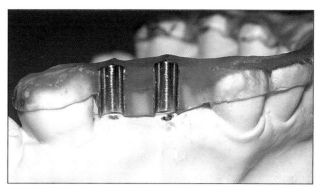

Fig 3-23a Section of completed maxillary implant placement guide (occlusal view). Additional acrylic resin has been placed around the metal slots, and the sticky wax used to temporarily secure the metal slot has been replaced with acrylic resin.

Fig 3-23b Section of completed maxillary implant placement guide (buccal view). Additional acrylic resin has been placed around the metal slots, and the sticky wax used to temporarily secure the metal slot has been replaced with acrylic resin.

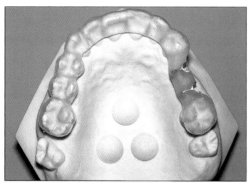

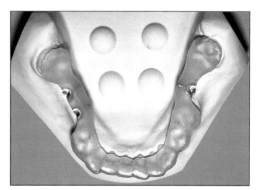

Figs 3-23c and 3-23d Completed maxillary and mandibular implant placement guides.

plant drill is not centered within the bony ridge, the angulation of the resin groove or metal slot is changed. The resin groove is changed by preparing each groove deeper at the coronal or apical end of the implant placement guide, depending on the desired change in angulation of the groove. The angulation of the metal slot is changed by heating the sticky wax used to temporarily position the metal slot, without changing its mesiodistal orientation, and tipping it to accommodate the drill orientation relative to the traced or mapped outline of the alveolar bone on the cast. Once the mesiodistal and buccolingual orientation of each metal slot has been established, the final position is fixed by flowing autopolymerizing acrylic resin or light-cured composite resin between each metal slot and the resin implant guide and curing appropriately. The sticky wax used to temporarily position the metal

slots in the guides is then removed, and additional resin is placed around the lugs to secure the metal slots in the guides (Figs 3-23a to 3-23d).

Finally, reference marks may be placed on the placement guides to assist the surgeon in placing each implant at the proper depth (Fig 3-24a). Depth of implant placement is particularly important in anterior sites where esthetics is involved. Horizontal lines can be drawn on the placement guides with a fine permanent-marking pen lateral to the drill grooves or metal slots/tubes. With the guides on the duplicate original casts on which the buccal/facial outline of each prosthetic tooth has been marked, the distance from each reference line and the outline of each corresponding prosthetic tooth is measured and recorded. To determine the optimal depth for each implant, this measurement is added to the desired distance of the implant head

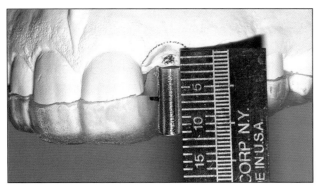

Fig 3-24a Section of an implant placement guide in maxillary left lateral incisor area with reference lines marked for determining desired depth of implant. Measurements can be recorded from the black horizontal reference line or apical end of metal slot.

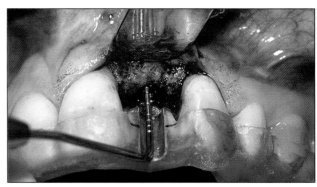

Fig 3-24b Placement of implant in maxillary left lateral incisor area at desired depth using reference marks on guide. Periodontal probe is used to measure desired distance. (Courtesy of Dr Michael Cohen.)

from the preferred level of marginal gingiva for each implant-supported prosthetic tooth. This distance may be recorded directly on the guide for reference during placement of the implant. The surgeon can place the head of each implant at the predetermined depth by measuring from the head of the implant to the reference line on the implant guide (Fig 3-24b). In esthetic areas, the head of the implant should be about 3 mm apical to the desired level of marginal gingiva facial to the prosthetic tooth to allow for the development of appropriate crown contours and emergence profile and the establishment of normal gingival architecture.

The apical end of each drill groove or slot also can serve as the reference point for determining the optimal depth for each implant in lieu of pre-marked reference lines. The coronal end of each groove or slot should not be used for reference, as it may need to be reduced in height to facilitate preparation of an implant site. If the height of the guide needs to be reduced, the reference point will be lost. Reference lines marked in the middle of the guides or at the apical end of each guide groove or slot are unaffected by any reduction in guide height.

The preceding steps allow fabrication of implant placement guides that dictate the location and angulation (mesiodistal and buccolingual) of each implant preparation and subsequent placement of the

implant. The resulting implants are well positioned and parallel to one another. Guides with grooves or slots are preferred over those with tubes for ease of placing the surgical drills in the guides and better visibility of the surgical sites. This is particularly true in posterior areas of the mouth where limited height or access is available. Metal slots in guides are preferred over grooves in acrylic resin because they have less tolerance and further restrict any unintended variability in implant placement. Many surgeons may feel uncomfortable using implant guides that are as restrictive as the ones recommended here. Implant guides that have been fabricated without as much information regarding the position and orientation of implants relative to adjacent teeth and underlying bone have generated this reaction; however, once the surgeon realizes how the recommended guides are developed and the accuracy of implant placement that can be achieved, confidence in using the guides will return. Implants that are well placed will allow subsequent orthodontic and prosthodontic treatment to be easier, more efficient, and more predictable in achieving the desired treatment result.

Implant placement may proceed after fabrication of the surgical placement guides has been completed; the quality and quantity of bone at the implant sites have been assessed; and the size and type of implants to be placed have been deter-

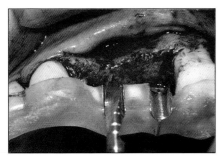 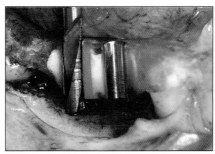 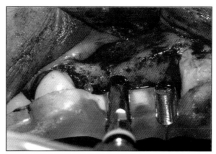

Figs 3-25a and 3-25b Preparation of maxillary and mandibular implant sites with surgical drill placed in one of the metal orientation grooves/slots to direct orientation of drill during implant site preparation. (Courtesy of Dr Michael Cohen.) Hybrid 3-mm–2-mm drill (Deplaque) is being used for initial site preparation.

Figs 3-25c Alignment of larger surgical drill buccal to guide slot during implant site preparation for proper orientation. Implant placement guide is removed lingually without disturbing orientation of larger surgical drill. Drill is then moved over initial hole preparation while desired angulation is maintained. Hole is then enlarged to appropriate size for placement of implant.

mined. It is advisable to place the implant guides in the patient's mouth after disinfection prior to the actual surgical date to make sure they fit and that adequate clearance exists to allow the dental handpiece with surgical drill in place to be properly positioned. It is quite likely that extended-length surgical drills will be needed to facilitate implant site preparation and/or the height of the implant guide will need to be reduced to facilitate the procedure. Excessive reduction in the height of implant guides should be avoided, however, as the resulting drill grooves or slots may be too short to direct proper placement of the implants.

Placement of Implants

During implant site preparation, the implant placement guide is positioned on the appropriate teeth after the bony ridge has been exposed. The surgical drill is positioned in the guide groove or metal slot to prepare the initial hole for each implant (Figs 3-25a and 3-25b). The holes are drilled to the desired depth. It is advisable to confirm the accuracy of the initial holes prepared by taking a periapical and/or panoramic radiograph with the initial drill or guide pin positioned in each hole. Once accurate angulation of the prepared sites has been confirmed, the holes are sequentially enlarged with larger drills according to the size and type of implants being used. The implant placement guide should be repositioned in the patient's mouth to facilitate proper orientation of the larger drills. Although only the initial drill usually fits into the groove or metal slot, larger drills can be aligned next to the guide (Fig 3-25c). Guides with 3-mm grooves or slots, especially in conjunction with a stepped 3-mm–2-mm drill, are preferable. The implant placement guides should be used throughout the surgical procedure to align successive drills, taps, and implants for accurate placement. The guides can be removed lingually without disturbing the orientation of the larger drill. The larger drill is then moved lingually over the initially prepared hole without changing its orientation. Each hole is then enlarged.

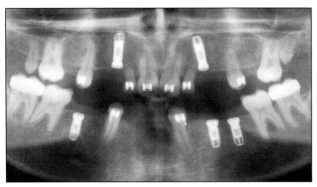

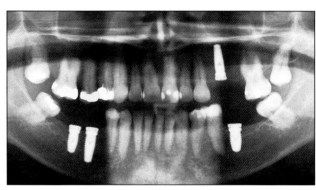

Fig 3-26a Panoramic radiograph showing implants placed prior to orthodontic treatment using implant placement guide with drill grooves prepared in acrylic resin. (Courtesy of Dr Ralph Yuodelis.) Compare with images of *wires* used in preoperative panoramic radiograph (Fig 3-20b).

Fig 3-26b Panoramic radiograph showing implants placed prior to orthodontic treatment using implant placement guide with metal drill slots. (Courtesy of Dr Michael Cohen.) Compare with images of *metal slots* used in preoperative panoramic radiograph (Fig 3-21f).

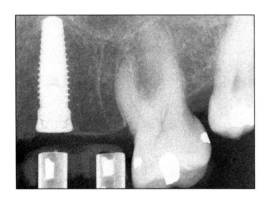

Fig 3-26c Periapical radiograph of implant replacing maxillary first premolar, showing the metal slot of the implant placement guide. (Courtesy of Dr Michael Cohen.) Note excellent alignment of implant and metal slot of guide. Periapical radiographs can clarify any apparent disparities in angulation of implants occasionally seen in panoramic radiographs as a result of distortion.

An alternative method for maintaining proper orientation during enlargement of the implant site preparation is to leave the initial drill in the prepared hole while positioning the larger drill parallel to it. The initial drill can then be removed and the larger drill moved over the prepared hole and drilled to the desired depth. Successive drills, taps, and implants can be oriented using the preceding drills as well. If needed, panoramic and periapical radiographs can be obtained after the implants have been placed and compared with preoperative radiographs to confirm the accuracy of implant placement (Figs 3-26a to 3-26c). Implants that are positioned incorrectly should be removed as soon as possible before osseointegration occurs.

Implant registration

Provisional implant restorations are fabricated on stone master casts with laboratory analogs of the implants.[45,46] The stone casts are produced from transfer registrations that record the position of the implants within the jaws. Transfer registrations usually are obtained with some type of elastomeric impression material at the time of implant exposure after osseointegration of the implants has occurred. Implant transfer copings are placed on the implants, and appropriate impressions are taken according to the manufacturer's recommendations.

It is often better, however, to obtain these registrations at the time of implant placement (depending

Fig 3-27 Section of implant analog master cast with resilient reproduction of residual ridge around implant analogs.

on the type of implant system being used).[47] Recording the positions of the implants at the time of implant placement has several advantages over recording implant positions during subsequent exposure of the implants after osseointegration. It allows for fabrication of the provisional implant restorations while the implants are undergoing osseointegration. The provisional restorations can then be placed on the implants at the time of exposure, providing the patient with a functional and esthetic alternative to the placement of metal healing abutments. The established contours of the provisional restorations with appropriate emergence profile allow the surrounding soft tissue to heal around the restorations and establish normal gingival contours.

Registrations may be obtained at the time of implant placement by attaching transfer copings or mounts placed on the implants to modified implant placement guides. The guides are modified by enlarging the drill grooves to accommodate the increased width of each transfer coping or mount. Self-curing or light-cured resin is used to attach the transfer copings or mounts to the modified guides. Implant placement guides with metal drill slots are more difficult to modify for this purpose, as the metal slots need to be removed. It usually is preferable to fabricate a separate appliance for this procedure or take an impression.

The master casts are made after transfer registrations of the implant positions have been recorded and implant analogs have been attached to the transfer copings/mounts of the transfer registrations. Master casts produced from transfer registrations obtained via impressions after osseointegration of the implants has occurred should have removable, resilient reproductions of the residual ridges around the implant analogs to facilitate the fabrication of provisional restorations (Fig 3-27). This is done by placing additional impression material around the base of each transfer coping and attached head of the implant analog. Lubrication of the impressions with petrolatum in the appropriate areas prior to the injection of additional impression material will prevent adhesion of the additional material to the impressions. It is advisable to block out the lingual area of the lower impression with alginate impression material to prevent excess stone accumulation in the lingual region of the cast. The impressions are then poured in dental stone, allowed to set, trimmed appropriately, and mounted on an articulator.

Provisional implant restorations

Provisional implant restorations are placed on the implants after osseointegration has been established to facilitate optimal tooth movement. These restorations simplify the attachment of orthodontic appliances, restore occlusal function, improve esthetics, provide posterior vertical support, and serve as templates for the fabrication of definitive implant restorations after orthodontic treatment is completed. To serve these functions, the restorations should be the same size and shape of the teeth they are to replace, with appropriate embrasures for the interdental papillae and access for oral hygiene. These requirements should be determined by the diagnostic waxing of the prosthetic teeth on the orthodontic setup casts. The provisional restorations should be relatively easy to fabricate from a material that is esthetic, color-stable, nonirritating to the surrounding periodontal tissues, easy to clean, and strong enough to resist breakage or abrasion from occlusal forces.[48–51] They also should be fabricated on nonrotating implant abutments. The use of manufactured "orthodontic" implant abutments in place of provisional implant restorations within the dental arches usually is inappropriate and not recommended. Typically, these are cylinder-shaped devices that are designed and promoted for ease of placement; however, they provide none of the desired functions of provisional implant restorations. For example, the size and shape of the teeth to be replaced are not reproduced, so optimal tooth position and appropriate spaces for eventual replacement of the missing teeth are difficult to achieve. Moreover, occlusal function is not restored, the desired level of the occlusal plane is difficult to establish, and posterior vertical support is not provided. Esthetics also is compromised, as the abutments are metal and normal crown contours are absent. The use of these so-called orthodontic abutments may be appropriate outside the dental arches, where the implants are placed only for orthodontic anchorage, and not for the prosthetic replacement of missing teeth.

Fabrication of the provisional implant restorations is facilitated by the use of molded forms of the prosthetic teeth that can be made on the composite casts produced from the orthodontic setup and diagnostic waxing casts and used to fabricate the implant placement guides.[52] The molded forms are made on the Biostar machine using Copyplast material (Great Lakes Orthodontics), which, unlike the Bioacryl II resin material used to fabricate the radiographic/implant placement guides, does not stick to the resin material used to fabricate the provisional restorations. The Copyplast molded forms are trimmed to include the prosthetic teeth and one or two adjacent natural teeth, which provide support and proper orientation of the molded forms during fabrication of the provisional restorations. It is important to note that movement of any teeth adjacent to implants that will be used to support the Copyplast forms should not begin until fabrication of the provisional implant restorations is complete. Such movement would prevent proper orientation of the forms relative to the implant analogs and compromise or preclude fabri-

cation of the provisional restorations that accurately relate to the implants, as planned.

Appropriate abutments are attached with retaining screws to the implant analogs of each master cast to provide support for the provisional restorations (Fig 3-28a). The fit of each abutment is checked on the master casts to make sure they are completely seated on the implant analogs (Fig 3-28b). The removable, resilient residual ridges around the implant analogs of the master casts, if present, are temporarily removed to facilitate evaluation of abutment fit and allow preparation of finish lines or undercuts on the abutments, if indicated. After proper fit is confirmed and abutment preparation is complete, the resilient residual ridges are replaced on the master casts. The abutments are then altered in height, if needed, to fit within the contours of the prosthetic teeth (Fig 3-28c). The Copyplast molded forms of the prosthetic teeth are used to facilitate this process. Clearance of at least 3 mm between the top of the abutment and the occlusal/incisal surface of the provisional restoration is usually needed to provide adequate bulk of resin veneering material to minimize the incidence of subsequent fracture from occlusal forces. This is necessary whether the provisional implant restorations are retained by engaging prepared or manufactured undercuts on the abutments or they are cemented on tapered abutments, depending on the implant system being used. Opaque material may be applied to metal abutments to mask the metal and improve esthetics (Fig 3-28d).

The contours of the provisional restorations are established using the Copyplast molded forms. The forms are replaced on the master casts and attached with sticky wax to stabilize their position (Fig 3-28e). For screw-retained provisional restorations, holes are prepared through the occlusal surface of the molded forms over the abutment retaining screw to allow the placement of longer (waxing) screws that facilitate the formation of screw access holes during the veneering process. Cemented provisional restorations do not require holes in the occlusal surfaces of the molded forms. An additional hole is prepared through the facial or lingual surface of each molded form in the cervical area to provide access for the injection of appropriate ve-

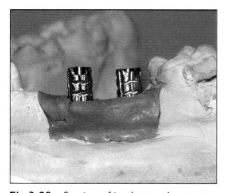

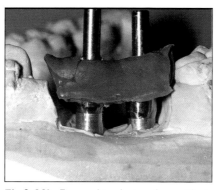

Fig 3-28a Section of implant analog master cast with implant abutments. (Note that Figs 3-28 to 3-30, showing fabrication of provisional implant restorations, are of a different patient.) Retention grooves (undercuts) have been prepared on abutments to retain veneering material.

Fig 3-28b Exposed implant analogs with attached abutments to evaluate fit of abutments on analogs.

Fig 3-28c Molded forms of prosthetic teeth on master casts produced from composite casts on Biostar machine using Copyplast material. Molded forms are used initially to assess abutments for desired height.

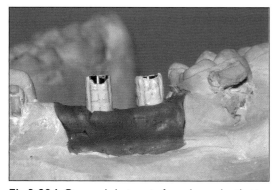

Fig 3-28d Opaqued abutments for enhanced esthetics.

Fig 3-28e Holes prepared in Copyplast molded forms of prosthetic teeth to allow for the injection of veneering material and the use of long abutment retaining screws to establish an abutment screw access hole in each provisional implant restoration. The forms are attached to the cast with sticky wax to prevent movement during the veneering process.

neering material. The master casts with attached forms of the prosthetic teeth are inverted to facilitate the injection process (Figs 3-28f and 3-28g).

Light-cured polymer glass resin (ceromer) is the restorative material of choice for fabrication of provisional implant restorations. Polymer glass resin is denser than acrylic resin, more resistant to wear, and more color stable. Curing of the resin with visible light is easy, fast, and efficient. Polymer glass resin does tend to fracture more readily than acrylic resin, so adequate bulk of material is needed to re-

duce this possibility. Sinfony veneering resin (ESPE America) is preferred because of its low viscosity, which allows it to easily flow into the molded forms of the prosthetic teeth. The resin is injected into the Copyplast forms through the prepared holes until the forms are completely filled. The resin is then cured with visible light according to the manufacturer's recommendations. After the resin has been cured, the filled forms are removed from the master casts to complete the fabrication of provisional restorations. The Copyplast forms are

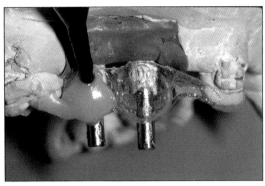

Fig 3-28f Injection of light-cured polymer glass veneering resin (Sinfony) into molded forms of prosthetic teeth. Cast is inverted to facilitate veneering process.

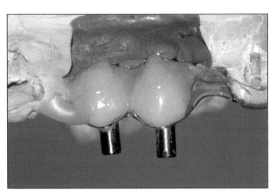

Fig 3-28g Injected polymer glass veneering resin (Sinfony) forms of prosthetic teeth. Resin is then cured with visible light.

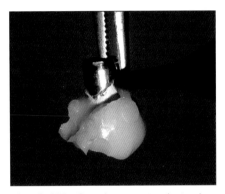

Fig 3-28h Cured provisional implant restoration removed from analog master cast to fill any deficiencies that exist with additional resin.

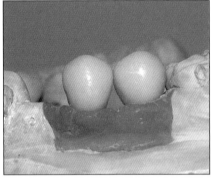

Fig 3-28i Completed provisional implant restorations on analog master cast. Size and shape of restoration are reproduced from initial diagnostic waxing of prosthetic teeth (Fig 3-28j) through use of the composite casts.

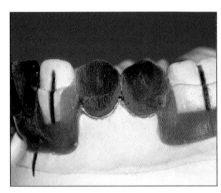

Fig 3-28j Wax prosthetic teeth on orthodontic setup cast.

removed from the provisional restorations, and resin is added to any deficient areas and then cured (Fig 3-28h). Usually, such deficiencies occur between the finish line of the abutment and the resin that was injected into the form. Any excess veneering material is removed, and the provisional implant restorations are polished according to the manufacturer's recommendations. After polishing, the provisional restorations are placed back on the master casts for final evaluation and adjustment as needed (Fig 3-28i). Screw-retained restorations are attached with appropriate retaining screws. Restorations to be cemented should easily slide onto the corresponding abutments attached to the implant analogs of the master casts. Proximal contours are adjusted for proper contact. Occlusal con-

tacts usually do not require adjustment if the occlusal plane established during the orthodontic setup was accurate and maintained throughout the transfer process and fabrication of provisional restorations. Contacts from any overerupted opposing teeth can be managed with a temporary anterior biteplate to disclude the posterior teeth until the occlusal plane is leveled. The biteplate may be removable or fixed, depending on the clinician's preference. Provisional implant restorations are facsimiles of the wax prosthetic teeth created during the initial planning and will be duplicated for the fabrication of definitive implant restorations after orthodontic treatment has been completed (Fig 3-28j).

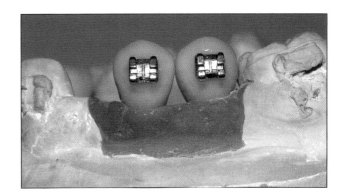

Fig 3-29 Orthodontic brackets placed indirectly on provisional implant restorations.

Orthodontic Appliance

Orthodontic brackets may be attached to the provisional implant restorations directly or indirectly, depending on the orthodontist's preference (Fig 3-29). Accurate positioning of brackets is important to facilitate optimal and efficient positioning of the teeth. The buccal/facial contours of the provisional restorations should facilitate accurate bracket placement. The slot for the arch wire in an edgewise appliance should be horizontal to allow rectangular wires to be passively placed, thereby preventing any undesirable movement of adjacent natural teeth. Bonding of brackets indirectly with unfilled, light-cured composite resin is the preferred method of attaching brackets. The same resin used to fabricate the provisional restorations also may be used. Accurate bracket placement is relatively easy and efficient. Autopolymerizing composite resin may be used, although it makes accurate bracket placement more difficult to achieve, especially if multiple adjacent implant restorations exist. Adjacent implant restorations require simultaneous bracket placement to ensure that the brackets are properly aligned, level, and passive, since the implant-supported provisional restorations will not move and adjust to dissimilar bracket positions. A segmental piece of edgewise wire placed in the bracket slots during bonding will facilitate proper positioning of the brackets. Bands usually are inappropriate for attaching brackets to provisional implant restorations since

they are not as easy to place and align properly for passive engagement of the arch wire. More important, bands require space between the teeth that should not exist between provisional implant restorations. It would be undesirable to create space for bands by reducing the proximal contours of the implant restorations. Bands also would prevent movement of adjacent natural teeth to contact the implant restoration and adversely affect optimal space appropriation as dictated by the orthodontic setup.

The provisional implant restorations are placed intraorally on the respective implants after the implants have osseointegrated and the provisional restorations have been fabricated. If registration of implant position was recorded after osseointegration of the implants occurred, the healing abutments placed by the surgeon after exposure of the implants are removed to allow attachment of the provisional restorations and supporting abutments. The retaining screws of the abutments are tightened according to the manufacturer's recommendations. Screw access holes, if present, are partly filled with cotton to facilitate subsequent access to the retaining screw and sealed with light-cured composite resin. Provisional restorations on tapered abutments are seated and cemented into place with appropriate permanent cement after attachment of the abutments to the corresponding implants. Direct placement of orthodontic brackets, if not done previously using the indirect method, can occur once the provisional restorations have been placed.

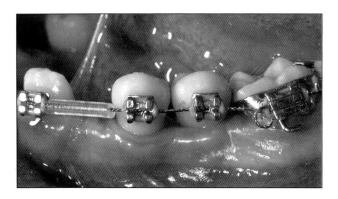

Fig 3-30 Provisional implant restorations with attached orthodontic appliances placed intraorally on implants.

Orthodontic Treatment

Orthodontic treatment can begin without delay after placement of the provisional implant restorations and the placement of orthodontic brackets on the remaining natural teeth (Fig 3-30). No waiting period is necessary. Appropriate arch wires can be placed that apply sustained light loads. Placement of nickel-titanium or copper-nickel-titanium arch wires initially is recommended. Since orthodontic forces are relatively light, no adverse effects to the implants would be expected. Orthodontic forces may actually contribute to favorable progressive loading of implants and enhance osseointegration through the application of light loads over time.[11] It is not uncommon for screw-retained provisional restorations to loosen during the course of orthodontic treatment. This usually is noticeable at the first progress appointment after treatment has begun. Loose implant restorations compromise the efficiency of orthodontic treatment and may lead to inflammation of the soft tissue surrounding the implant restoration. Chronic soft tissue inflammation can adversely affect implant osseointegration. It is important, therefore, to retighten loose provisional restorations to prevent the occurrence or persistence of any problems and to provide stable anchorage. Access to the screw is achieved by removing the composite resin sealing the access hole and the cotton plug in the hole. The screw is tightened again according to the manufacturer's recommendations. Placement of cotton in the hole and composite resin over the cotton reseals the screw access hole.

Orthodontic treatment with implant anchorage can progress in a traditional manner with sequential arch wires up to standard stainless steel edgewise wires once the teeth are aligned and level. Space appropriation can then begin with movement of teeth along the arch wires according to the orthodontic setup completed during the initial planning phase of treatment. The mechanotherapy used with implants providing anchorage within the dental arches usually is no different than that used with conventional toothborne anchorage. The efficiency of the mechanotherapy used, however, is significantly different with movement of teeth that would be difficult or impossible without implant anchorage. Any limitations to tooth movement using toothborne anchorage are all but eliminated using implant anchorage.

Implant Placement After Orthodontic Treatment

After orthodontic treatment is completed, any additional implants for replacement of missing teeth can be placed in the appropriate spaces established, and definitive restorations can be placed on the implants. The remaining implants to be placed are those that could not be placed before orthodontic treatment due to the presence of natural teeth at the desired sites. Movement of these teeth during treatment will allow appropriate spaces to be established for subsequent implant placement. Tooth movement also may develop edentulous sites for implants through apposition of bone in deficient areas by moving away from eventual implant sites or slowly erupting com-

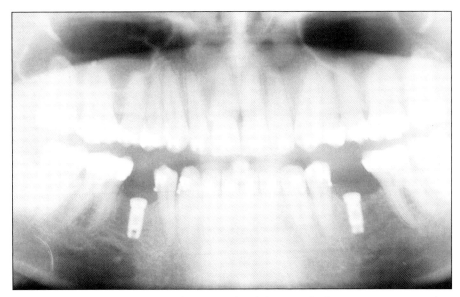

Fig 3-31a Panoramic radiograph of implants placed during orthodontic treatment to replace missing mandibular second premolars.

promised teeth with bony defects to extraction. Bony augmentation of other deficient sites may be necessary to allow implant placement. These areas commonly occur where no teeth ever developed or where compromised teeth were previously extracted.

Placement of Definitive Restorations

Placement of definitive restorations is facilitated by the existing provisional implant restorations used during orthodontic treatment. Since they were produced from the initial diagnostic waxing of the prosthetic teeth, they provide the correct relationship for fabrication of the definitive implant restorations relative to the size and shape of the teeth to be replaced. Fabrication and placement of the definitive restorations is relatively easy once correction of the malocclusion has been completed. The restorative/prosthetic dentist need only take appropriate impressions of the teeth with provisional implant restorations in place and transfer impressions of the implants with provisional restorations removed, produce and cross-mount casts of the impressions, and have the dental laboratory technician fabricate the restorations. The definitive restorations can be fabricated on master casts with implant

analogs using silicone molds of the provisional implant restorations obtained from the cross-mounted postorthodontic casts of the final tooth position with provisional implant restorations in place. The contours of the provisional restorations should make fabrication of the definitive restorations relatively easy. Information from the initial planning is used throughout treatment to the final result.

Placement of Implants Without Adequate Planning

Placement of implants before or during orthodontic treatment for orthodontic anchorage and/or replacement of missing teeth without appropriate determination of proper implant location through an orthodontic setup of the existing teeth and diagnostic waxing of the prosthetic teeth usually leads to compromised treatment results. The implants placed are usually malpositioned and prevent correction of the malocclusion with proper positioning of the teeth. The compromised orthodontic result precludes optimal replacement of the missing teeth by the restorative/prosthetic dentist. Figures 3-31a to 3-31e show the results of implants placed at incorrect positions. Complete correction of the malocclusion was pre-

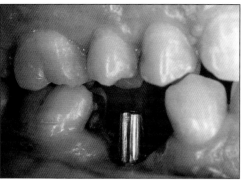

Fig 3-31b Clinical view of implant abutment on right side at completion of orthodontic treatment. Complete correction of malocclusion was prevented by implant aberrantly positioned 2 to 3 mm distal to desired position. As a result, molar relationship is end-to-end Class II.

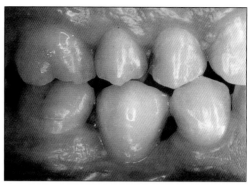

Fig 3-31c Clinical view of restored implant in aberrant position. Definitive implant restoration is oversized for second premolar replacement from excessive space in area.

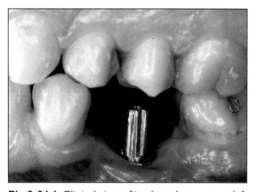

Fig 3-31d Clinical view of implant abutment on left side at completion of orthodontic treatment. Complete correction of malocclusion was prevented by implant aberrantly positioned 4 to 5 mm distal to desired position. As a result, molar relationship is Class II.

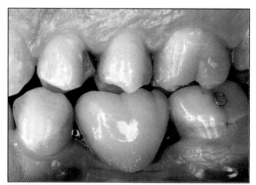

Fig 3-31e Clinical view of restored implant in aberrant position. Definitive implant restoration is too large, especially for the size of the implant supporting the restoration. A premolar-sized prosthetic tooth would have been more desirable.

vented by the malpositioned implants. Replacement of the missing teeth was compromised with oversized restorations on standard-sized implants that should have had premolar-sized restorations. The occlusion of the teeth and implant restorations is compromised as well. These unfavorable results occurred because no orthodontic setup of the teeth was done. The implants were placed without adequate information related to the postorthodontic tooth position or the use of an appropriate implant placement guide fabricated from information related to an orthodontic setup of the existing natural teeth and diagnostic waxing of the prosthetic teeth. Although implant an-

chorage was not needed to correct this malocclusion, the optional use of implant anchorage to assist in the correction of malocclusions can be done, but only if the appropriate planning is completed. In those situations, a determination needs to be made whether the planning necessary for implant anchorage is worth the time and expense if correction of the malocclusion is possible without it. Factors other than the lack of adequate toothborne anchorage need to be considered to make this determination. Elimination of patient compliance necessary for correction of a malocclusion could certainly be an acceptable indication.

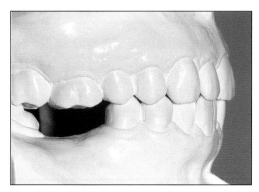

Fig 3-32a Original casts showing malocclusion with Class II tendency (end-to-end) and tipped mandibular third molar. Mandibular first and second molars are missing.

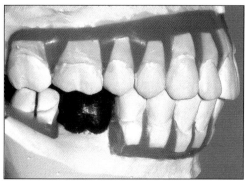

Fig 3-32b Orthodontic setup and diagnostic waxing of prosthetic replacement of mandibular first molar. Mandibular anterior teeth and premolars were moved forward into solid Class I relationship. Mandibular third molar was moved into second molar position. Implant placed in area of planned first molar position would provide support for replacement of missing tooth and anchorage to move adjacent teeth into position as determined by orthodontic setup.

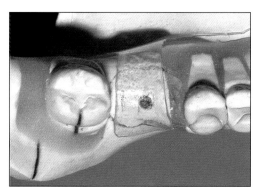

Fig 3-32c Section of mandibular setup cast with wax prosthetic tooth removed and location of implant marked within center of outlined tooth.

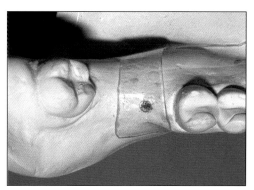

Fig 3-32d Section of duplicate original mandibular cast with implant location transferred to cast.

Communication Between Treating Clinicians

Communication between the clinicians or team members providing care also is essential to achieving optimal results. Lack of adequate communication, like inadequate planning, will usually lead to implants placed at undesirable sites and/or angled so as to compromise or prevent proper correction of the malocclusion. The prosthetic treatment will then be compromised as well. Figures 3-32a to 3-32j illustrate the inappropriate placement of an implant despite appropriate planning and fabrication of an implant placement guide that was sent to the surgeon prior to placement of the implant. From the position of the implant relative to the drill groove of the implant placement guide, it is readily apparent that the surgeon did not use the guide to place the implant. In addition, the implant placed was of standard size when a large diameter implant was desired and the edentulous ridge was wide enough to accommodate a larger implant. The orthodontic setup indicated that the dentition anterior to the implant on the mandibular right side

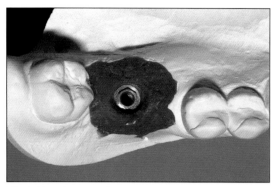

Fig 3-32e Section of implant analog master cast poured from transfer impression of implant after osseointegration of implant has occurred. Note implant analog is centered in space.

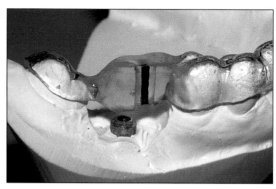

Fig 3-32f Section of implant analog master cast with implant placement guide on existing teeth and resilient reproduction of residual ridge removed. Note implant analog is positioned about 4 mm distal to desired location indicated by implant placement guide. Surgeon apparently did not use guide during placement of implant.

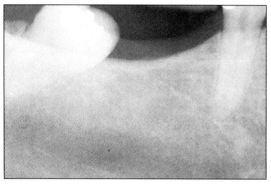

Fig 3-32g Periapical radiograph of area before treatment.

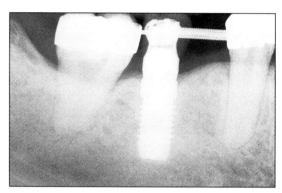

Fig 3-32h Periapical radiograph of aberrant implant used during orthodontic treatment to move teeth as much as possible according to plan of treatment. Third molar was moved forward considerably, as were anterior teeth. Implant was eventually removed and replaced with larger implant at proper location to facilitate complete correction of malocclusion.

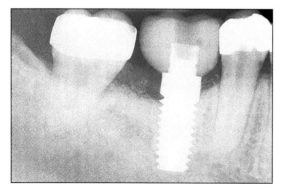

Fig 3-32i Periapical radiograph of new implant placed at optimal position to complete correction of malocclusion. Final tooth position can now be achieved with further mesial movement of teeth.

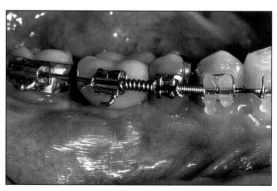

Fig 3-32j Clinical view of provisional implant restoration used to complete correction of malocclusion.

needed to move forward 2 to 3 mm to establish a Class I canine relationship and the third molar needed to move forward into the second molar position with establishment of a molar-sized space for implant-supported replacement of the first molar. The diagnostic waxing of the prosthetic tooth indicated that the implant needed to be placed near the second premolar to facilitate optimal tooth movement and the desired treatment goals. With the implant actually placed in the center of the space, the tooth movement necessary to correct the malocclusion could not be accomplished. Since the implant was osseointegrated when its aberrant position was discovered, it was used during the orthodontic treatment to move the adjacent teeth as much as possible. The implant was eventually removed and replaced with a larger-diameter implant in the correct position using an implant placement guide. Subsequent orthodontic treatment was then completed as planned to correct the malocclusion and position the teeth properly for definitive replacement of the missing molar. Although the aberrant implant in this situation was used for anchorage and then removed, it is preferable to remove any incorrectly placed implants before osseointegration occurs. Replacement of the removed implant may need to wait until the aberrant implant site has healed if its proximity is close to the correct site; otherwise it may be replaced at the same time. Appropriate communication between all members of the team providing care, in addition to the planning required for implant anchorage, will prevent problems related to incorrect placement of implants as illustrated in these figures.

Summary

Endosseous implants provide stable and efficient anchorage for tooth movement. In partially edentulous patients lacking sufficient toothborne anchorage, implants may be placed in edentulous areas to provide skeletal anchorage to facilitate correction of any existing malocclusion. They also will provide support for the prosthetic replacement of the missing teeth during and after orthodontic treatment. To achieve acceptable results, the implants need to be optimally placed to allow proper correction of the malocclusion and replacement of the missing teeth. Knowing where the existing teeth will be at the end of orthodontic treatment is essential to determining the location and orientation of the implants. This requires an orthodontic setup of the existing teeth and a diagnostic waxing of the missing teeth to be replaced. An implant placement guide can then be fabricated to direct the surgeon where to place the implants. Once the implants have been placed, provisional implant restorations can be fabricated and placed on the implants to facilitate orthodontic treatment. Appropriate communication between the clinicians providing care is essential to achieving optimal results. Without adequate communication, the treatment provided, regardless of the extent of initial planning, will fall short of the desired result. A combination of adequate planning and communication will allow the desired goals of treatment to be met and an optimal result of treatment to be achieved that will benefit all involved, but most of all the patient who is the recipient of our care.

Acknowledgments

The author thanks Dr Michael Cohen and Dr Ralph Yuodelis for their surgical expertise and treatment in the placement of implants, Dr Arturo Blanco for assistance in the fabrication and placement of provisional implant restorations, and Dr Duane Eng for his expertise in treatment planning and restorative management of the principal patient discussed in this chapter. The author also thanks his family and office staff for their support and understanding during preparation of this chapter.

Some of the information and figures presented in this chapter were previously published in the *Journal of Esthetic Dentistry* 1995;7, nos 2 and 4.

References

1. Roberts WE, Smith RK, Zilberman Y, et al. Osseous adaptation to continuous loading of rigid endosseous implants. Am J Orthod Dentofac Orthop 1984;86:95–111.

2. Roberts WE, Helm FR, Marshall KJ, Gongloff RK. Rigid endosseous implants for orthodontic and orthopedic anchorage. Angle Orthod 1989;59:247–256.

3. Turley PK, Kean C, Schur J, et al. Orthodontic force application to titanium endosseous implants. Angle Orthod 1988;58:151–162.

4. Ödman J, Lekholm U, Jemt T, et al. Osseointegrated titanium implants: A new approach in orthodontic treatment. Eur J Orthod 1988;10:98–105.

5. Kraut RA, Hammer HS, Wheeler JJ. Use of endosteal implants as orthodontic anchorage. Compendium 1988;9:796–801.

6. Van Roekel NB. Use of Brånemark system implants for orthodontic anchorage: Report of a case. Int J Oral Maxillofac Implants 1989;4:341–344.

7. Roberts WE, Marshall KJ, Mozsary PG. Rigid endosseous implant utilized as anchorage to protract molars and close an atrophic extraction site. Angle Orthod 1990;60:135–152.

8. Linder-Aronson S, Nordenram A, Anneroth G. Titanium implant anchorage in orthodontic treatment: An experimental investigation in monkeys. Eur J Orthod 1990;12:414–419.

9. Higuchi KW, Slack JM. The use of titanium fixtures for intraoral anchorage to facilitate orthodontic tooth movement. Int J Oral Maxillofac Implants 1991;6:338–344.

10. Hannaes HR, Stenvik A, Sterner B-O, et al. The efficacy of two-stage titanium implants as orthodontic anchorage in the preprosthodontic correction of third molars in adults. A report of three cases. Eur J Orthod 1991;13:287–292.

11. Wehrbein H, Diedrich P. Endosseous titanium implants during and after orthodontic load: An experimental study in the dog. Clin Oral Implant Res 1993;4:76–82.

12. Ödman J, Lekholm U, Jemt T, Thilander B. Osseointegrated implants as orthodontic anchorage in the treatment of partially edentulous adult patients. Eur J Orthod 1994;16:187–201.

13. Southard TE, Buckley MJ, Spivey JD, et al. Intrusion anchorage potential of teeth versus rigid endosseous implants: A clinical and radiographic evaluation. Am J Orthod Dentofac Orthop 1995;107:115–120.

14. Prosterman B, Prosterman L, Fisher R, Gornitsky M. The use of implants for orthodontic correction of an open bite. Am J Orthod Dentofac Orthop 1995;107:245–250.

15. Block MS, Hoffman, DR. A new device for absolute anchorage for orthodontics. Am J Orthod Dentofac Orthop 1995;107:251–258.

16. Schweizer CM. Endosseous dental implants in orthodontic therapy. Int Dent J 1996;46:61–68.

17. Kokich VG. Managing complex orthodontic problems: The use of implants for anchorage. Semin Orthod 1996;2:153–160.

18. Valerón JF, Velázquez JF. Implants in the orthodontic and prosthetic rehabilitation of an adult patient: A case report. Int J Oral Maxillofac Implants 1996;11:534–538.

19. Akin-Nergiz N, Nergiz I, Schulz A, et al. Reactions of peri-implant tissue to continuous loading of osseointegrated implants. Am J Orthod Dentofac Orthop 1998;114:292–298.

20. Wehrbein H, Glatmaier J, Yildirim M. Orthodontic anchorage capacity of short titanium screw implants in the maxilla. An experimental study in the dog. Clin Oral Implants Res 1997;8:131–141.

21. Schneider G, Simmons K, Nason R, Felton D. Occlusal rehabilitation using implants for orthodontic anchorage. J Prosthodont 1998;7:232–236.

22. Wehrbein H, Merz BR, Diedrich P. Palatal bone support for orthodontic implant anchorage: A clinical and radiological study. Eur J Orthod 1999;21:65–70.

23. Smalley WM, Shapiro PA, Hohl TH, et al. Osseointegrated titanium implants for maxillofacial protraction in monkeys. Am J Orthod Dentofac Orthop 1988;84:285–295.

24. Smalley WM. Implants for tooth movement: Determining implant location and orientation. J Esthet Dent 1995;7:62–72.

25. Reynolds MJ. Abutment selection for fixed prosthodontics. J Prosthet Dent 1968;19:483–488.

26. Wheeler RC. Wheeler's Atlas of Tooth Form. Philadelphia: Saunders, 1984.

27. Blustein R, Jackson R, Rotskoff K, et al. Use of splint material in the placement of implants. Int J Oral Maxillofac Implants 1986;1:47–49.

28. Edge MJ. Surgical placement guide for use with osseointegrated implants. J Prosthet Dent 1987;57:719–722.

29. Engelman MJ, Sorenson JA, Moy P. Optimum placement of osseointegrated implants. J Prosthet Dent 1988;59:467–473.

30. Burns DR, Crabtree DG, Bell DH. Template for positioning and angulation of intraosseous implants. J Prosthet Dent 1988;60:479–483.

31. Johnson CM, Lewandowski JA, McKinney JF. A surgical template for aligned placement of the osseointegrated implant. J Prosthet Dent 1988;59:684–688.

32. Cowan PW. Surgical templates for the placement of the osseointegrated implant. Quintessence Int 1990;21:391–396.

33. Orenstein IH. The surgical template: A prescription for implant success. Implant Dent 1991;2:182–184.

34. Perel ML. Stabilized template for implant insertion. Dent Implantol Update 1991;2:85–87.

35. Neidlinger J, Lilien BA, Kalant DC. Surgical implant stent: A design modification and simplified fabrication technique. J Prosthet Dent 1993;69:70–72.

36. Lima Verde MAR, Morgano SM. A dual-purpose stent for the implant-supported prosthesis. J Prosthet Dent 1993;69:276–280.

37. Lazzara RJ. Effect of implant position on implant restoration design. J Esthet Dent 1993;5:265–269.

38. McGivney GP, Haughton V, Strandt JA, et al. A comparison of computer-assisted tomography and data gathering modalities in prosthodontics. Int J Oral Maxillofac Implants 1986;1:55–59.

39. Schwarz MS, Rothman SLG, Rhoades ML, Chafetz N. Computed tomography. Preoperative assessment of the mandible for endosseous surgery. Parts 1 and 2. Int J Oral Maxillofac Implants 1987;2:137–141, 142–148.

40. Rothman SLG, Chafetz N, Rhoades ML, Schwartz MS. Computed tomography in the preoperative assessment of the mandible and maxilla for endosteal implant surgery. Radiology 1988;168:171–176.

41. Schwartz MS, Rothman SLG, Chaftez N, Rhoades M. Computed tomography in dental implant surgery. Dent Clin North Am 1989;33:565–597.

42. Smith JP, Borrow JW. Reformatted CT imaging for implant planning. Oral Maxillofac Surg Clin North Am 1991;3:805–825.

43. Wilson DJ. Ridge mapping for determination of alveolar ridge width. Int J Oral Maxillofac Implants 1989;4:41–43.

44. ten Bruggenkate CM, de Rijcke TB, Kraaijenhagen HA, Oosterbeck HS. Ridge mapping. Implant Dent 1994; 3:179–182.

45. Parel SM, Sullivan DY. Esthetics and Osseointegration. Dallas: Osseointegration Seminars, 1989:97–112.

46. Rosenstiel SF, Land MF, Fujimoto J. Contemporary Fixed Prosthodontics, ed 2. St Louis: Mosby, 1995:289–291, 325–357.

47. Reiser GM, Dornbush JR, Cohen R. Initiating restorative procedures at the first stage implant surgery with a positional index: A case report. Int J Periodont Rest Dent 1992;12:278–293.

48. Krug RA. Temporary resin crowns and bridges. Dent Clin North Am 1975;19:311–320.

49. Yuodelis RA, Faucher R. Provisional restorations: An integrated approach to periodontics and restorative dentistry. Dent Clin North Am 1980;24:285–303.

50. Kaiser DA, Cavazos E Jr. Temporization techniques in fixed prosthodontics. Dent Clin North Am 1985;29: 402–412.

51. Vahidi F. The provisional restoration. Dent Clin North Am 1987;31:363–381.

52. Smalley WM. Implants for tooth movement. A fabrication and placement technique for provisional restorations. J Esthet Dent 1995;7:150–154.

4 | Implant Anchorage in Orthodontic Treatment

Birgit Thilander, LDS, Odont Dr

In recent years the demand for orthodontic treatment in adults has increased significantly, mainly because patients today are more aware of their dental health and require the result to be an esthetic improvement. Furthermore, dentists are more aware of the problems of occlusion and tooth alignment in overall treatment planning. Some obvious differences exist between the orthodontic treatment of adults and that of children due to basic biological concepts as well as biomechanical principles of force and anchorage.

Adult patients who are partially edentulous often need preprosthetic orthodontics and, in those patients, anchorage problems may arise. Regular orthodontic patients with full dentitions are also subject to anchorage problems in special situations, as when teeth are to be moved en bloc in a posterior or anterior direction. Thus, anchorage problems in both orthodontic-prosthetic patients and regular orthodontic patients are of vital concern. Are there indications for the use of implants as anchorage units in these two groups? A review of published results based on experimental and clinical studies, discussed in this chapter, will help us answer that question.

Anchorage Principles

Orthodontic treatment involves the use and the control of forces acting upon the teeth and associated structures. An understanding of several fundamental mechanical concepts is necessary to appreciate the clinical relevance of biomechanics to orthodontics. Definitions of therapeutic forces differ for reasons of tradition, and it is apparent in modern orthodontics that complicated interactions exist between combinations of forces. The fact that any force will create a reaction in the opposite direction is a problem, ie, all active unit force systems deliver equal and opposite forces to the reactive system (the anchor-

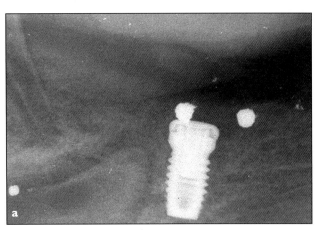 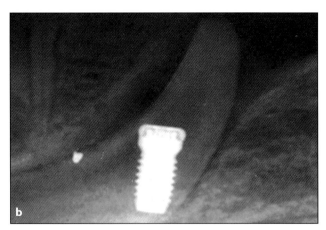

Fig 4-1 Radiographs of an erupting mandibular canine in a growing pig. (a) Canine in contact with an implant. (b) Five months later, the eruption path has deviated in the lingual direction because of the stable implant.

age unit). It is crucial to respect the need for anchorage and to monitor the force according to the reaction of the tissues. All force systems are in equilibrium, and if the forces implicit in the equilibrium are not acceptable, special consideration must be given to the anchorage. It is therefore important to consider how the reactive unit can be kept stable. The orthodontist must know how to use both components and, when impossible, how to counteract or dissipate unwanted reactions. Planned tooth movement is often realized by including more and larger teeth in the anchorage unit, thus increasing the number of resisting root surfaces and decreasing the strain or distortion of the periodontal structures within the anchorage unit. In this way the reactive force will elicit little or no tissue change in the supporting tissues of the anchoring teeth, while the force is optimal for movement of the desired teeth. Sequential mandibular anchorage preparation, initiated by tipping the second molar to a 15-degree distal inclination, has also been recommended in special cases. Traditional anchorage reinforcement methods, eg, headgear and transpalatal bars, may be suitable. However, adult patients will hardly tolerate a headgear 24 hours a day, and lack of cooperation may spoil the treatment result. In partially edentulous jaws the orthodontic treatment may be difficult to perform. To overcome such problems, the use of osseointegrated implants has been suggested.

Experimental Studies

In a number of experimental studies, orthodontic forces have been applied to endosseous implants of various types and installed in different species (rabbits, dogs, monkeys) at different sites (femur, mandible, maxilla). In some studies the force has been applied from implant to implant to test their stability under such loading[1–10] or for sutural expansion[11,12] and orthopedic movement of the maxilla.[10,13] Other studies used one implant to move a tooth or group of teeth.[14–16]

Furthermore, it has been demonstrated that titanium implants inserted in growing jaws of pigs behaved like ankylosed teeth,[17–19] results which have also been verified in a clinical study of adolescents.[20] Figures 4-1 and 4-2 show radiographs and ground sections from an implant installed in the canine region of the mandible of a growing pig. When the erupting canine came into contact with the implant, it had changed its eruption path and caused resorption of the bone-implant interface; ie, there was no bone involvement in the contact area.

Fig 4-2 Ground sections from implants and adjacent erupting teeth (toluidine blue stain; bar = 1 mm). (a) Tooth in contact with the implant. (b) No bone involvement in the contact area. (c) Changed morphology of the hard tissue of the developing tooth germ. (d) Even the enamel has been formed within the implant threads.

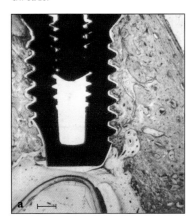
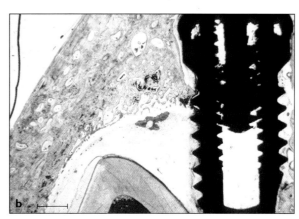
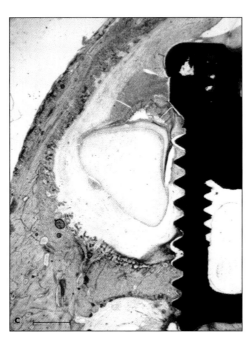
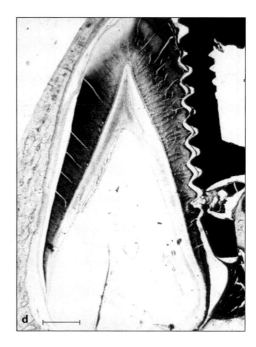

A changed morphology of the tooth germ in close contact with the implant was observed. In one specimen even the enamel was malformed and outlined in accordance with the threads of the implant, which may exemplify the good biocompatibility of the implant material. The bone interface of this implant was only 19.6%, but it could still withstand the pressure from the huge erupting canine, which was displaced lingually.

All of these experimental studies have shown that implants, exposed to eruptive forces from ad-

jacent teeth or loaded with orthodontic forces, remained stable (ankylosed anchorage). Although the observation period in these experiments was short, expectations concerning the use of osseointegrated implants as anchorage units for tooth movement in orthodontic patients have been raised.

Two categories of orthodontic patients are typical candidates for implant anchorage units: partially edentulous patients and regular orthodontic patients who need tooth movement en bloc.

Partially Edentulous Patients

In patients with several missing teeth, tooth movement using conventional methods may be impossible. The use of osseointegrated implant anchorage may solve the problem, however, as has been shown in some clinical studies. Another advantage is that the implants initially used as anchorage for tooth movement later can serve as abutments for fixed restorations. Results from such a treatment procedure have been presented in the following papers:

- Ödman et al[21] used implants as anchorage units for extrusion of an impacted maxillary canine
- van Roekel[22] used implants for lingual movement of a mandibular canine
- Roberts et al[23] used implants for mesial movement of two mandibular molars in one patient
- Haanaes et al[24] used implants for correction of mandibular impacted molars in three patients
- Higuchi and Slack[25] placed implants bilaterally in the mandibular third molar region for protraction or retraction of the incisor segment in seven patients
- Stean[26] used implants for alignment of the mandibular right premolars in one patient
- Ödman et al[27] used implants as orthodontic anchorage to perform tipping, torquing, intrusion, extrusion, rotation, and bodily movements in nine patients
- Wehrbein[28] used implants in the mandible for alignment of the dental arch in two patients
- Sorenson[29] used maxillary implants for Class II elastic anchorage in one patient
- Prosterman et al[30] used implants for correction of an open bite
- Kokich[31] used implants in the mandible for alignment of the dental arch in three patients.

The number of patients described in these reports is limited, varying between one and nine cases, and the tooth movements were performed in different directions. The observation period after the orthodontic treatment varied between 0 and 6 years. Nevertheless, the results indicate that the implants remained stable during the orthodontic treatment period on average 1.5 to 2 years and in a few cases even 3 years. However, it is of obvious interest to evaluate the long-term effect of loading during and after orthodontic treatment, including the retention period, on the implant area.

Case Presentations

Nine patients treated by our team in Göteborg will be presented with regard to type of malocclusion and number of missing teeth (classification according to FDI). The treatment planning in all cases was done by an interdisciplinary team composed of an orthodontist, an oral surgeon, a prosthodontist, and a radiologist. All implants were of commercially pure titanium (Brånemark); the characteristics of each will be given below. A brief description of the orthodontic treatment of each patient will be provided, and our experiences from this kind of treatment will be summarized. Three representative cases (Angle Class I; Class II, division 1; and Class III) will also be documented by illustrations.

Patient 1

A 48-year-old woman with Angle Class II, division 1 malocclusion, a deep bite, a scissors bite, a narrow mandibular arch, and tipped mandibular third molars. Missing teeth: 12, 47, 46, 45, 35, 36, 37 (Fig 4-3).

Treatment planning: Surgical correction of the malocclusion was discussed, but the patient preferred the other alternative presented: orthodontic treatment with osseointegrated fixed partial dentures for anchorage.

Treatment procedure: Six implants (7-mm standard) were placed in regions 37, 26, 25 and 47, 46, 45. After implant insertion and a healing period of 4 months, the temporary implant-supported fixed partial dentures were constructed. Orthodontic treatment with the standard edgewise technique started immediately after placement of the prosthetic constructions for correction of the narrow

Fig 4-3 Patient 1, a 48-year-old woman with an Angle Class II, division 1 malocclusion, a deep bite, a scissors bite, a narrow mandibular arch, and tipped mandibular third molars. (a-c) Frontal and lateral views of the deep bite. The right maxillary lateral incisor is missing; the incisors are damaged by caries; a provisional fixed partial denture is present on the right side. (d,e) Occlusal view of the narrowed mandibular arch and tipped third molars before placement of the implants and after orthodontic expansion and uprighting of the third molars using the provisional implant-supported fixed partial dentures as anchorage units. (f,g) Periapical radiographs of the implants (right and left sides) before orthodontic treatment. (h-k) Intraoral views of the dentition 3 years later with permanent fixed partial dentures in the mandible. After orthodontic alignment and space closure of the maxillary arch, a single implant-supported crown was placed in the lateral incisor region. (l) Schematic drawing of superimposed before- and after-treatment cephalograms, illustrating the large tooth movements. The numbers 1 to 6 correspond to the implants that were placed, which are now stable. Incorrect positioning of the patient´s head in the cephalostat explains the minimal change in inclination of some implants. Dotted line designates start of treatment; solid line designates end of treatment. (m,n) Periapical radiographs of the implants (right and left sides) after orthodontic treatment. (o-q) Intraoral views of the dentition 5 years after the prosthetic constructions. (r,s) Periapical radiographs of the implants (right and left sides) at the last observation period (8 years after placement) showing no change in the marginal bone level.

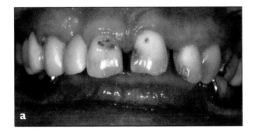
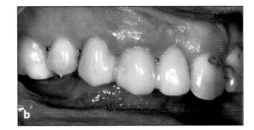
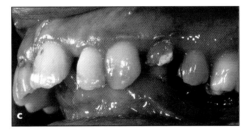
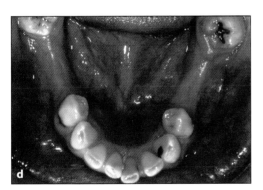
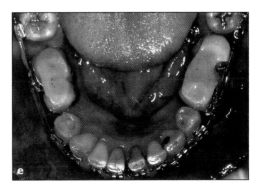

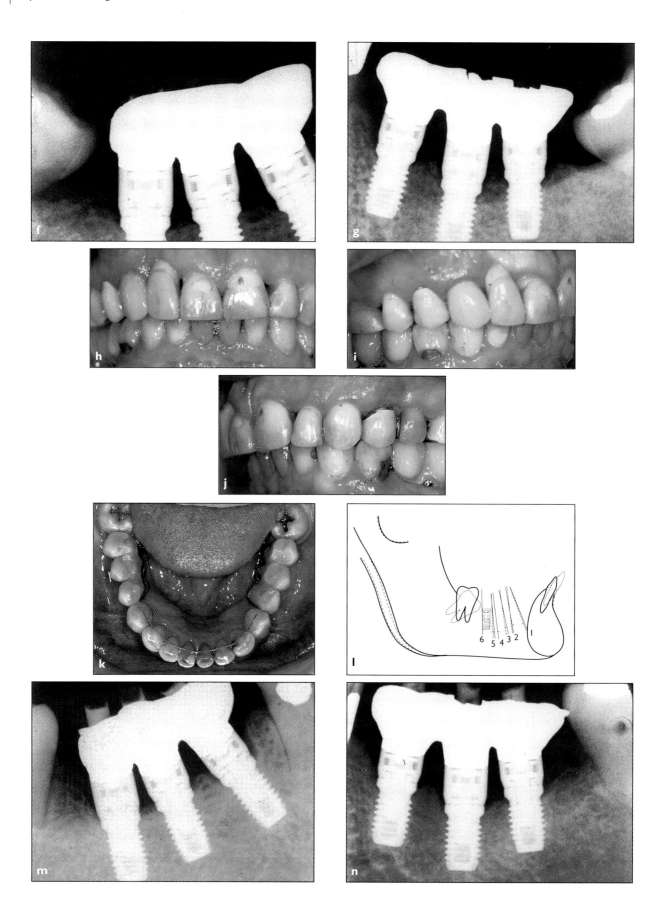

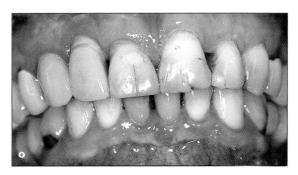

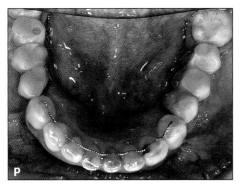

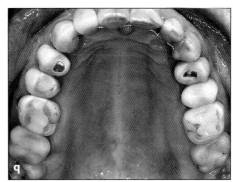

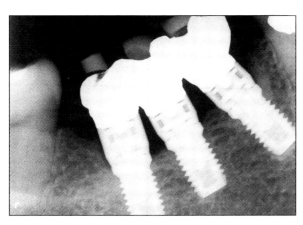

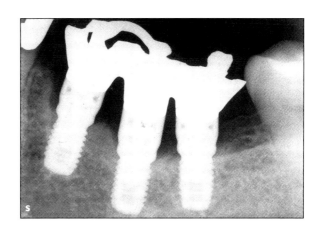

mandibular dental arch and uprighting of the mandibular third molars. In the meantime, orthodontic alignment of the maxillary arch was performed to gain space for the missing lateral incisor which, after treatment, was replaced by an implant-supported crown. After an orthodontic treatment period of 22 months, lingual retainers in the maxillary and mandibular anterior regions were bonded; the implants now served as abutments for a permanent prosthetic construction.

Result: Five years later, the patient was very satisfied and happy not to have been subjected to maxillofacial surgery.

Patient 2

A 54-year-old woman with Angle Class II, division 1 malocclusion, 15-mm overjet, a narrow maxilla, a crowded mandibular anterior, and rotated maxillary anterior teeth. Missing teeth: 17, 16, 15, 14, 23, 24, 25, 26, 27 and 47, 44, 34, 37.

Treatment planning: The patient declined orofacial surgery and preferred orthodontic treatment, even though the overjet could be reduced to only half the size. Therefore, expansion of the maxillary dental arch and alignment and retroclination of the maxillary incisors, using implant-supported crowns as anchorage, and prosthetic reconstruction in the mandible (without orthodontic treatment) were planned.

Treatment procedure: Three implants (15-mm self-tapping) were placed in regions 15 and 24, 25. After insertion and a healing period of 4 months, the implants were supplied with crowns, and orthodontic treatment with the standard edgewise technique was started. Nine months later a lingual retainer was bonded.

Result: The overjet was reduced to 6 mm, with improvement of the soft profile. The patient was satisfied.

Patient 3

A 47-year-old woman with Angle Class II, division 1 malocclusion, an anterior open bite, supraocclusion of 12, a mesially tipped 13, and rotated 13, 11, 21, 22. Missing teeth: 17, 16, 15, 14, 27 and 47, 46 mesial root, 36, 37.

Treatment planning: The patient had been treated for periodontitis. Her dental hygiene was now good. Alignment of the maxillary dental arch using implants for anchorage needed to be performed; the implants were to be used for prosthodontic construction after orthodontic treatment. No orthodontic treatment in the mandible—only prosthodontic constructions—was planned.

Treatment procedure: One implant (13-mm standard) was placed in region 14 and two implants (10-mm standard) in regions 15, 16. After implant insertion and a healing period of 6 months, the provisional implant-supported fixed partial denture was adapted, and orthodontic treatment with standard edgewise technique was started. After a treatment period of 13 months, a lingual retainer was bonded in the incisor region and a permanent prosthetic construction was placed, using the implants as abutments.

Result: Three years later, the patient's oral hygiene is still satisfactory.

Patient 4

A 53-year-old man with Angle Class III malocclusion, anterior and bilateral buccal crossbites, and spacing in the maxillary and mandibular incisor regions (Fig 4-4). Missing teeth: 17, 16, 15, 24, 26, 27 and 48, 46, 45, 35, 36, 37, 38.

Treatment planning: Various signs and symptoms of TMD, eg, bruxism, frequent headache, pain on movement of the mandible, and TMJ clicking, necessitated a treatment that could produce a stable occlusion.

Treatment procedure: Two implants (7-mm standard) were placed in regions 35, 36. After a healing period of 6 months, the implant-supported crowns were produced and orthodontic treatment with the standard edgewise technique was started to close the anterior diastemas in the mandibular incisor region. In the meantime, alignment of the maxillary dental arch with closure of the diastemas was performed. After a treatment period of 21 months, the anterior and buccal crossbites, as well as the bimaxillary anterior spacing, were eliminated.

Result: After a follow-up period of 4 years, the TMD signs and symptoms have been eliminated. There is now also an osseointegrated single-tooth replacement in the maxillary left first premolar region.

Patient 5

A 39-year-old woman with Angle Class I malocclusion; a deep bite; supraocclusion of 24, 25; a scissors bite 24; and attrition. Missing teeth: 17, 16, 23, 26, 27 and 47, 46, 36, 37.

Treatment planning: Intrusion of the supraerupted maxillary premolars, using a single-tooth implant and a small third molar as orthodontic anchorage. The patient refused treatment in the mandibular molar regions.

Treatment procedure: One implant (15-mm standard) was placed in region 23. After 8 months of healing, it was equipped with a crown; then orthodontic treatment with a sectional arch, inducing forces of approximately 30 cN, was started. The scissors bite was eliminated and the premolars were intruded in stable occlusion 15 months later.

Fig 4-4 Patient 4, a 53-year-old man with an Angle Class III malocclusion, anterior and bilateral buccal crossbites, and spacing in the maxillary and mandibular incisor regions. (a,b) Intraoral views of the anterior crossbite and spacing in the maxillary and mandibular anteriors. (c,d) Left side of the maxilla and mandible before and after placement of the osseointegrated implant-supported temporary crowns. (e,f) Intraoral view after orthodontic treatment. A permanent prosthesis has been constructed in the mandibular left region and a single implant-supported crown has been placed in the maxillary left first premolar region. (g) Superimposition of cephalograms from the start (*dotted line*) and end (*solid line*) of orthodontic treatment, showing no movement of the anchorage units but lingual tipping of the mandibular incisors.

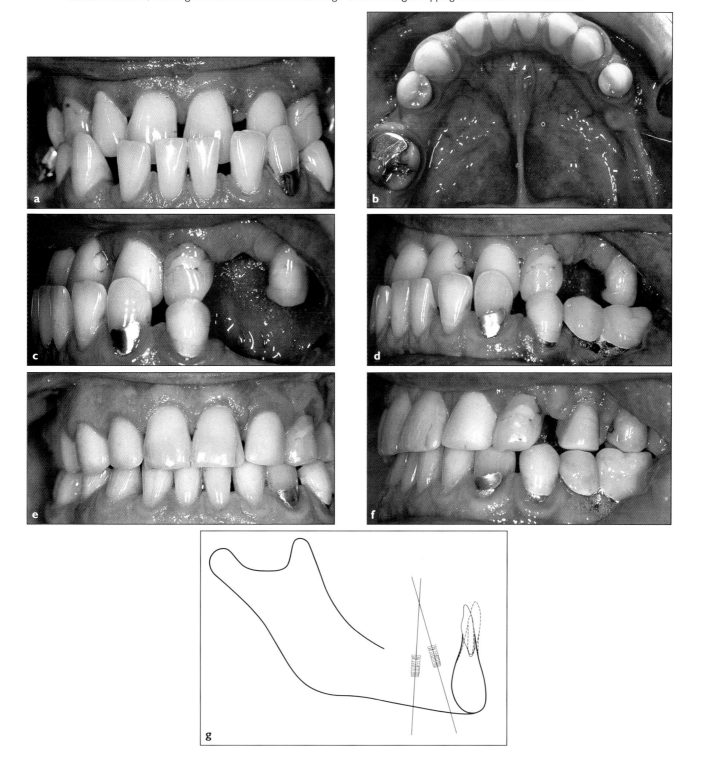

Result: Three years later at the follow-up, good occlusal stability was observed.

Patient 6

A 20-year-old woman with Angle Class I malocclusion, a median diastema, mesially migrated and rotated maxillary first molars, and a tipped 46. Missing teeth: 17, 15, 14, 12, 22, 24, 25 and 47, 45, 35, 36, 37.

Treatment planning: Orthodontic treatment in the maxilla had just been finished. Therefore, the following were planned: osseointegrated single tooth replacement for the maxillary lateral incisors; prosthetic construction bilaterally in the maxillary arch after distalization of the first molars; in the mandible, distalization of the right first molar using a single implant as anchorage; prosthetic construction on the left side.

Treatment procedure: One implant (10-mm self-tapping) was placed in region 45. After a healing period of 8 months, the implant was equipped with a crown, and orthodontic treatment with a sectional arch, inducing a force of 50 cN, was started. After a period of 4 months, the molar was upright and in contact with the implant-supported crown.

Result: At the control 5 years later, a good result was observed.

Patient 7

A 58-year-old man with Angle Class I malocclusion, proclination and spacing of mandibular anterior teeth, an impacted 44, and an ankylotic and impacted 43. Missing teeth: 17, 21, 22, 23, 24, 25, 26 and 48, 47, 46, 45, 42, 35, 36, 37.

Treatment planning: Osseointegrated prosthetic constructions in the maxillary left side (21 to 26) and the mandibular right side (45 to 48); extrusion of the impacted mandibular right first premolar and ankylotic canine, using a single implant as anchorage.

Treatment procedure: One implant (7-mm standard) was placed in region 46. After a healing pe-

riod of 9 months, it was supplied with a crown, and orthodontic treatment with a sectional arch, inducing forces of 50 cN, was started. The impacted 44 was moved into a vertical position and good occlusion after an orthodontic treatment period of 30 months. The impacted and ankylotic 33, however, which showed no signs of movement during a treatment period of 7 months and an increased force of 100 cN, was surgically removed. The short single implant withstood the forces for a long period, which clearly demonstrates the value of osseointegrated implants as orthodontic anchorage.

Result: Observation 2 years later verified that conclusion.

Patient 8

A 39-year-old man with Angle Class I malocclusion, a crowded mandibular anterior region, and a blocked-out 31. Missing teeth: 17, 24 and 47, 46, 45, 35, 36, 37.

Treatment planning: A partial denture in the mandible, which had caused great problems when chewing, needed to be replaced with osseointegrated implant-supported fixed partial dentures on the right and left sides. Space gaining for 31 and alignment of the mandibular anterior segment, using the bilateral osseointegrated implant-supported fixed partial dentures as anchorage units, were planned.

Treatment procedure: Four implants (10-mm self-tapping) were placed in regions 35, 36 and 45, 46. After a healing period of 6 months, implant-supported fixed partial dentures with a 2-mm increased occlusal plane were constructed. The orthodontic treatment, with the standard edgewise technique, aimed to distalize 33, 32, 44, 43, 42, 41 and to gain space for the blocked-out 31. Treatment period was 7 months.

Result: Control 2 years later showed a very good esthetic result and a possibility for the patient to follow the prescribed hygiene program.

Fig 4-5 Patient 9, a 64-year-old woman with an Angle Class I malocclusion and a palatally impacted maxillary right canine. (a) Radiographic survey of the dentition showing an impacted right canine (*arrow*). (b) Impacted right canine. (c,e) Occlusal view of the maxillary arch before and after implant placement. (d) Two implants placed in the maxillary right side. (f,g) Periapical radiographs of the implants at the start of orthodontic treatment. (h-j) Exposure of the impacted canine and orthodontic extrusion combined with distobuccal movement for final placement in the alveolar process. (k) Occlusal view of the canine in desired position; provisional fixed partial denture. (l) Periapical radiograph of the implants 3 years after the orthodontic-prosthetic procedure. (m,n) Intraoral view and radiographic survey of the dentition 3 years after prosthetic reconstruction in the maxilla and mandible.

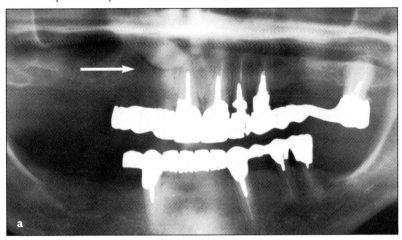
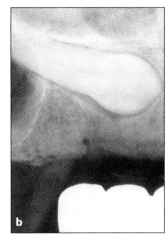
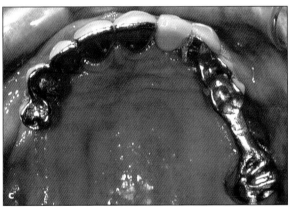
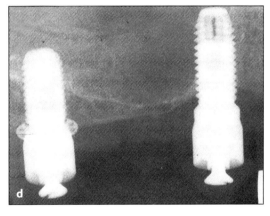

Patient 9

A 64-year-old woman with Angle Class I malocclusion and a palatally impacted maxillary right canine. Missing teeth: 18, 17, 16, 15, 14, 12, 24, 25, 26 and 38, 37, 36 distal root, 34, 32, 31, 41, 42, 44, 45, 46, 47, 48 (Fig 4-5).

Treatment planning: From the prosthodontic aspect, it was of greatest value to extrude the impacted canine for a later abutment in a fixed partial denture in the maxilla, so prosthetic constructions in the mandible could be performed.

Treatment procedure: One implant (7-mm flange) was placed in region 16 and one implant (10-mm self-tapping) in region 14. After a healing period of 6 months, an implant-supported fixed partial denture was constructed, serving as an anchorage unit for extrusion of the impacted canine. After surgical exposure, a sectional arch, inducing forces of 25 to 30 cN, was used for extrusion and tooth movement in the buccal and distal directions. After a treatment period of 33 months, the canine was in the desired position and could be used as an abutment in the fixed partial denture 13 to 27.

Result: Control 3 years later showed a good result, and the patient was very satisfied with both the esthetic and functional improvement.

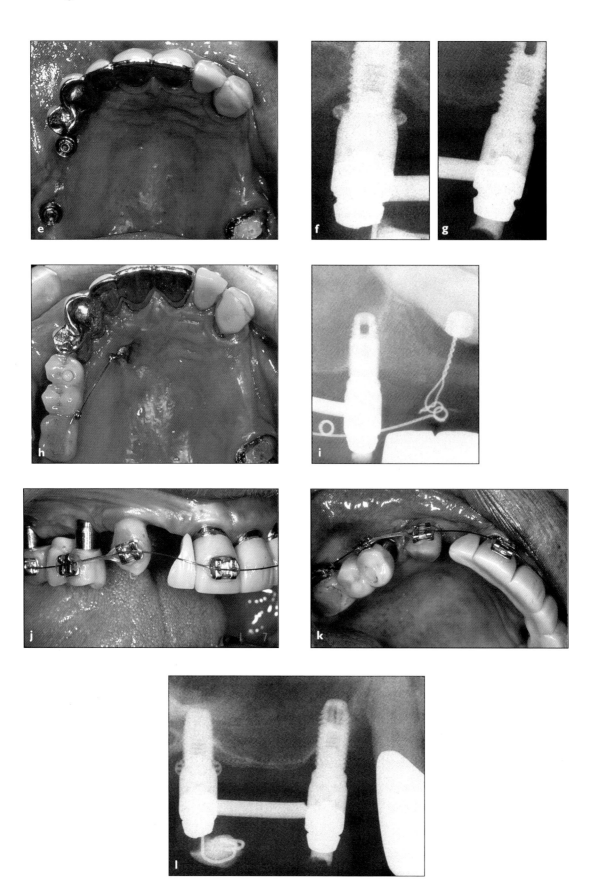

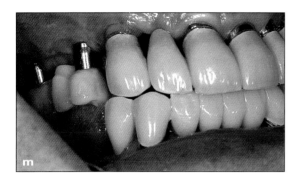

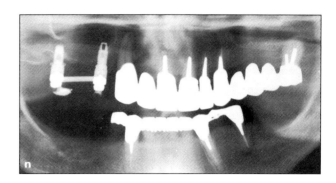

Summary of the Clinical Cases

The findings from the nine patients (mean age 47 years) treated in our clinic can be summarized as follows: The stability of all 23 implants was constant both during the orthodontic treatment (mean 17 months) and during the follow-up period (mean 37 months). It was possible to achieve the individual treatment objectives for all patients by means of the implants serving as anchorage units for different types of tooth movements (tipping, torque, rotation, intrusion, extrusion, and bodily movement). The anchorage units were loaded with orthodontic forces induced by standard procedures with the standardized edgewise technique or sectional arches (25 to 100 cN). They were able to resist forces from movements of up to 10 teeth with an amount of bone support around the moved teeth ranging between 44% and 85% (mean 72.9%), calculated as the relationship of alveolar bone height to root length (Fig 4-6). Even if the bone-root ratio was high, it was not difficult to perform the required movements with the aid of the osseointegrated implants. The marginal bone level, assessed at the mesial and distal surfaces of each implant, showed a change of only 0 to 0.2 mm during the total follow-up period, a value much less than that reported during the first year of conventional implant function.[32]

By means of a coordinate machine, the three-dimensional movements were recorded for individual teeth (Fig 4-7). The directions of the tooth movements in the X-Y plane (close to the occlusal plane) together with the space vector (3-D movement) for each patient are shown in Fig 4-8. For a single measuring point on a tooth, the mean movement in space was 3.9 mm (range 0.6 to 18.7 mm); the largest movement was recorded for a maxillary impacted canine (patient 9), and in one patient (patient 1), the total movements of all measuring points of the teeth amounted to 55.7 mm. Regardless of the extensive tooth movements and the long duration of loading of the osseointegrated anchorage units, no change in the implant position was recorded when the cephalograms from the start and end of orthodontic treatment were superimposed.

It was obvious that the implants remained stable in their original positions, thereby indicating that they maintained a direct bone anchorage during the orthodontic treatment. This is in agreement with the findings of Roberts et al,[23] Higuchi and Slack,[25] and Sennerby et al.[19] The orthodontic forces used in the clinical studies referred to were obviously weaker than those used in previous experimental trials,[6,9,10] but the orthodontic load lasted for a longer period than in the experimental studies. The superimposition of pre- and posttreatment tracings still did not show any movement of the implants. The bone thus seems to resorb the load and can apparently maintain its rigid attachment to the implant by continuous remodeling of portions of the interface, which also has been suggested by Roberts et al.[23] The minimal loss of marginal bone height at the implants during the time they were used as orthodontic anchorage indicates that orthodontic treatment did not seem to jeopardize the use of the implants as abutments for permanent prosthetic reconstructions afterward.

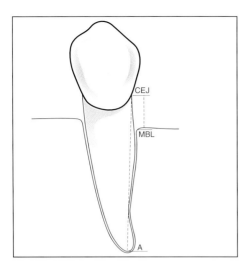

Fig 4-6 Schematic drawing of a tooth in its root socket illustrating the bone support of the orthodontically moved tooth, calculated as the percentage of root length within bone (MBL-A) in relation to total root length (CEJ-A). (MBL = marginal bone length; CEJ = cementoenamel junction.)

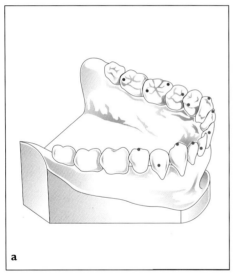

a

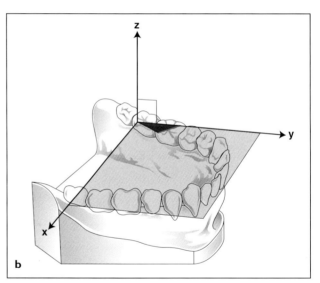

b

Fig 4-7 Schematic drawings illustrating the reference plane and measuring points in the coordinate system used for evaluating tooth movement (space vector 3-D). (a) Reference points (*red dots*) and measuring points (*blue dots*) placed on the implant anchorage unit indicate examples of the teeth that are to be moved orthodontically. (b) Reference plane between reference points (*red area*). The X-Y plane (*light grey*) is an extension of the reference plane. The origin of the coordinate system has been placed at one of the reference points. The Z-axis is perpendicular to the X-Y plane. The study casts made of each patient at the start and end of orthodontic treatment formed a cast pair. The cast pairs were placed in the coordinate machine (Mitutoyo FJ 406). The degree of movement of each tooth was given as the difference between the measurements before and after treatment for each measuring point related to the origin of the X, Y, and Z coordinates. The total magnitude of movement (space vector) could then be calculated.

Fig 4-8 Tooth movement of the nine patients, studied via changes of X, Y, and Z coordinates. Arrows indicate direction of plane vectors for the teeth-measuring points (*blue dots*). Shading shows the location of the anchorage units. The magnitude of the space vector (3-D) in each patient is given in millimeters.

Patient 1

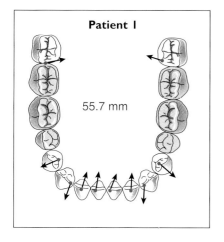

55.7 mm

Patient 2

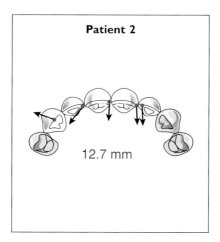

12.7 mm

Patient 3

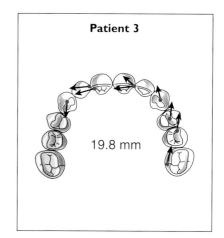

19.8 mm

Patient 4

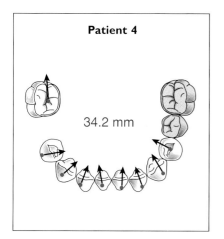

34.2 mm

Patient 5

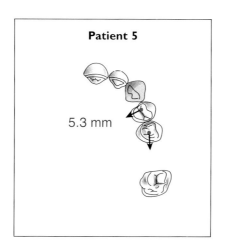

5.3 mm

Patient 6

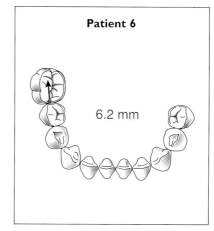

6.2 mm

Patient 7

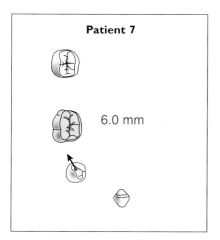

6.0 mm

Patient 8

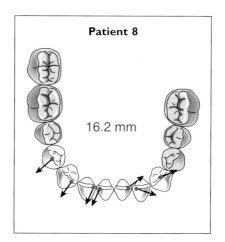

16.2 mm

Patient 9

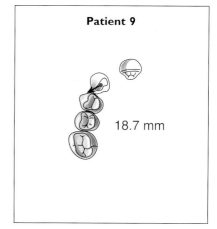

18.7 mm

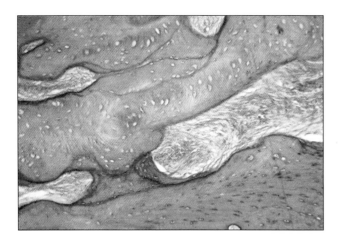

Fig 4-9 Photomicrograph showing partial fusion of the intermaxillary suture in a 25-year-old man (Mayer's hemalum-eosin stain; original magnification ×250).

Thus, it can be stated that dental implants resist tooth movements in all planes of space, hence function excellently as orthodontic anchorage units. After orthodontic treatment, the implants can also serve as abutments for permanent prosthetic reconstructions of missing teeth. The use of dental implants is a very important complement in orthodontic-prosthetic treatment, especially in cases with a great number of missing teeth that could not have been orthodontically treated without implant anchorage.

Regular Orthodontic Patients

Implants as orthodontic anchorage in regular orthodontic patients have been discussed during the last few years, especially in relation to the maxilla. In these patients, there are problems other than those in orthodontic-prosthetic patients due to a full dentition, in which the anterior segment is to be moved en masse in an anterior or posterior direction and in which the patient cannot accept extraoral anchorage. The anchorage units must be placed in regions other than in the alveolar bone, eg, in the palate.

Due to the thin bone height in the palate, an endosseous implant must have small dimensions, especially in length, so as not to perforate the palate and penetrate the nasal cavity. Different types of implants are available and a few experimental studies have been published, eg, with endosseous titanium flat-screw implants,[33,34] endosseous re-

sorbable implant anchorage,[35] and subperiosteally applied titanium alloy disks coated with hydroxyapatite.[36] Another type of pure titanium onplant (Brånemark) is undergoing clinical testing. Also, Wehrbein et al[34] have reported clinical experience in the use of a newly developed endosseous orthodontic anchor system for palatal anchorage in a 16-year-old patient (Straumann).

The palatal anchorage implants are usually placed in the midline, and there is always a risk of interference with the palatal sutures. Most sutures ossify when cranial growth ceases, and our own histologic studies in humans from 15 to 35 years of age have shown that the extent and course of the fusion process of the palatal sutures vary between individuals.[37,38] Palatal sutures may show obliteration during the juvenile period, but a marked degree of closure is rarely found until the third decade of life (Fig 4-9). Besides variations in the degree of closure between sutures, variations also exist between different parts of the same suture. For instance, the intermaxillary suture starts to close more often in the posterior part than in the anterior. Due to individual variations in suture closure, it must be questioned whether sufficient interface between bone and onplant will occur if the onplant is placed over a suture area with incomplete bone bridging. Thus, it seems that this type of anchorage can best be used in adult patients.

Another disadvantage of palatal implants, as described in the literature, is the fact that they must be removed after orthodontic treatment, with the risk of bony defects. In this respect, the use of subperiosteal onplants seems to be preferable. However, the technical procedure implies at least three-stage surgery: implant placement, abutment connection, and removal of the onplant after the orthodontic treatment. Before starting orthodontic treatment, a long process awaits the patient, ie, a healing period of approximately 4 months after the first-stage surgery and another healing period of the soft tissue after second-stage surgery. Management of the palatal mucosa must be reduced to a relatively simple level when placing and removing the implant to allow adequate postoperative tissue healing. Then follows preparation for the orthodontic appliance, ie, transfer of molar bands and the abutment position to a working plaster or stone cast and adaptation of the transpalatal bar and cylinder to the bands and abutment replica, placement of the transpalatal bar and cylinder, and final adjustment. The patient must be informed of all details before this procedure and he or she must indeed be motivated.

Conclusions

Dental implants resist orthodontic tooth movements, making them excellent orthodontic anchorage units, and the future use of dental implants in orthodontic-prosthetic cases is a very important complement. In regular orthodontic cases, however, there is need for more research and development of new implants and implant components, together with positional stability. Manufacturers must be made aware of the clinical problems such as choice of site for implant placement, reliable fixture of orthodontic wires and handling simplicity, and—last but not least—the importance of minimizing strain on the patient.

Finally, it must be stated that, although we now fully realize the importance of interdisciplinary cooperation between those in basic science and in different clinical specialities, it is important to define how the planning and performance of this treatment should be organized in the future. The orthodontist will have an important place in this interdisciplinary team.

References

1. Paige S, Clark A, Costa P, et al. Orthodontic stress application to bioglass implants in rabbit femurs. J Dent Res 1980;59A:445.

2. Oliver S, Mendez V, Evans C, et al. Change in position of vitrous carbon implants subjected to orthodontic forces. J Dent Res 1980;59A:280.

3. Oliver S, Mendez-Villamil C, Heely J, Shulman L. Orthodontic stresses and peri-implant alveolar bone in baboons. J Dent Res 1982;61A:281.

4. Gray J, Steen M, King G, Clark A. Studies on the efficacy of implants as orthodontic anchorage. Am J Orthod 1983;83:311–317.

5. Roberts E, Smith RK, Zilberman Y, et al. Osseous adaptation to continuous loading of rigid endosseous implants. Am J Orthod 1984;86:95–111.

6. Roberts E, Helm F, Marshall K, Gongloff R. Rigid endosseous implants for orthodontic and orthopedic anchorage. Angle Orthod 1989;59:247–256.

7. Turley P, Roth P. Orthodontic force application to vitallium subperiostal implants. J Dent Res 1983;62A:282.

8. Turley P, Gray J, Kean C, Roberts E. Titanium endosseous and vitallium subperiosteal implants as orthodontic anchors for tooth movement in dogs. J Dent Res 1986; 63A:156.

9. Turley P, Kean C, Schur J, et al. Orthodontic force application to titanium endosseous implants. Angle Orthod 1988;58:151–162.

10. Smalley W, Shapiro P, Hohl T, et al. Osseointegrated titanium implants for maxillofacial protraction in monkeys. Am J Orthod Dentofac Orthop 1988;94:285–295.

11. Movassaghi K, Altobelli D, Zhou H. Frontonasal suture expansion in the rabbit using titanium screws. J Oral Maxillofac Surg 1995;53:1033–1042.

12. Parr A, Garetto L, Wohlford M, et al. Sutural expansion using rigidly integrated endosseous implants: An experimental study in rabbits. Angle Orthod 1997;67:283–290.

13. Turley P, Shapiro P, Moffett B. The loading of bioglass-coated aluminium oxide implants to produce sutural expansion of the maxillary complex in the pigtail monkey (Macaca nemestrina). Archs Oral Biol 1980;25:459–469.

14. Linder-Aronson S, Nordenram Å, Anneroth G. Titanium implant anchorage in orthodontic treatment: An experimental investigation in monkeys. Eur J Orthod 1990; 12:414–419.

15. Wehrbein H, Diedrich P. Endosseous titanium implants during and after orthodontic load: An experimental study in the dog. Clin Oral Implants Res 1993;4:76–82.

16. Southard T, Buckley M, Spivey J, et al. Intrusion anchorage potential of teeth versus rigid endosseous implants: A clinical and radiographic evaluation. Am J Orthod Dentofac Orthop 1995;107:115–120.

17. Ödman J, Gröndahl K, Lekholm U, Thilander B. The effect of osseointegrated implants on the dentoalveolar development. A clinical and radiographic study in growing pigs. Eur J Orthod 1991;13:279–286.

18. Thilander B, Ödman J, Gröndahl K, Lekholm U. Aspects on osseointegrated implants inserted in growing jaws. A biometric and radiographic study in the young pig. Eur J Orthod 1992;14:99–109.

19. Sennerby L, Ödman J, Lekholm U, Thilander B. Tissue reactions towards titanium implants inserted in growing jaws: A histological study in the pig. Clin Oral Implants Res 1993;4:65–75.

20. Thilander B, Ödman J, Gröndahl K, Friberg B. Osseointegrated implants in adolescents: An alternative in replacing missing teeth? Eur J Orthod 1994;16:84–95.

21. Ödman J, Lekholm U, Jemt T, et al. Osseointegrated implants: A new approach in orthodontic treatment. Eur J Orthod 1988;10:98–105.

22. van Roekel N. The use of Brånemark system implants for orthodontic anchorage: Report of a case. Int J Oral Maxillofac Implants 1989;4:341–244.

23. Roberts E, Marshall K, Mozsary P. Rigid endosseous implant utilized as anchorage to protract molars and close an atrophic extraction site. Angle Orthod 1990;60:135–152.

24. Haanaes H, Stenvik A, Beyer-Olsen E, et al. The efficacy of two-stage titanium implants as orthodontic anchorage in the preprosthodontic correction of third molars in adults: A report of three cases. Eur J Orthod 1991;13:287–292.

25. Higuchi K, Slack J. The use of titanium fixtures for intraoral anchorage to facilitate orthodontic tooth movement. Int J Oral Maxillofac Implants 1991;6:338–344.

26. Stean H. Clinical case report: An impoved technique for using dental implants as orthodontic anchorage. J Oral Implantol 1993;19:336–340.

27. Ödman J, Lekholm U, Jemt T, Thilander B. Osseointegrated implants as orthodontic anchorage in the treatment of partially edentulous adult patients. Eur J Orthod 1994;16:187–201.

28. Wehrbein H. Enossale Titanimplantate als orthodontische Verankerungselemente. Experimentelle Untersuchungen und klinische Anwendung. Fortschr Kieferorthop 1994;55:236–250.

29. Sorenson N. Case report. Use of maxillary intraosseous implants for Class II elastic anchorage. Angle Orthod 1995;65:169–173.

30. Prosterman B, Prosterman L, Fisher R, Gornitsky M. The use of implants for orthodontic correction of an open bite. Am J Orthod Dentofac Orthop 1995;107:245–250.

31. Kokich V. Managing complex orthodontic problems: The use of implants for anchorage. Semin Orthod 1996;2:1–8.

32. Adell R, Lekholm U, Rockler B, Brånemark P-I. A 15-year study of osseointegrated implants in the treatment of the edentulous jaw. Int J Oral Surg 1981;10:387–416.

33. Triaca A, Antonini M, Wintermantel E. Ein neues Titan-Flachschrauben-Implantat zur orthodontischen Verankerung am anterioren Gaumen. Inf Orthod Kieferorthop 1992;24:251–257.

34. Wehrbein H, Glatzmaier J, Mundwiller U, Diedrich P. The Orthosystem: A new implant system for orthodontic anchorage in the palate. J Orofac Orthop/Fortschr Kieferorthop 1996;57:142–153.

35. Glatzmaier J, Wehrbein H, Diedrich P. Die Entwicklung eines resorbierbaren Implantatsystems zur orthodontischen Verankerung. Fortschr Kieferorthop 1995;56:175–181.

36. Block M, Hoffman D. A new device for absolute anchorage for orthodontics. Am J Orthod Dentofac Orthop 1995;107:251–258.

37. Persson M, Thilander B. Palatal suture closure in man from 15 to 35 years of age. Am J Orthod 1977;72:42–52.

38. Persson M, Magnusson B, Thilander B. Sutural closure in rabbit and man: A morphological and histochemical study. J Anat 1978;125:313–321.

5 | Orthodontic Loading of Implants: Biomechanical Considerations

John B. Brunski, MS, PhD
James M. Slack, DDS, MS

In 1991, Higuchi and Slack[1] reported the first prospective study in which osseointegrated implants were used as intraoral orthodontic anchorage. Single implants were placed bilaterally in the retromolar region of the dentitions of seven patients. The retruded dentitions of six of these patients were protracted using implants as anchorage, while in the seventh patient, implants were used to retract teeth from a Class III dental malocclusion. Of the 14 implants placed, all remained stable and integrated in position throughout treatment. Recently eight more patients were treated with 19 implants; all but 1 remained stable and in position. In this group, six adult patients with mutilated dentitions received implants that would be used as anchorage to align teeth and then as abutments for prosthetic restoration of missing teeth to restore function. In some of these patients, who were missing multiple posterior teeth and had severe malocclusion, treatment would have been difficult or impossible without the anchorage provided by implants. In all, 15 patients with 33 implants were treated in both groups. One implant was lost after treatment, but the patient has adequate function without it. No implants were lost as a result of orthodontic loading. Initially, only light forces were placed on the implants.

What follows in this chapter are some examples of the orthodontic use of implants to facilitate different types of tooth movement. Most of the cases demonstrate more than one type of movement.

Nature of Orthodontic Anchorage

When dealing with osseointegrated implants, restorative dentists consider the term *anchorage* differently than do orthodontists. The goal of anchorage in surgical and prosthetic terms is functional and esthetic replacement of missing dental, skeletal, and soft tissue anatomy. However, orthodontists view anchorage as the ability of teeth and implants to resist movement while other structures are being deliberately moved during orthodontic therapy. For instance, Proffit[2] defines anchorage as resistance to unwanted tooth movement. The basis of this problem is Newton's Third Law, which states that "the actions of two bodies upon each other are always equal and directly opposite."[3] Unless the treatment is properly designed, reactive forces will cause undesirable movement in the group of teeth that is supposed to act as stable anchorage for delivering the orthodontic loading. Anchorage can therefore be operationally defined as the resistance to reactive forces provided by teeth or structures outside the mouth, eg, headgear. Anchorage must be considered whenever teeth are to be moved or, for that matter, whenever orthodontists plan extractions or treatments.

Orthodontic anchorage can be increased by *(1)* pitting groups of teeth against one or two teeth that are to be moved; *(2)* using extraoral reinforcement, such as headgear; or *(3)* using osseointegrated implants. Until implants were tested for this purpose, no predictable source of rigid intraoral anchorage was available. Because of the nature of the osseointegrated bone-implant interface—which does not involve a periodontal ligament—an osseointegrated implant does not move when subjected to reactions inherent in the anchorage system. A number of studies have shown that osseointegrated implants ad modum Brånemark can provide an excellent source of intraoral anchorage for tooth movement (Higuchi and Slack,[1] Roberts et al,[4] Ödman et al[5]).

In view of the above, the main purpose of this chapter is to characterize the biomechanical nature of the orthodontic loading to which the implants are subjected, using clinical case studies as examples.

Background

Review of biomechanical concepts

It is appropriate to start with a review of the macroscopic, clinic-level biomechanical concepts underlying conventional orthodontics because these same concepts form the basis of therapy with osseointegrated implants. The following synopsis of principles of mechanics is fundamental to understanding the analyses of clinical cases that are presented later in the chapter.

Mass versus force. In lay terms, a force can be thought of as a push or a pull. The most common units of force are the pound (lb) and the newton (N). Unfortunately, some orthodontic textbooks confuse the issue by using *mass* units such as ounces or grams when *force* is being discussed. For example, sometimes it is stated that an orthodontist applies force of so many grams or ounces. Strictly speaking, this is incorrect usage because these are not units of force; they are units of mass. To explain further, the following conversion may help: 1 ounce (oz, avoirdupois) = 28.3495 grams (g). At sea level, under the earth's gravitational pull, a 1-ounce mass (28.3495 g) weighs (is attracted by the earth with a force of) 0.278 N. The operative equation is of the form, $W = mg$, where W is weight in newtons, m is mass in kilograms, and g is acceleration due to gravity in m/sec[2]. (Note that $W = mg$ is a form of $F = ma$.) Therefore, when an orthodontist speaks of a 1-ounce "force," what is really meant is a force of 0.278 N.

Force as a vector quantity. Another important characteristic of a force is that it is a *vector* quantity. A vector quantity has both magnitude and direction. It follows that two forces might be equal in magnitude but unequal in direction. For instance, two equal-magnitude forces might act on a tooth in different directions, one intrusive and the other buccolingual. Here the two forces do not have the same effect on the tooth even though their magnitudes are equal.

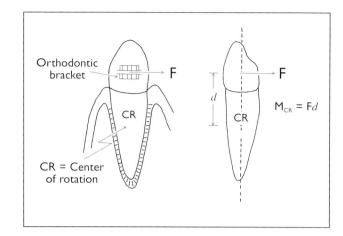

Fig 5-1 An orthodontic force *F* applied to a tooth at the bracket will produce a moment of magnitude $M_{CR} = Fd$ at the center of resistance CR, which is located at a perpendicular distance *d* from the line of action of force *F*.

Moment. In orthodontics it is essential to recognize that a force on a body such as a tooth or implant can produce a moment (or torque) about a point. A *moment* is a vector quantity that tends to produce rotation of a body about an axis. For example, a screwdriver applies a moment to the head of a screw that tends to rotate the screw about its central axis. Likewise, a torque wrench for tightening an implant's abutment screw applies a force through a lever arm, creating a moment (torque) at the head of the screw; this tends to rotate the screw about its long axis as it advances.

A concept related to moment is the idea of a *couple* or *couple-moment*. This is a special case of a moment. A couple can be represented as a pair of equal, noncollinear parallel forces of opposite sense acting on a body but separated by a perpendicular distance; classic examples of couples are two hands turning a steering wheel, and the thumb and forefinger unscrewing a bottle cap. The unique aspect of a couple is that it has zero resultant force, yet it produces an effect on the body–the twisting action due to the moment on the body.

In orthodontics, a force is sometimes applied to a tooth to make it tip (or rotate) about an axis. In the simplified two-dimensional situation shown in Fig 5-1, a horizontal force *F* acts at the orthodontic bracket and tends to tip the tooth about its center of resistance, or center of rotation (CR). Here the tipping, or rotating, tendency is expressed by a

moment. The moment's magnitude is computed as follows: the magnitude of the moment (M_{CR}) of the force *F* about the point CR is *Fd*, where *d* is the perpendicular distance between the line of action of *F* and the point CR.

It follows from the foregoing that the dimensions of a moment are force times distance. Common units for a moment in the orthodontic literature include N·m, N·cm, N·mm, oz·in, and in·lb, depending on the system of units (metric or English) and convention (oz·in are actually incorrect units for moment because ounce is a mass unit rather than a force unit, as discussed previously). To help determine the direction of the moment vector, one can define the axis about which tipping occurs as a line perpendicular to the page through the point CR in Fig 5-1, having a direction pointing into the page along the axis of rotation, with a magnitude *Fd*.

Of course, what happens in clinical orthodontics can be considerably more complicated than that. In general, the moment produced by an orthodontic force about a point CR in a tooth or implant will be a three-dimensional moment vector having three nonzero components. (This 3-D moment would have to be computed by vector methods involving the vector cross-product, which falls outside the scope of this chapter but is explained in any introductory mechanics text.) Typically, an orthodontic moment on a tooth or implant will tend to produce tipping or rotation about three mutually perpendicular axes. For example, if one defined a Cartesian coordinate system with x, y, and z axes along the mesiodistal, buccolingual, and occluso-apical directions in the mouth, a three-dimensional moment vector could, in the most general case, have nonzero components about each of these axes: one component of the moment vector could cause tipping mesiodistally, another could cause tipping buccolingually, and a third could cause rotation about the tooth's long axis. For analysis purposes, it is often the case that we may be interested in the nature of only one of the components, such as the one that causes tipping.

Another complication that arises in "real" orthodontics is the friction at the contact surfaces where the arch wire interacts with the bracket.[6] We will not discuss this topic further.

Equivalent force-moment system, or resultant force and moment at a point. Another clinically relevant concept involving forces and moments is the idea of an *equivalent force-moment system,* or *resultant force and moment at a point.* This concept is well known in basic mechanics, although by slightly different terminology. Its significance is that it is possible (and often helpful) to reduce a complicated system of forces and moments acting at multiple points on a body to a simpler, statically equivalent force-moment system acting at a single point. This can be best illustrated by an example in orthodontics.

In Fig 5-1, consider the applied force F acting on a tooth at the orthodontic bracket. At the point CR, the equivalent force-moment system (or resultant force and moment at the point CR) consists of two quantities: *(1)* the force vector F and *(2)* the moment vector that F (at the bracket) produces about point CR. In other words, a convenient, equivalent way of representing the effect of F on the tooth at the point CR is to state that there exists a force F and a moment Fd at CR. Actually, in this description one should list both the force and the moment as vectors, not just magnitudes. Also, if additional forces besides F acted on the tooth at other points, these could be handled the same way by moving each of them to, say, CR and then

adding the moments that each produced about CR. If couple-moments also existed on the tooth, they could be moved to CR and added vectorially to the other moments, since couple-moments are free vectors.

Equivalent force-moment systems are critical in answering the following question that represents a fundamental problem in clinical orthodontics: An orthodontic force F at the bracket tends to tip a tooth about its center of rotation. What loading would have to be applied at the bracket if one wanted only to translate the tooth, ie, move the tooth bodily? The answer involves the notion of an equivalent force-moment system (Fig 5-2, modified from Smith and Burstone[7]).

First note that one cannot apply an orthodontic force F at CR to translate the tooth because that point is physically inaccessible inside the root, but F applied by itself at the bracket will tend to tip the tooth. Therefore, to move the tooth bodily, one must apply something besides just the force F at the level of the bracket.

The solution is to apply not only the desired force F at the bracket but also a couple-moment that will counteract, ie, act equal and opposite to, the moment Fd which develops at CR due to the force F at the bracket. Note that if one applies this couple-moment at the bracket that is equal and opposite to the moment Fd, then the resultant force and moment at CR consists of F plus a net moment of zero, allowing us to create conditions for pure translation. Figure 5-3 is a numerical example: To achieve a translatory force of 150 g only at CR (Fig 5-3a), we should apply 150 g at the bracket plus a couple-moment equal to 150 g × 8 mm = 1200 g·mm in a counterclockwise direction (Fig 5-3b). It should be apparent that the equivalent force-moment system at CR for Fig 5-3b is indeed just the 150 g force to the left.

Static equilibrium. As will be seen in the following analyses of orthodontic treatments with implants, the importance of an equivalent force-moment system is that it gives us a convenient way to summarize the loading of an implant used as anchorage. It also helps clarify the meaning of static equilibrium of a rigid body. For example, in Fig 5-

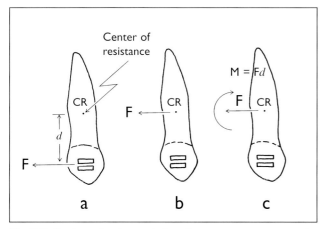

Fig 5-2 By the rules for equivalent force-moment systems, the loading in case A is equivalent to that shown in case c, consisting of the force *F* acting at the point CR, as well as the moment *M* = *Fd*. Note that the loading in case b is not equivalent to that in either case a or case c. (From Smith and Burstone.[7] Reprinted with permission.)

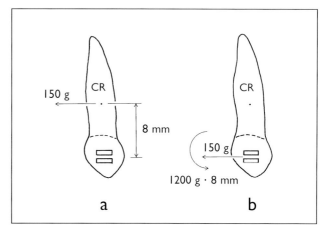

Fig 5-3 A numerical example of equivalent force-moment systems: To obtain only a translatory force of 150 g acting to the left at point CR, apply 150 g to the left at the bracket and a counterclockwise couple-moment equal to 8 mm × 150 g × 1,200 g•mm at the bracket. The purpose of the counterclockwise couple-moment is to counteract the clockwise moment at CR due to the force *F* at the bracket. (From Smith and Burstone.[7] Reprinted with permission.)

2, the equivalent system at CR is *F* to the left and a moment *Fd*, tending to cause clockwise rotation about CR. The opposite of this system—*F* to the right and a counterclockwise moment of magnitude *Fd*—is the net reaction that the bone supplies about this point to keep the implant in equilibrium. Static equilibrium of a rigid body means that the sum of all forces equals zero and the sum of all moments about any point must also be zero.

Biomechanical Analyses of Clinical Cases

The following cases illustrate some of the ways implants have been used successfully to supply orthodontic anchorage. The purpose of the accompanying biomechanical analyses is to reveal the magnitudes and directions of the forces and moments on implants and to compare these loadings with those encountered during conventional use of implants, for example, during support of conventional prostheses.

Patient RH

Geometrical and biomechanical analyses. Implants in the retromolar pad area were used as anchorage to protract the lower dentition (Figs 5-4a and 5-4b), thereby closing space from congenitally missing premolars. In step 1 of the treatment plan (Fig 5-4c), open coil springs pushed the first molars mesially (protraction). Each spring was anchored to a rigid wire (BC) connected to a bracket (C) on the buccal aspect of each osseointegrated implant in the distal region. Each spring was nominally set to exert 12 to 15 oz (3.3 to 4.2 N) force, with the force's line of action along line AB.

By Newton's law of action-reaction, the force protracting the first molar at A must be equal and opposite to the reactive force supplied by the anchorage at B. Assuming that wires BC are rigid as well as rigidly attached to each implant, the force from spring AB is applied at point B, with a line of action determined by the orientation of spring AB. Let F_1 and F_2 be these spring forces on the left and right sides of the jaw, respectively (Fig 5-5). (F_1 and F_2 could be equal in magnitude if both springs were set identically, which we assume later when

Fig 5-4 Treatment to protract the lower dentition so as to close space created by congenitally missing premolars in patient RH. (a) Cast of dentition showing the posterior position of the implants and the rigid attachment to the first molars, which effectively transfers anchorage from the implant to the first molars. (b) Periapical radiograph showing attachment of the implant to the dentition. (c) Diagram of occlusal view of the clinical treatment. Implants at C support rigid wires BC and the open coil springs AB, which push the molars mesially in step 1.

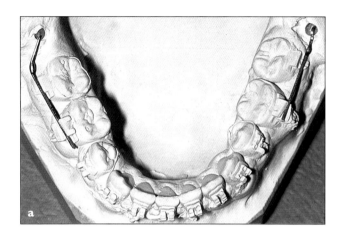

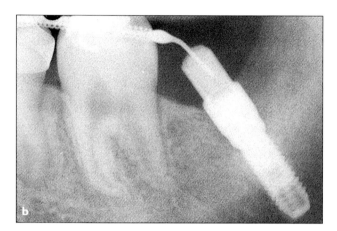

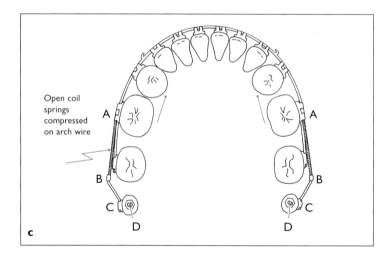

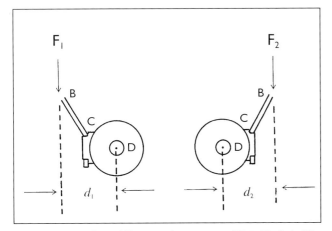

Fig 5-5 Forces F_1 and F_2 come from springs AB in Fig 5-4c. The lines of action of these forces are at perpendicular distances d_1 and d_2 from the centers of the implants.

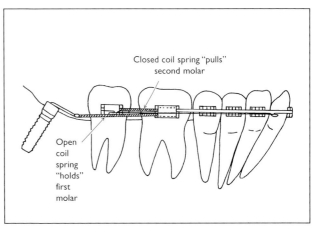

Fig 5-6 Lateral view of patient RH. In reality, force from the spring AB acts at an angle to the long axis of the implant, but this does not appreciably change the general conclusions about the level of loading of the implants (see text).

we estimate numerical results for this analysis.) Distances d_1 and d_2 are perpendicular distances between the lines of action of forces F_1 and F_2 and the top-center of each implant (D). Although the actual geometry of this case was more complicated than that depicted in Fig 5-5 (with angulated implants, Fig 5-6), this fact does not appreciably change the approach and the numerical results.

The loading on each implant is as follows. The implant and rigid wire BC are treated as a single rigid body. This body is subjected to an equivalent system consisting of a force and a moment, the moment being computed about, for example, point D at the top of the implant (Fig 5-5). That is, we describe the net loading of each implant using the concept of an equivalent force-moment system at the top-center of the implant.

Based on the estimated spring forces and distances d_1 and d_2 from the patient's plaster casts, the typical force on each implant is about 4 N, with a moment of about 4 N·cm when d_1 and d_2 are estimated at 1 cm. A more detailed analysis of the case—based on more precise measurements of distances and vector computations of the moment—indicates that for each implant, one compo-

nent of the moment vector tends to tip the implant toward the distal while another component tends to rotate it about its long axis.

In a later step of the treatment (Fig 5-7), which occurred after the first molars had been successfully protracted, the first molars and the teeth anterior to them were anchored in position facially by open coil springs AB, which were also anchored to the implants. Then, using this anchorage, closed coil springs EF pulled the second molars anteriorly. In this step, the biomechanical purpose of the implants was to help anchor the first molars and the rest of the arch. However, without more information about the mechanical properties of the teeth and implants, one cannot reliably predict the exact loading on the implants during this step because the anchorage arises from an uncertain mixture of contributions from the implants and rest of the arch. Figures 5-7b and 5-7c show pre- and posttreatment panoramic radiographs, while Figs 5-7d and 5-7e show pre- and posttreatment photographs of the anterior dentition. The posttreatment photograph also demonstrates implants with prosthetics in the lateral incisor location.

Fig 5-7 (a) General scheme of step 3 in the treatment of patient RH. (b) Panoramic radiograph showing the placement of implants prior to any tooth movement. Note the congenitally missing mandibular second premolars and the maxillary lateral incisors. (c) Posttreatment view of unilateral tooth movement. Compare the distance from implant to second molar in (b) and (c). The dentition was effectively protracted. (d) Pretreatment appearance of anterior dentition. (e) Posttreatment appearance of anterior dentition.

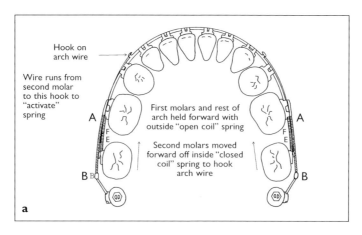

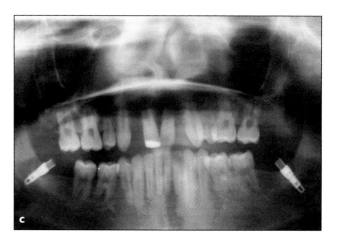

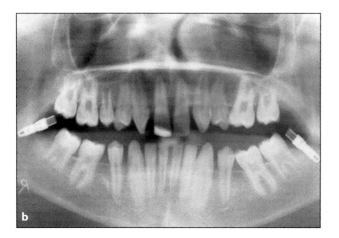

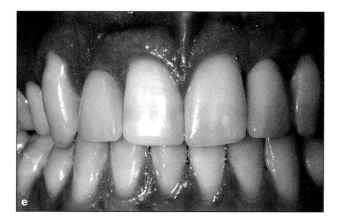

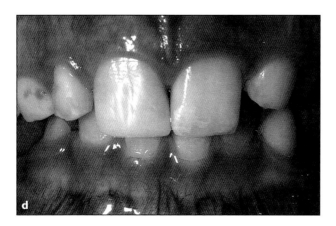

Patient LE

Geometrical and biomechanical analyses. The analysis of this case is similar to the one described above. In step 1 of the treatment, coil springs at A and A' pushed the anterior teeth forward (Figs 5-8a and 5-8d). New springs were inserted between the molars and premolars to push the premolars forward. However, because the teeth and implants served as anchorage, it is difficult to predict what loads would occur on the implants during this step. For example, if the teeth were rigid, they would supply nearly all the anchorage, the implants doing relatively little. Alternatively, if the teeth were "soft" while the implants were held firmly in bone, the opposite would occur, ie, the implants would support most of the load. Without more information about the properties of the teeth and implants, quantitative analyses are impossible.

In step 2 (Fig 5-8b), closed coil springs at B and B' pushed the first molars anteriorly with 12 to 15 oz (3.4 to 4.2 N) while the implants served as anchorage on each side of the arch. Here the implants may be idealized as rigid bodies subjected to loading via springs B and B'. Given the dimensions of the live condition, each implant experienced a distally directed force of about 4.2 N delivered at C and C' parallel to the line of the springs B and B'. By the principles of equivalent systems, the force system at the top-center point of each implant (D and D') will reduce to a force of 4.2 N directed distally and a moment of magnitude of 2 N·cm. The moment tends to cause each implant to tip distally and rotate about its center axis.

In step 3 (Figs 5-8c and 5-8d), coil springs at E and E' pulled the second molars forward. This action would not require any appreciable anchorage by the implants if the anterior dentition were assumed to be rigid. The pre- and posttreatment cephalometric headfilms in Figs 5-8e and 5-8f illustrate the anterior movement of the mandibular dentition. Figure 5-8g shows the patient early in treatment with an overjet and lingually tipped mandibular incisors. Figure 5-8h shows the final dentition from the anterior view.

Patient JP

Geometrical and biomechanical analyses. This case is another example of anteroposterior movement in the mandibular arch. The patient had bilateral mandibular edentulous areas and retroclined mandibular incisors (Fig 5-9). Implants were placed in the mandibular saddle areas bilaterally, creating the necessary anchorage to protract the remaining mandibular anterior dentition (Fig 5-9a). Afterward, the implants were used to restore prosthetic function.

Looped arch wires exerting a force of approximately 10 oz (2.8 N) on the teeth along direction AA' were used to protract the dentition, thereby eliminating appliance friction (Figs 5-9a and 5-9c). A diagram (Fig 5-9b) illustrates that a force F acts on the wire at B; this force is equal and opposite to that acting on the teeth. Measurements of distances involved in the study allow estimates of the numerical values of the equivalent system at point CR. There is a distal force of magnitude 2.8 N and a moment of magnitude 3.6 N·cm. The moment vector has major components tending to tip the implant distally and rotate it about its occlusoapical axis.

Figures 5-9d and 5-9e show the pre- and posttreatment headfilms. Note the dentition and profile improvement with anterior protraction of the dentition. With no posterior teeth in the mandibular posterior quadrants, such protraction would have been difficult if not impossible. Figures 5-9f and 5-9g show the pre- and posttreatment anterior dentition. Even in these views, it is possible to see a more anterior position of the patient's dentition.

Patient MB

Geometrical and biomechanical analyses. This is another example of anteroposterior tooth movement aided by implants, which were placed unilaterally in the maxillary arch. The implants provided excellent anchorage to unilaterally retract the maxillary anterior teeth, after which they were used to restore function.

Fig 5-8 Treatment of overjet and lingually tipped mandibular incisors in patient LE. (a) Step 1: open coil springs at A and A' push the anterior teeth forward, with anchorage provided by the distal implants. New springs were inserted between the molars and premolars to push the premolars forward. (b) Step 2: closed coil springs at B and B' push the first molars anteriorly, with anchorage provided by the implants. (c) Step 3: closed coil springs at E and E' pulled the second molars anteriorly. This action would not require significant anchorage by the implants if the anterior dentition were assumed to be rigid. (d) Method of attaching implant to first molar. This arrangement effectively moved the anchorage from the implant to the first molar lingually. (e) Pretreatment headfilm. The position of the lower dentition is shown prior to protraction. (f) Posttreatment headfilm. Reduction of the overjet has been achieved by protraction of the mandibular dentition. (g) Overjet prior to protraction of the mandibular dentition. (h) Reduction of the overjet and overbite.

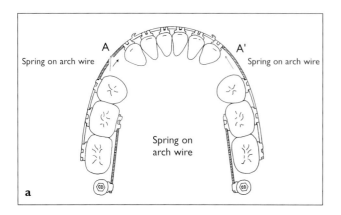

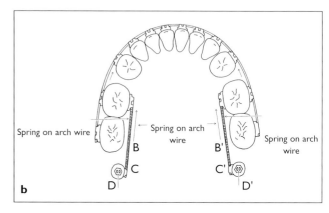

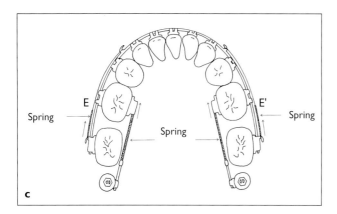

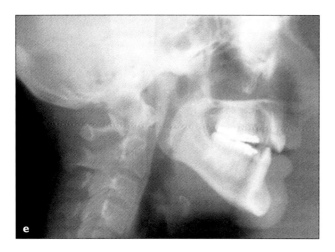

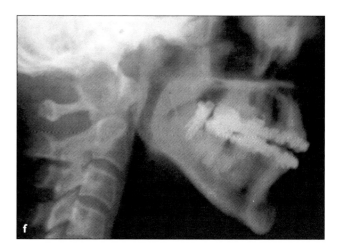

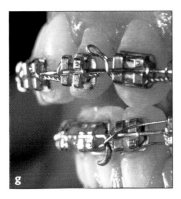

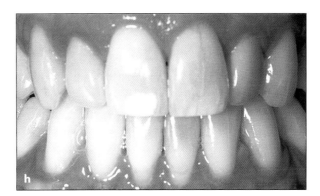

Fig 5-9 Treatment of retroclined mandibular incisors in patient JP. (a) Looped arch wires were used to protract the dentition. (b) Diagram showing the force *F* on the loop; an equal and opposite force *F* acts on the teeth (not shown). (c) Looped arch wire used to protract the mandibular dentition. (d) Pretreatment headfilm showing retruded dentition. (e) Posttreatment headfilm showing protraction of the maxillary and mandibular dentition by means of posterior implants and looped arch wires in the mandibular arch. Protracting the mandibular arch and the use of elastics allowed protraction of the maxillary arch, reduction of the overbite, and a decrease in the interincisal angle. (f) Pretreatment photograph of retruded dentition. (g) Posttreatment photograph showing marked decrease in overbite.

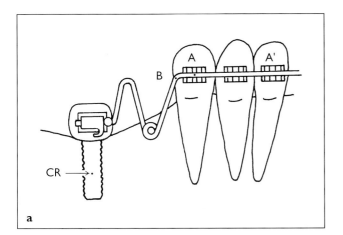

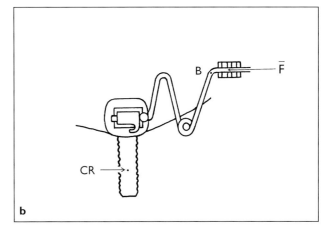

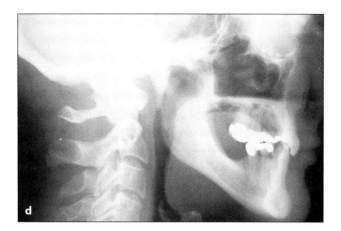

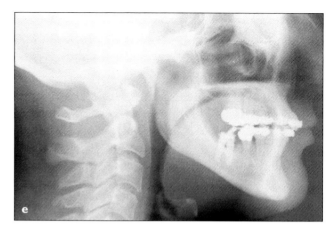

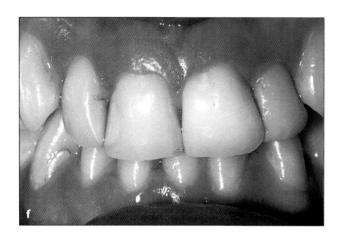

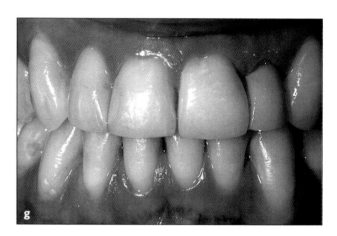

Implants (1, 2, and 3 in Figs 5-10a and 5-10b) were linked rigidly together (Fig 5-10d) so that they could provide group anchorage. A retraction force of 12 to 15 oz (3.3 to 4.2 N) was applied to the anterior teeth by means of a closed coil spring. By Newton's law of action-reaction, an equal and opposite force must develop at the implant anchorage. Because all three implants are linked together, it is difficult to predict exactly what loading will exist on any one implant; more information is needed about the nature of their fixation in bone. Under the extreme assumption that only one of the implants—say implant 1—would provide the entire anchorage, then the equivalent loading on that implant would be as follows. At a point CR near the apex of the implant (Fig 5-10c), there would be an anteriorly directed force of 3.3 to 4.2 N plus a

moment of about 3 to 4 N·cm. This patient had a Class II relationship on the left. Fortunately, this was the side where multiple teeth were missing. Implants were placed after a diagnostic waxup to determine their positions and were then used to correct the Class II malocclusion.

Patient JS

Geometrical and biomechanical analyses. This is a more complex case involving leveling and aligning an arch. Implants were placed in the mandibular posterior edentulous areas, which helped eliminate rotations, allowed leveling of the arch, and corrected the transverse discrepancies. The case also illustrates anteroposterior movement.

Fig 5-10 (a) In the treatment of MB, three implants were rigidly linked together to provide group anchorage for retraction of the maxillary anterior teeth. (b) Occlusal view of (a). (c) Analysis of a hypothetically extreme case. All the anchorage would be provided by just one of the three implants. In this case, maximal loading at CR would be a force *F* and a moment about the point CR. (d) Unilateral retraction of anterior teeth anchored by three implants in the maxillary left quadrant. (e) Panoramic radiograph of the implants in place.

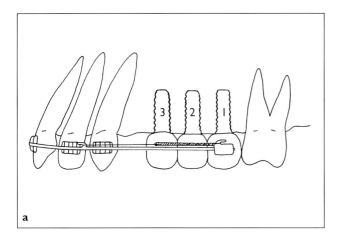

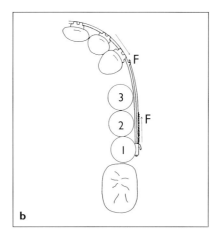

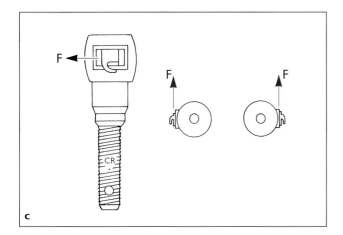

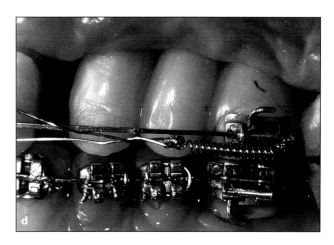

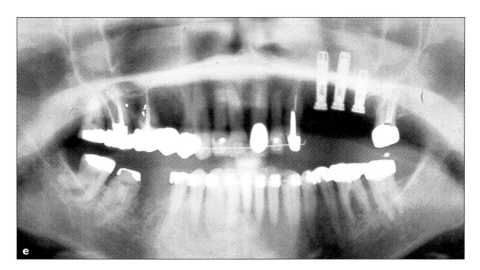

Fig 5-11 Treatment of a rotated and malaligned mandibular dentition and a Class III dental malocclusion in patient JS. (a) Step 1: an implant in the right posterior region was used to anchor a wire that produced lingual forces on the malpositioned teeth in the premolar region. (b) Later steps: the lateral view shows diagrammatically the use of Jasper Jumpers. (c) Study cast showing rotations and malalignment of the mandibular dentition. (d) Posterior implants can greatly enhance alignment and leveling of teeth. Without the implants, tooth alignment would be both time consuming and difficult. (e) A Jasper Jumper was used to protract the maxillary anterior dentition in this Class III dental malocclusion. (f) Panoramic radiograph showing mutilated dentition and lack of anchorage, particularly in the mandibular arch. (g) Panoramic radiograph showing the use of implants as anchorage units. (h) Pretreatment Class III malocclusion. (i) Posttreatment correction of Class III malocclusion.

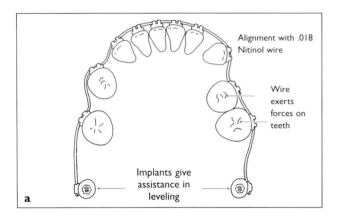

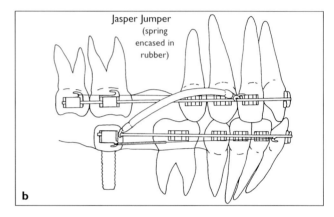

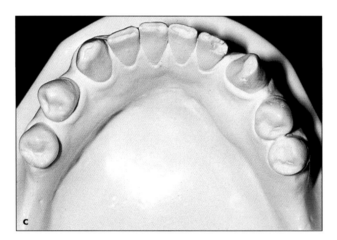

In step 1 of the treatment (Figs 5-11a and 5-11c), the implant in the right posterior region was used to anchor an 0.018-inch Nitinol wire that delivered a lingually directed force of about 2 to 3 oz (0.56 to 0.83 N) to malpositioned teeth in the premolar region. At this stage, the reactive loading of the implant is relatively small, consisting of a force of 0.56 to 0.83 N and a moment of magnitude of roughly 1.1 to 1.7 N·cm.

In later stages of the treatment, Jasper Jumpers (American Orthodontics) were used bilaterally between the maxillary and mandibular arches, as were closed coil springs (Figs 5-11b, 5-11d, and 5-11g). This meant that each implant was subjected to a combination of loading from the Jasper Jumpers and the closed coil springs. The moment of magnitude from each type of loading was about 1 to 2 N·cm.

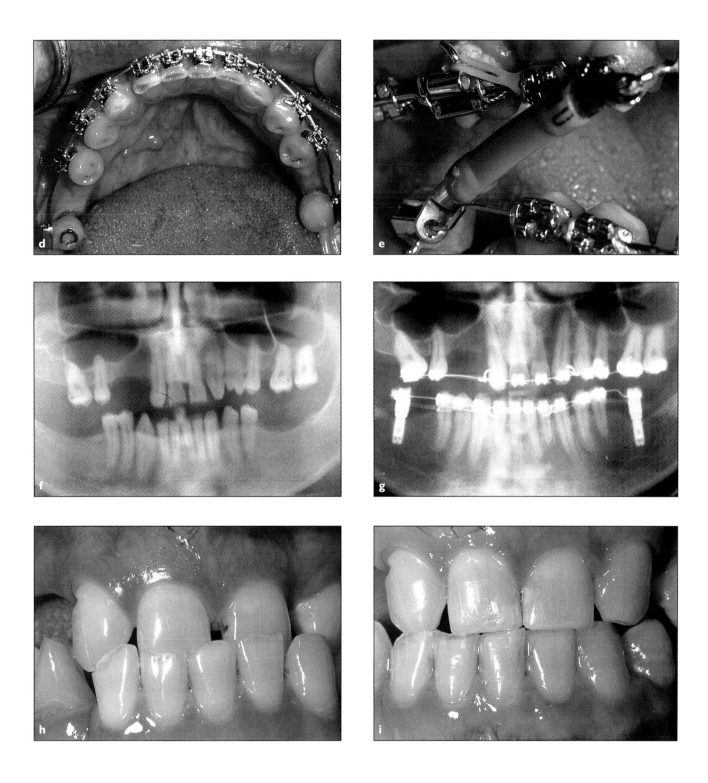

Figures 5-11c and 5-11d show the effect of the implants in facilitating alignment and leveling of the mandibular arch. The implants were then used to retract the mandibular anterior teeth and protract (with elastics and Jasper Jumpers [Fig 5-11e]) the maxillary anteriors to correct the Class III malocclusion. Figures 5-11f and 5-11g show the implants in place in panoramic films; figs 5-11h and 5-11i show the pre- and posttreatment straight-on dental photographs.

Fig 5-12 Treatment of severe Class II, division 2 malocclusion with minimal posterior occlusion in patient EU. (a) Step 1: bilateral distal implants anchored a rectangular wire used to level the anterior teeth via intrusive loading. (b) Step 2: protraction of the teeth via open coil springs. (c) In the maxillary arch, molars were intruded via a rectangular wire designed to deliver an intrusive load on the teeth. The equivalent load system on the implants is reduced to an applied force *F* and a moment at a point of interest, say, P. (d) Pretreatment photograph of crippling Class II, division 2 malocclusion with little or no posterior anchorage available. (e) Posttreatment photograph of corrected Class II, division 2 malocclusion using implants, without which correction of deep bite would not have been possible. One periodontally involved mandibular incisor was lost in treatment and the space closed with protraction off the posterior implants. (f) Implants in place prior to tooth movement. Note extruded maxillary first molar. (g) In-treatment photograph showing completed leveling and alignment. Note bite opening and intrusion of maxillary molar.

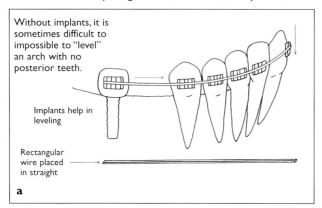

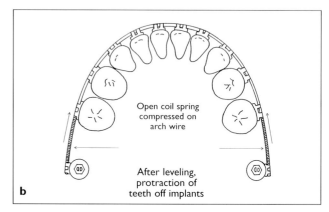

Patient EU

Geometrical and biomechanical analyses. This case demonstrates all forms of tooth movement with the use of implants. The main goal was closure of posterior open bites. Implant locations were determined from a diagnostic waxup. Pre-implant orthodontics was performed to open space for the predetermined implant locations, after which the implants were placed and allowed to integrate.

Bilateral posterior implants were used to anchor a rectangular arch wire that was connected to the anterior teeth to achieve leveling. The wire was placed without adjustment and therefore exerted an intrusive load of 2 oz (0.56 N) on the teeth (Fig 5-12a). The loading on the implants consisted of the same force that the rectangular wire exerted on the teeth (0.56 N) plus a moment of about 1 to 2 N·cm, tending to cause implant tipping toward the distal and rotation about the occlusoapical axis.

Once leveling had been achieved, protraction of the teeth was accomplished using open coil springs (Fig 5-12b) at 15 oz (4.2 N). This loading produces an equivalent system of 4.2 N acting distally on the

implants plus a moment of approximately 0.8 N·cm, having a tendency to rotate the implant about its long axis and tip it distally.

The maxillary molars were intruded by the use of an implant-anchored appliance of an .018 × .025-inch stainless steel rectangular wire (Fig 5-12c). This device was designed to deliver an intrusive loading of about 2 oz (0.56 N) on the maxillary molar. For the given geometrical conditions, the equivalent force-moment system at point P near the implants is a force of 0.56 N and a moment of magnitude of 0.83 N·cm.

The patient had a mutilated dentition with no significant posterior anchorage. Treating her Class II, division 2 malocclusion (Figs 5-12d and 5-12e) would have been difficult—if not impossible—without implants for anchorage. Her maxillary incisors impinged on her mandibular anterior gingiva and her mandibular incisors impinged on the roof of her mouth. Figures 5-12f and 5-12g show how the dentition was leveled. Note intrusion of the maxillary molar during leveling, the most significant effect of the implants in the course of treatment.

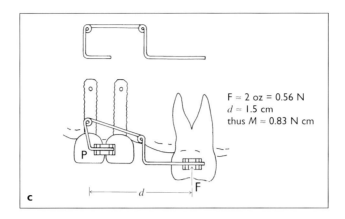

$F \approx 2$ oz $= 0.56$ N
$d \approx 1.5$ cm
thus $M \approx 0.83$ N cm

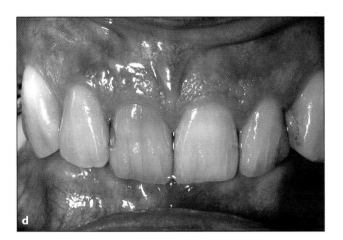

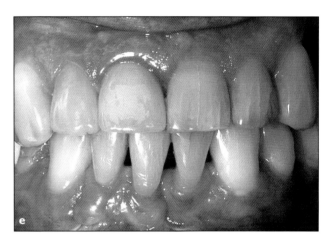

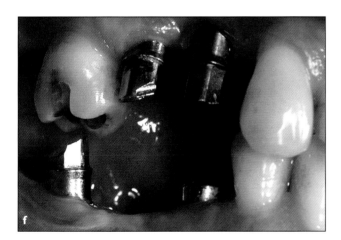

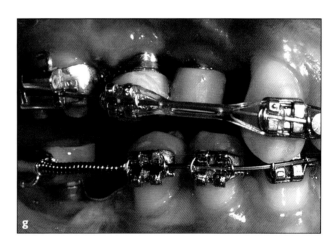

Patient EV

Geometrical and biomechanical analyses.
This case is an example of extrusion-intrusion mechanics as well as anteroposterior movement in the maxillary and mandibular arches. Implants were placed in both the posterior maxilla and mandible. After space was created, the implants were placed in accordance with a diagnostic waxup, then subsequently uncovered and used for protraction of the posterior mandibular molars, as well as extrusion of posterior molars to close lateral open bites (Figs 5-13a and 5-13b). Implants were placed distal to the maxillary right first premolar and distal to the left canine. Three implants were placed in the mandibular arch: two distal to the right canine and one distal to the left canine. The maxillary implants were used to extrude the molars, while the mandibular implants served to extrude molars as well as protract the posterior molars. In terms of forces and moments on the implants, the protraction is similar to that seen in previous examples. Figure 5-13c shows the initial open bite and Fig 5-13d shows the open bite closed. Figure 5-13e shows the occlusal view of the mandibular arch during space closure. (Note the difference in heights between the implants in Figs 5-13d and 5-13e.) Forces to extrude these teeth were from 8 to 10 oz (2.2 to 2.8 N). Figure 5-13f shows the extrusion effects on the molars apically. Bone apposition can also be seen distal to the right mandibular molars and distal to the left mandibular premolar and molars, demonstrating unilateral tooth movement.

Implant Loading in Orthodontic Versus Masticatory Activities

The foregoing analyses reveal that the typical levels of forces and moments on implants in all the clinical orthodontic cases examined here are small compared with levels during mastication. For example, according to our analyses—which are based on spring forces and dimensional data from the cases—the forces on implants in orthodontic therapy rarely exceed a few N. On the other hand, in vivo measurements of bite forces during mastication (eg, Graf[8]; Carlsson and Haraldson[9]; van Eijden[10]; Osborn and Mao[11]) show vertical components as large as 800 N. Moreover, theoretical models of implant loading (Brunski and Skalak[12]; Brunski[13]; Mailath-Pokorny and Solar[14]; Prabhu and Brunski[15,16]; Stegaroiu et al[17]) as well as direct in vivo measurements of forces on implants (Glantz et al[18]; Rangert et al[19]; Mericske-Stern et al[20]; Richter[21]) indicate that forces on implants can equal or exceed the biting force, depending on the exact geometrical conditions in the prosthetic design. Likewise, the same research shows that moments on implants can be in the range of 10 to 40 N·cm, which is about 10 times as large as the moments estimated here for implants used as orthodontic anchorage.

At no time during the courses of treatment described above was there any evidence of implant failure, bone loss, or implant movement. This result is consistent with other research on load levels associated with failures of implant hardware and/or interfacial bone. A review of that subject appears in a recent chapter by Brunski and Skalak,[22] but to develop an estimate of the maximum load-bearing capabilities of the interface, consider the following. The horizontal and lateral force levels needed to cause single-cycle overload failure of the bone-implant interface depend on many factors, for example, whether the implant is in cortical or in cancellous bone. As a rule of thumb, single-cycle failure forces with Brånemark implants are reported to be in the range of 1,000 to 1,500 N for the axial direction and 200 to 300 N for the lateral direction.[23] Likewise, torque-to-failure studies with Brånemark implants report failure in the range of 16 to 77 N·cm for implants in rabbit tibiae for 1 to 6 months[24] and 45 to 48 N·cm in one human volunteer at second-stage surgery.[25] Even allowing for wide variability in such features as healing conditions and bone quality, these failure limits exceed the load levels in the treatments discussed in this chapter by 10 to 100 times.

Fig 5-13 Treatment of lateral open bites in patient EV. (a,b) Diagrams showing the use of springs and arch wire appliances to both extrude and protract teeth while using implant anchorage. (c) Significant posterior open bite. The maxillary premolar and mandibular first premolars are prostheses attached to implants. (d) Extrusion of posterior teeth accomplished using implants. (e) Occlusal view of space closure accomplished using implants as anchorage. (f) Panoramic radiograph of the extrusion that has occurred in the posterior quadrants. Note level of implants in relation to the posterior teeth. The posterior molars, particularly in the mandible, show the effects of extrusion periapically.

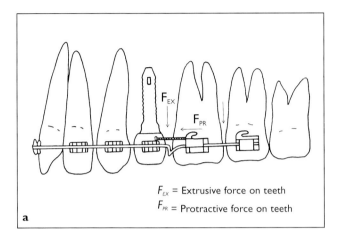

F_{EX} = Extrusive force on teeth

F_{PR} = Protractive force on teeth

a

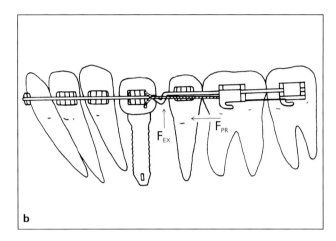

b

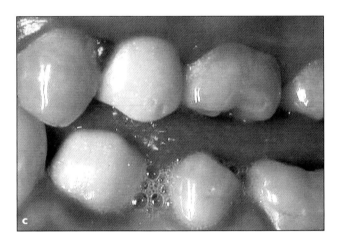

c

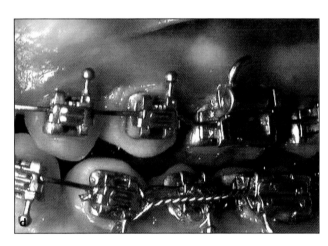

d

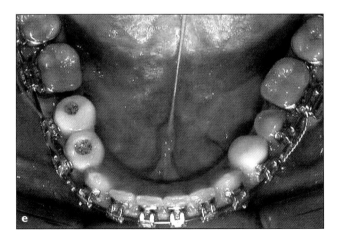

e

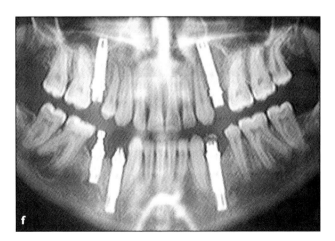

f

Acknowledgments

The authors would like to thank Rensselaer Polytechnic Institute students S. Cowell and E. Pastecki for assistance in making measurements and calculations involving plaster casts of the orthodontic cases discussed in this paper.

References

1. Higuchi KW, Slack JM. The use of titanium fixtures for intraoral anchorage to facilitate orthodontic tooth movement. Int J Oral Maxillofac Implants 1991;6:338–344.

2. Proffit WR, Fields HW Jr, Ackerman JL, et al. Contemporary Orthodontics, ed 2. St Louis: Mosby-Year Book, 1986.

3. Mach E. The Science of Mechanics, ed 9. La Salle, IL: Open Court, 1942.

4. Roberts WE, Marshall KJ, Mozary PG. Rigid endosseous implant utilized as anchorage to protract molars and close an atrophic extraction site. Angle Orthod 1990;60:135–152.

5. Ödman J, Lekholm U, Jemt T, Thilander B. Osseointegrated implants as orthodontic anchorage in the treatment of partially edentulous adult patients. Eur J Orthod 1984;16:157–201.

6. Schlegel V. Relative friction minimization in fixed orthodontic bracket appliances. J Biomech 1996;29:483–491.

7. Smith RJ, Burstone CJ. Mechanics of tooth movement. Am J Orthod 1984;85:294–307.

8. Graf H. Occlusal forces during function. In: Rowe NH (ed). Occlusion: Research on Form and Function. Ann Arbor: Univ of Michigan Press, 1975:9–11.

9. Carlsson GE, Haraldson T. Functional response. In: Brånemark P-I, Zarb GA, Albrektsson T (eds). Tissue-Integrated Prostheses. Chicago: Quintessence, 1985:155–163.

10. Van Eijden TMGJ. Three-dimensional analyses of human bite-force magnitude and moment. Arch Oral Biol 1991;36:535–539.

11. Osborn JW, Mao J. A thin bite force transducer with three-dimensional capabilities reveals a consistent change in bite force direction during jaw muscle endurance tests. Arch Oral Biol 1993;38:139–144.

12. Brunski JB, Skalak R. Biomechanical considerations. In: Worthington P, Brånemark P-I (eds). Advanced Osseointegration Surgery. Chicago: Quintessence, 1992:15–39.

13. Brunski JB. Biomechanics of dental implants. In: Block MS, Kent JN (eds). Endosseous Implants for Maxillofacial Reconstruction. Philadelphia: Saunders, 1995:22–39.

14. Mailath-Pokorny G, Solar P. Biomechanics of endosseous implants. In: Watzek G (ed). Endosseous Implants: Scientific and Clinical Aspects. Chicago: Quintessence, 1996:291–318.

15. Prabhu AA, Brunski JB. Finite element analysis of a clinical case involving overload of an oral implant interface. In: Chandran KB, Vanderby R Jr, Hefzy MS (eds). [Proceedings of the 1997 Bioengineering Conference BED, vol 35]. New York: American Society of Mechanical Engineers, 1997:575–576.

16. Prabhu AA, Brunski JB. An overload failure of a dental prosthesis: A 3D finite element nonlinear contact analysis. In: Simon B (ed). Advances in Bioengineering BED, vol 36. New York: American Society of Mechanical Engineers, 1997:141–142.

17. Stegaroiu R, Sato T, Kusakari H, Miyakawa O. Influence of restoration type on stress distribution in bone around implants: A three-dimensional finite element analysis. Int J Oral Maxillofac Implants 1998;13:82–90.

18. Glantz P-O, Rangert B, Svensson A, et al. On clinical loading of osseointegrated implants: A methodological and clinical study. Clin Oral Implants Res 1993;4:99–105.

19. Rangert B, Gunne J, Glantz P-O, Svensson A. Vertical load distribution on a three-unit prosthesis supported by a natural tooth and a single Brånemark implant. Clin Oral Implants Res 1995;6:40–46.

20. Mericske-Stern R, Assal P, Buergin W. Simultaneous force measurements in 3 dimensions on oral endosseous implants in vitro and in vivo: A methodological study. Clin Oral Implants Res 1996;7:378–386.

21. Richter E-J. In vivo horizontal bending moments on implants. Int J Oral Maxillofac Implants 1998;13:232–243.

22. Brunski JB, Skalak R. Biomechanical considerations for craniofacial implants. In: Brånemark P-I, Tolman DE (eds). Osseointegration in Craniofacial Reconstruction. Chicago: Quintessence, 1998:15–36.

23. Brånemark R. A Biomechanical Study of Osseointegration [dissertation]. Göteborg: Univ of Göteborg, 1996.

24. Johansson C, Albrektsson T. Integration of screw implants in the rabbit: A 1-year follow-up of removal torque of titanium implants. Int J Oral Maxillofac Implants 1987;2:69.

25. Sullivan DY, Sherwood RL, Collins TA, Krogh PH. The reverse-torque test: A clinical report. Int J Oral Maxillofac Implants 1996;11:179–185.

6 Orthodontic and Orthopedic Anchorage Using Subperiosteal Bone Anchors

Michael S. Block, DMD

This chapter is dedicated to my friend and codeveloper of the onplant, Dr David R. Hoffman, who died in 1996.

O rthodontists use anchorage to move teeth and bones. Integrated devices can serve as an absolute anchor for moving teeth and the bones of the craniofacial complex. Endosseous implants can serve as anchors for orthodontic movements,[1,2] including movement of the craniofacial complex.[3] However, endosseous implants require bone availability without the presence of a vital structure at the implant site. The presence of erupted or nonerupted teeth, the inferior alveolar nerve, the nasal and sinus cavities, and the thickness of the soft tissues may prevent the use of an endosseous implant as an orthodontic anchor.

Devices that can be used in the majority of patients require that it be placed on bone, not within bone. Anchoring devices, such as cervical headgear, can be useful in critical orthodontic anchorage situations. But headgear anchorage is active only when the headgear is worn; when not in place, anchorage is less controlled and undesired tooth movement can occur. Headgear devices are not ideal because of lack of patient compliance and questions about their safety.[4–8] Poor patient compliance complicates orthodontic treatment. An anchor that eliminates or significantly reduces the need for patient compliance devices (elastics, headgear, removable devices) helps the orthodontist provide predictable treatment for the patient.

Fig 6-1 (a) The onplant's superficial surface, made of smooth titanium, with the cover screw in place. (b) The onplant's textured, HA-coated undersurface, which is placed directly onto bone.

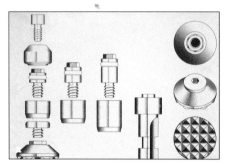 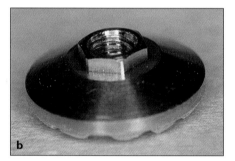

Fig 6-2 (a) Parts utilized with the onplant. (*From left*) Onplant with three transgingival abutments of different lengths and the abutment to which a 0.051-inch transpalatal wire is connected; the transfer coping; and three views of the onplant. (b) Onplant with the cover screw removed, revealing the external hex.

An orthodontic anchor should:

1. Not be placed into bone; therefore, it should not be an endosseous implant
2. Be relatively thin and have a low profile to avoid trauma to the structures of the mouth and provide patient comfort
3. Be noninflammatory and hence be biocompatible
4. Have a versatility of attachments
5. Have sufficient shear strength to resist orthodontic forces and withstand forces placed upon it
6. Be easy to place, remove, and utilize in the conventional orthodontic office
7. Be cost-effective for use within conventional orthodontic care.

The Onplant Device

Based on these criteria, the onplant was designed and tested by Block and Hoffman.[9] The term *onplant* reflects the position of this device on the surface of the bone, not within bone as is a conventional endosseous implant. The onplant is a relatively thin disc measuring approximately 8 mm in diameter and less than 3 mm in height. The surface that lies against the bone is textured and is coated with a thin layer of hydroxyapatite (HA) (Fig 6-1). This bioactive surface joins to the bone via a mechanically significant bond, termed *biointegration*.[10] The superficial surface of the onplant that lies against the periosteal soft tissue is smooth-surfaced titanium. It has an internally threaded hole with an external hexagonal head to accept a variety of attachments, depending on the needs of the case (Fig 6-2).

The abutment system for the onplant includes a transgingival component, which is secured to the onplant by a screw. For patients requiring anchorage of the posterior maxillary molars to retract the anterior maxillary dentition, an abutment with a 0.051-inch wire is placed onto the transgingival component. A transpalatal wire, included with the abutment, is then soldered to the molar bands.

The onplant is placed by the surgeon through a well-defined subperiosteal tunnel. A healing time of 3 to 4 months is allowed for HA-to-bone integration to occur. A small soft tissue trephine is used to remove a circular patch of tissue over the healing screw. An abutment of an appropriate length is screwed into place and protrudes through the tissue into the oral cavity.

The abutment is designed to accept several types of screw-retained attachments. For the use of transpalatal arch mechanics, the abutment has a 0.051-inch wire in place. Custom attachments may be designed to expand the use of this device for protraction, distraction osteogenesis device anchorage, and distalization procedures.

Establishment of the Efficacy of the Onplant Device

Study 1: Initial evaluation of the onplant's ability to withstand a constant orthodontic force[11]

Four mongrel dogs were used. After the animals were given general anesthesia, a full-thickness incision was made in the anterior portion of the palate, followed by the formation of two subperiosteal tunnels reaching the first molar locations. Tunnels were used to avoid placing the incision site directly over the onplant devices. Two onplants were placed into these tunnels, resulting in onplants placed on the right and left sides of the palate. After 10 weeks for integration of the bone to the HA surface of the onplants, one of the onplants was exposed by removing a circular patch of tissue over the onplant. The healing screw was then removed, and a ball-type abutment was placed into the threaded hole of the onplant. A hole was drilled through the maxillary second premolar on the opposite side of the maxilla and a spring was placed, attaching the onplant to the premolar.

The spring was activated between the tooth and the onplant to exert 11 oz of force. The spring was checked weekly and reactivated when needed. After 5 months, the premolar had moved toward the onplant, but the onplant had not moved in any direction as referenced from other teeth. The onplants and adjacent tissues were removed, fixed in 10% neutral buffered formalin, embedded in plastic, and sectioned at 30 μm thickness (Fig 6-3).

The onplants used in this dog study were prototypes with sharp margins. One onplant in one animal developed a large tissue dehiscence and was lost due to lack of integration. Of the remaining three onplants in function, one tooth was moved 4 mm and the other two teeth moved 8 mm toward the onplant device. There were minimal signs of tissue inflammation around the transgingival component of the onplant.

Histologic characteristics of the loaded and unloaded onplants were similar. Bone was found directly apposed to the HA surface (Fig 6-3c). In a few locations, dense bone was found connecting the onplant to the palatal bone, but in most regions trabecular bone connected the onplant to the palatal bone. Bone was present within the textures of the textured surface of the onplant. The HA coating was intact without the presence of osteoclasts or other multinucleated cells.

Study 2: Simulation of the use of the onplant for anchorage of teeth

The purpose of this study was to simulate an intended use of the onplant to anchor molars and retract the anterior dentition. Five adult monkeys (*Macaca fascicularis*) were used. One served as a control, with no onplant placed. The remaining four had one onplant placed onto the palatal bone opposite the maxillary first and second molars. To simulate the clinical situation, this animal model was designed such that the onplant was anchored to the maxillary first molar on one side and to the second molar on the contralateral side. The premolars anterior to the first molars were extracted, and the first molars were ligated to the canines by springs. The springs exerted a reciprocal 250 g force between the first molars and canines. The springs were calibrated weekly and replaced as needed to keep the forces constant throughout the study (Fig 6-4).

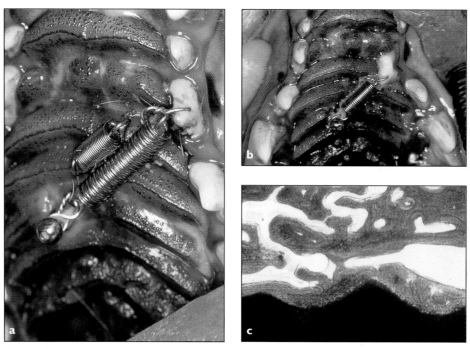

Fig 6-3 (a) In the dog, one onplant has been exposed and connected to the contralateral second premolar with a stainless steel spring activated to deliver 11 oz of force. The nonactivated spring shows the amount of activation. (b) Five months later, the second premolar has been moved 8 mm toward the onplant without movement of the onplant. (c) The textured HA-coated surface coated with bone from the bony palate. Specimen is an onplant loaded 5 months, demonstrating viable bone anchoring the device to the palate (Alizarin red, undecalcified; original magnification ×100).

Two of the monkeys had prosthetic abutments placed into the onplants. These abutments were transferred to a model by means of transfer copings for fabrication of a cast gold transpalatal bar. The cast bar was screw-retained into the onplant and soldered to molar bands on the first molar on one side and the contralateral second molar.

The two remaining monkeys had placed a custom abutment having a groove within it to engage a 0.051-inch transpalatal wire.[11] Impressions were taken, a cast was poured using plaster or stone, and a 0.051-inch wire was soldered to the molar bands and bent to engage the groove of the onplant abutment. The fifth animal, which served as the control, had a 0.051-inch transpalatal wire placed and soldered to the molar bands, without engagement of an onplant device. The monkeys were sacrificed after 6 months.

All onplants integrated. The soft tissue response to the taper-edged onplants was excellent, compared with an occasional soft tissue dehiscence from sharp-edged onplants.

The anchored molars moved anteriorly 1.2 ± 0.2 mm toward the central incisors. The nonanchored molars moved anteriorly an average of 4.1 ± 1.4 mm toward the central incisors ($P < .01$). The anchorage with the cast bar was slightly better than the 0.051-inch wire, due to settling of the wire into the groove in the abutment. The canines did not move differently between the anchored and nonanchored sides ($P > .01$). The control, nononplant dog's teeth showed no evidence of anchoring effects.

When the animals were sacrificed, the palatal soft tissue was removed and the onplants were removed by means of an osteotome and periosteal elevator. The bone was intact and resembled the texture of the onplant's textured surface (Fig 6-4g).

Fig 6-4 (a) Cast bar fabricated in the laboratory and secured to the onplant by a screw and bands cemented to the molars. The first molar on one side is anchored by the onplant, but the contralateral molar is not anchored. (b) Six months later, the anchored tooth has not moved, while the nonanchored first molar has moved toward the canine. (c) In this monkey, a 0.051-inch wire was soldered to the molar bands abutting the onplant. One first molar is anchored to the onplant, and the other (contralateral) is not. (d) Six months later, the anchored molar has moved only 1 mm, whereas the nonanchored molar has moved more than 4 mm. (e) Control animal with 0.051-inch wire placed as above, except no onplant was used. (f) Both teeth have moved the same amount, indicating that the transpalatal wire alone did not anchor the teeth. (g) The onplant was removed from the animal shown in (b) with the aid of an osteotome. Note the bone texture that formed, mirroring the texture of the onplant's surface.

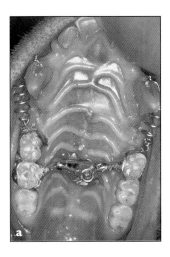

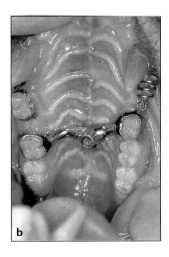

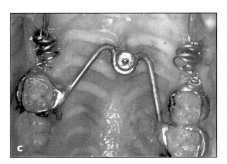

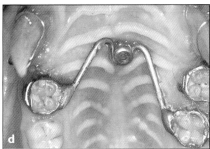

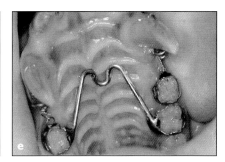

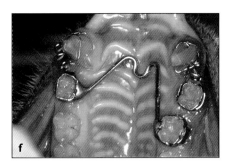

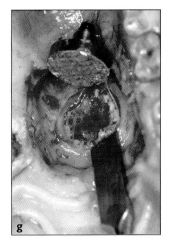

Fig 6-5 (a) One onplant was placed and an antirotational custom abutment was secured to it via a screw. An expansion device was soldered to a transpalatal bar and secured to the abutment on the onplant using a cast attachment. Cast crowns were soldered to the expansion device to securely control molar distalization. Gradual force was placed on the teeth to move them posteriorly. (b) The second molars were distalized bodily 6 mm in 11 months. The onplant served as the sole anchorage and did not move. (c) Defleshed specimen showing amount of distal bodily movement of molar without tipping.

Additional studies involving the onplant device

Molar distalization: An onplant was placed midpalatally opposite the maxillary second premolars. The maxillary third molars were extracted bilaterally. The right and left maxillary second molars were prepared for full-crown cast restorations, which were soldered to a rigid transpalatal bar. An expansion device was soldered to the transpalatal bar and secured to the abutment using a cast attachment (Fig 6-5). The spring expansion device was activated to provide 150 to 200 g of continuous distal force to the second molars. The cast crowns and rigid transpalatal bar ensured bodily movement. The second molars were bodily distalized 6.0 mm in 11 months. The onplant device remained stationary and did not migrate in reference to the remaining teeth in the maxilla. After sacrifice, the tissues were removed, demonstrating the bodily distalization of the maxillary second molar anchored only by the onplant device.

Tooth movements of this type are not easily achieved. The orthodontist may use the onplant to anchor distalizing forces, thus expanding treatment choices when dealing with maxillary dental protrusion, crowding, or Class II malocclusion.

Mechanical testing: Onplants were placed on the ramus and allowed to integrate. These onplants were tested for their ability to resist a shear force. The push-off forces for the onplants averaged 161 lb.

Mandibular lengthening using onplants to anchor the distraction device: Block and Zoldes (unpublished data) used two onplant devices unilaterally positioned on the lateral surface of a dog's mandible to anchor a distraction device. This was the first use of an intraoral device anchored by onplants to the mandible to distract the mandible and lengthen its corpus (Fig 6-6). The onplants were placed against the mandibular body after creation of a subperiosteal tunnel originating from the alveolar crest.

In the laboratory, a custom-cast L-shaped attachment was made to attach to the onplant by a screw into a prosthetic abutment. The vertical component of the custom attachment engaged the jaws of a small Howmedica mini-lengthener. At the time of creation of the osteotomy, the attachment was placed after the lateral aspect of the mandible was exposed.

After approximately 12 weeks for integration of the onplant, an incision was made on the crest and a split-thickness dissection was achieved. The healing screws of the onplants were removed and replaced by prosthetic abutments, and the custom-cast L-shaped attachment was placed. A bur was used to create a corticotomy along the buccal cortex, full thickness above and inferior to the inferior alveolar nerve canal. The lingual plate was gently fractured, preserving the integrity of the neurovascular bundle. The previously adjusted mini-lengthener was positioned. After 7 days for healing, dis-

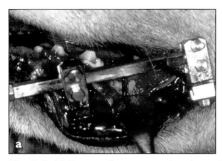
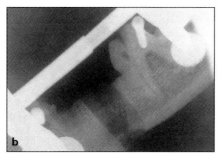
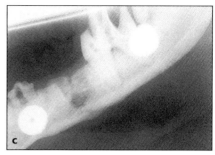

Fig 6-6 (a) Two onplants were placed on the lateral cortex of the mandible. After integration, a custom abutment attached to a mini-lengthener device from Howmedica was placed. An osteotomy was performed without trauma to the neurovascular bundle. (b) After 7 days of healing, the mandible was lengthened 0.5 mm twice each day for 10 consecutive days. (c) Bone filled in the gap by 8 weeks.

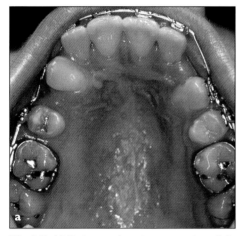
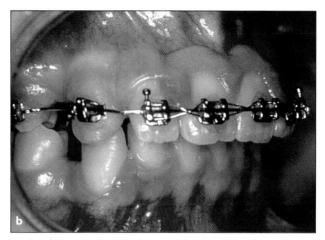

Fig 6-7 (a) Patient undergoing retraction of the anterior dentition with the aid of cervical headgear. This patient opted to use the onplant and eliminate the headgear. (b) Preoperative view showing the need to retract the dentition without anterior migration of the molar.

traction was accomplished 0.5 mm twice a day for 10 consecutive days, for a total of 10 mm of unilateral elongation. The inferior alveolar nerve was monitored throughout the experiment by the use of a jaw-jerk reflex without loss of nerve function. Radiographic evidence of bone formation within the distraction gap was present at 6 weeks.

The onplant is a device that can use any bone surface as the location of the anchor.

Clinical field testing: Four women participated in a pilot field evaluation using prototype devices. They were wearing orthodontic appliances, a headgear (albeit reluctantly), and had critical anchorage requirements, and they welcomed an alternative form of treatment. A single onplant was surgically inserted subperiosteally in the midpalatal region. After 4 months, the onplant was exposed and a grooved abutment was inserted. Stainless steel bands were fitted to the maxillary first molars, and a polyvinylsiloxane impression technique was used to transfer the bands and abutment location to a working cast. A 0.051-inch stainless steel wire rested against the posterior surface of the abutment and was soldered to the bands. See Figs 6-7 to 6-14 for case examples.

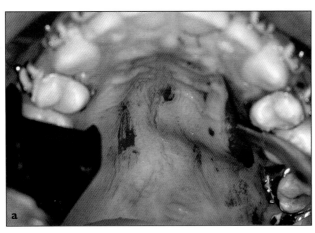

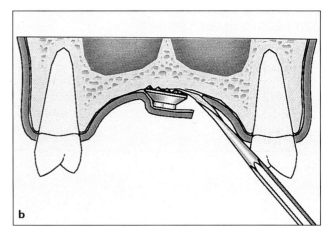

Fig 6-8 (a) Subperiosteal tunnel created through an incision adjacent to the teeth. A periosteal elevator was used to create the tunnel across the midline of the palate. It is important to place the onplant in the central portion, not the periphery of the palate. (b) Diagram showing placement of the onplant through the subperiosteal tunnel.

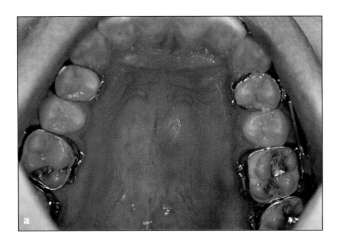

Fig 6-9 (a) Onplant in the middle of the palate prior to exposure. (b) The tip of a tissue punch plunger is placed into the central hole of the cover screw, and the punch is guided to remove a circular piece of gingiva, exposing the cover screw. (c) Diagram showing removal of the cover screw from the onplant.

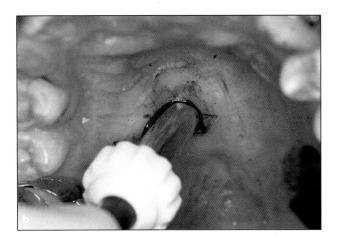

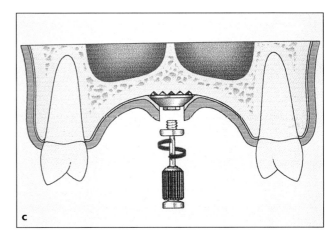

Fig 6-10 (a) Screw-retained transgingival abutment placed on the external hex of the onplant. (b) Transfer coping placed in the transgingival abutment. (c) After placement of the abutment, the transfer coping is placed and an impression is taken using an open-tray technique. (d) Onplant analog placed into the transfer coping. The cast is then poured. (e) Onplant analog attached to the transfer coping.

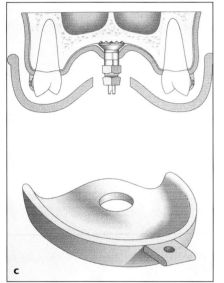

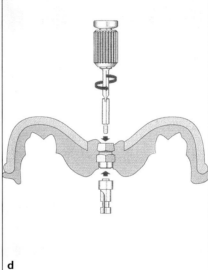

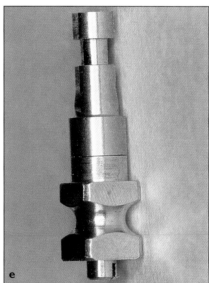

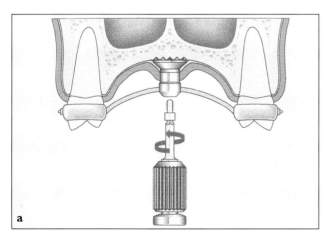

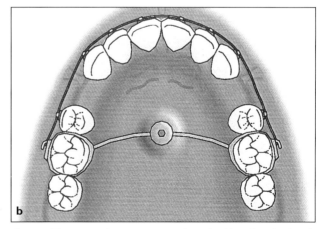

Fig 6-11 (a) Abutment with the laser-welded 0.051-inch wire placed on the cast. The wire is bent appropriately and soldered to the bands of the teeth to be anchored. The wire is then secured to the onplant with a screw and the bands are cemented to the teeth. (b) Onplant with transpalatal wire attached to the teeth. Conventional orthodontics is used to move the anterior teeth posteriorly as a unit, without loss of molar anchorage.

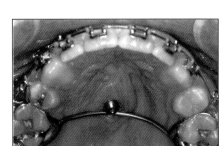 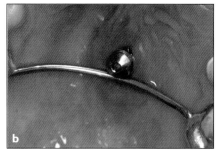 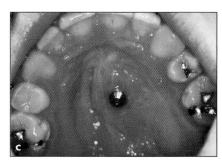

Fig 6-12 (a) Patient shown in Fig 6-7, with maxillary anteriors completely retracted without molar movement. (b) Soft tissues tolerate the transpalatal wire. (c) After the transpalatal wire is no longer needed, it is removed prior to removal of the onplant.

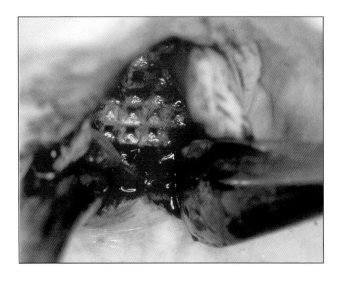

Fig 6-13 Using local anesthesia, a small incision is made along the edge of the onplant. The onplant is elevated from the bone using a small periosteal elevator or an osteotome. Note the texture of the palatal bone, which mirrors the textured surface of the onplant.

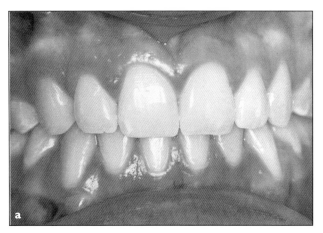 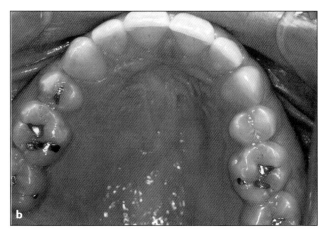

Fig 6-14 (a) Final occlusion of the patient in Fig 6-7. (b) Six months after removal of the onplant, minimal evidence of it remains.

The anterior maxillary teeth were bodily retracted as a unit, without the aid of elastics or headgear. The onplant provided the sole means of anchorage for the dental movements. After the anterior teeth had been retracted into their new positions, the transpalatal wire and the onplants were removed. Removal of the onplants required local anesthesia, a small incision on the anterior 120 degrees of the onplant's circumference, and a periosteal elevator to separate the onplant from the palatal bone. The underlying bone had developed a textured pattern to match the undersurface of the onplant. In all four patients the palatal tissues were closed and healed without adverse effects.

It is significant that all six anterior teeth were retracted simultaneously. In many conventional orthodontic treatment schemes, the canines are retracted before the incisors. Theoretically, this technique of "divide and conquer" reduces the strain on the posterior units. These sequential methods create large diastemas between the canines and lateral incisors during conventional treatment, which can be a serious deterrent for prospective patients. Esthetics is a powerful motivational factor in the decision to tolerate orthodontic treatment. Although the spaces are transient, solutions that avoid the problem offer an advantage.

The implanting and retrieval procedure of the onplant was atraumatic. The cost of including the onplant therapy can be offset by the reduction in treatment time. Elimination of the compliance factor and control of the result simplify the orthodontist's task, and the hazards of extraoral devices are avoided.

Conclusion

Orthodontics is poised at the dawning of a great expansion of its abilities to treat many types of malocclusion. Animal research has clearly proved the absolute stability of implants subjected to orthodontic and orthopedic force levels. Thus far, the use of implants in humans has been limited. As with much of this book, the explosion of knowledge will soon dwarf this chapter. Even though the orthodontist's dream of absolute anchorage control and pure orthopedic intervention has been realized, we should set our sights higher to consider matters beyond our horizons.

References

1. Roberts WE, Helm FR, Marshall KJ, Gongloff RK. Rigid endosseous implants for orthodontic and orthopedic anchorage. Angle Orthod 1989;59:247–256.

2. Roberts WE, Marshall KJ, Mozsary PG. Rigid endosseous implant utilized as anchorage to protract molars and close atrophic extraction site. Angle Orthodont 1990;60:135–152.

3. Smalley WM, Shapiro PA, Hohl TH, et al. Osseointegrated titanium implants for maxillofacial protraction in monkeys. Am J Orthod Dentofac Orthop 1988;94:285–295.

4. Holland GNM, Wallace DA, Mondino BS, et al. Severe ocular injuries from orthodontic headgear. Arch Ophthalmol 1985;103:649–651.

5. Booth-Mason S, Birnie D. Penetrating eye injury from orthodontic headgear—A case report. Eur J Orthod 1988;10:111–114.

6. Seel D. Extra oral hazards of extra oral traction. Br J Orthodont 1980;7:53.

7. Postlethwaite K. The range and effectiveness of safety headgear products. Eur J Orthod 1989;11:228–234.

8. Postlethwaite K. Orthodontic materials update and product news. Br J Orthod 1990;17:329–332.

9. Block MS, Hoffman DR. A new device for absolute anchorage for orthodontics. Am J Orthod Dentofac Orthop 1990;107:251–258.

10. Block MS, Kent JN, Kay J. Evaluation of hydroxylapatite-coated titanium dental implants in dogs. J Oral Maxillofac Surg 1987;45:601–607.

11. Hoffman DR. Implants and orthodontics. In: Block MS, Kent JN (eds). Endosseous Implants for Maxillofacial Reconstruction. Philadelphia: Saunders, 1995:382–400.

7 | Restorative Considerations in Combined Orthodontic-Implant Therapy

Frank M. Spear, DDS, MSD

For the restorative dentist, orthodontics plays a key role in two significant elements of interdisciplinary implant therapy. The first element is function: the orthodontist can significantly influence occlusal relationships by determining whether natural teeth or implants will provide eccentric occlusal guidance and by influencing the angle of contact used for guidance through alteration of the overbite and overjet. The second element is esthetics: the orthodontist can affect the overall esthetic result by altering the location and width of the edentulous spaces where implants are to be placed. The purpose of this chapter is to address these two elements of combined orthodontic-implant therapy.

The goal of all implant restorations is long-term, maintenance-free, functional, and esthetic tooth replacement with osseointegrated implants. To define the orthodontist's role in this treatment, it is necessary to review how implants differ from natural teeth and what causes them to fail.[1,2]

Principles of Function

The single most significant clinical difference between an implant and a natural tooth is the absence of a periodontal ligament around the implant and, consequently, the absence of all the advantages a periodontal ligament provides.[3] On a natural tooth, the periodontal ligament serves several important functions. Proprioceptors within the ligament provide feedback about tooth contact and loading, something implants lack. The nature of the ligament provides the tooth with the ability to adapt to overloading. If the alveolar housing is altered, creating a wider ligament space, the tooth will become mobile without losing attachment. After these excessive forces are managed, bony apposition occurs and the ligament returns to a normal width

Fig 7-1 Perhaps the worst type of implant failure: loss of integration following completion of the final restoration. The failure may or may not have been related to an occlusal problem.

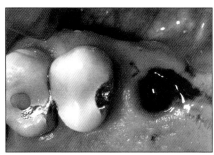

Fig 7-2 Patient complained of a loose second premolar crown that was supported by an implant. With light pressure, the crown and coronal third of the implant body, having fractured, came out.

Fig 7-3 The crown and fractured implant from Fig 7-2. This type of structural failure is almost always the result of occlusal overloading. In this case, the patient was a severe bruxer.

with an accompanying decrease in tooth mobility. An implant, in contrast, has almost no adaptability to overloading; once osseointegration is lost, it will not return by correcting the excessive force. Finally, the periodontal ligament also provides the tooth with shock absorption, which is a decided advantage for relatively fragile dental materials such as porcelain. The amount of shock absorption is determined by the width of the ligament space and the relative tooth mobilities. The implant, however, has essentially no shock absorption, placing dental materials under greater loads with a higher likelihood of fracture.[4] Because of these factors, the goal of occlusal treatment planning on implants is to minimize the risk of overloading the appliances and the attached restorations.

It is also important to understand the three primary types of failures that occur in implant therapy. The first type of failure occurs when the implant fails to integrate after stage-one surgery. This is relatively uncommon and rarely involves the orthodontist or the restorative dentist. The second type of failure is the loss of integration following placement of the prosthesis (Fig 7-1), which is extremely frustrating for the patient as it may mean starting the treatment over again. There are two known causes for this type of failure. One is a microbiological cause, in which periodontal disease develops around the implant resulting in peri-implantitis.[5] The other is the result of occlusal trauma in which the load being applied is greater than the ability of the alveolar bone to resist it. It has been

postulated that occlusal trauma is always the predecessor to microbiologic breakdown. Inasmuch as the occlusion may play a critical role in the loss of integration, the orthodontist and restorative dentist can have a profound influence on the long-term success of the implant. The third and most common type of failure is structural in which either a failure of the implant components occurs, such as a fractured or loose abutment or retaining screws, or the implant body itself fails (Figs 7-2 and 7-3).[6,7] The fracture of dental materials used in the fabrication of the restoration is also included in this category. Structural failures are almost always due to faulty occlusion, unless the patient has been involved in a traumatic accident. Therefore, the orthodontist and the restorative dentist play critical roles in setting up the occlusion to minimize the risk of structural failure.

In order to plan a patient's treatment from the perspective of a restorative dentist, the dentist should address the occlusion first and then the esthetics. The two questions to consider in beginning a treatment plan are:

1. How did the patient lose his or her teeth?
2. Is there evidence of parafunctional activity on the remaining teeth?

It is helpful to know how the patient's teeth were lost because it can help predict what the future may hold for the remaining natural teeth. For example, if the teeth were lost as a result of severe caries or periodontal disease, the patient will be more likely to lose more teeth in the future from these causes than would a patient whose teeth were missing congenitally or lost in an accident. This will influence the decision whether to keep questionable teeth or to remove them and use more implants.

It is critical to know if there is parafunctional activity on the remaining teeth because abnormal function could adversely affect the longevity of the implant restoration. In fact, the type of function may determine whether orthodontics or orthognathic surgery is required in the treatment plan. For patients without evidence of parafunction, the occlusal management of implants is very similar to that of natural teeth, so that even if a canine implant is guiding the lateral movements, it is unlikely that it will cause any long-term maintenance problems. The patient who has moderate to severe bruxism, however, is much more difficult to treat; therefore, the remaining functional consideration of implant therapy will focus on the management of the patient with evidence of parafunctional activity.

For the patient who shows evidence of parafunction, either by wear, mobility, or fractured teeth, it is important to follow a logical process in developing the overall treatment plan. The first step is to diagnose, if possible, the etiology of the parafunction,[8] of which there are two major categories. Parafunctional activity that is completely unrelated to any occlusal relationship is called *central nervous system (CNS) parafunction.* Parafunctional activity that has an occlusal component is called *occlusal parafunction,*[9,10] and it follows that an alteration in the occlusion may alter the parafunctional activity.

It is important to diagnose which of these two etiologies is causing the patient's parafunction prior to developing the final treatment plan. If the occlusion is the primary cause of the bruxism, the predictability of treatment and occlusal management are greatly simplified. If CNS bruxism is the cause, then a very specific occlusal scheme will be required.[11,12] Diagnosing the type of parafunction is a two-step process.

The first step is to identify any occlusal findings that in some patients may trigger bruxism. The specific findings to look for are temporomandibular joints that are painful or have unstable intracapsular

disorders, interferences in the arc of closure from centric relation to intercuspal position, and eccentric interferences in protrusive and lateral movements. The presence of these findings alone does not mean that they are responsible for the bruxism; it is necessary to confirm their significance.

To do this, a second step, trial therapy, is necessary. This involves trying to eliminate all the potential causes of bruxism and then seeing if the activity continues. The most common form of trial therapy is an occlusal appliance that eliminates the occlusal findings listed above.[13] After 12 weeks, during which the appliance is worn typically at night and during the 6 to 8 most stressful hours of the day, the surface of the appliance is evaluated. If severe wear facets are present, the assumption is that the primary etiology of the patient's bruxism is CNS parafunction and that appropriate occlusal management is necessary (Fig 7-4). If by 12 weeks no wear facets—or only a few—are found, then occlusal therapy to eliminate the causes of the bruxism is undertaken.

For the patient who has CNS bruxism, there are critical questions that must be addressed in the treatment planning. The first is the nature of the parafunction (bruxism). There are two types of bruxism: horizontal and vertical. In horizontal bruxism, the patient bruxes in a broad, grazing pattern, using a wide range of mandibular movements. It can be identified by evaluating the incisal edges and buccal cusps of the maxillary teeth. In horizontal bruxers, the wear extends across the edges of the teeth, resulting in decreased overbite as the teeth wear away (Fig 7-5). Whether the patient has a Class II malocclusion with a deep overbite or a Class III open bite, it is critical to assess if he or she bruxes in a broad range of movement. The second type of bruxism is vertical bruxism. In this type, the patient uses a very small range of mandibular motion. It typically results in wear on the lingual of the functional surfaces of the maxillary teeth and on the facial of the functional surfaces of the mandibular teeth. As this wear progresses, the centric holding areas are lost and the teeth supraerupt. Since the incisal edges do not wear away as the posterior teeth wear and erupt, the overbite increases (Fig 7-6).

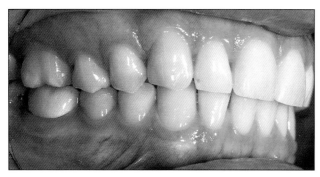

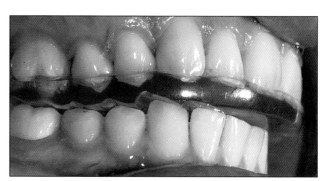

Fig 7-4a Lateral view of a 27-year-old patient with evidence of significant bruxism. Her temporomandibular joints are pain free and functionally normal. She does, however, have eccentric interferences and an interference with the arc of centric closure.

Fig 7-4b Patient shown in Fig 7-4a wearing an appliance that was fabricated in centric relation with anterior guidance. After 12 weeks, she has worn away the canine rise and created grooves in the posterior portion of the appliance. This patient would be diagnosed as having CNS parafunction (bruxism), which would not be altered by an occlusal change.

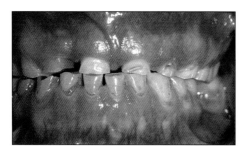

Fig 7-5 Typical appearance of a patient with horizontal bruxism. The broad mandibular movements have resulted in a wearing away of the incisal edges of the teeth and a subsequent reduction in overbite.

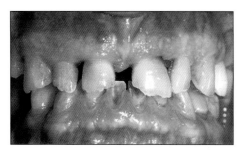

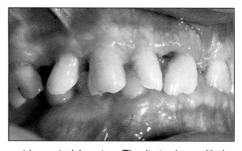

Figs 7-6a and 7-6b Typical appearance of a patient with vertical bruxism. The limited mandibular movements during bruxism have resulted in a wearing away of the lingual of the maxillary anteriors and the facial of the mandibular anteriors and a subsequent deepening of the overbite.

The occlusal management of these two types of bruxism is very different. In all cases of parafunction, however, the basic rule is to get the teeth out of the way of the bruxing activity. In horizontal bruxers this is far more difficult because of the broad range of motion during bruxism. In general, the horizontal bruxer will require a shallow overbite to allow the mandible to move. In some patients this may require orthodontics and orthognathic surgery to produce the minimal overbite prior to restoration. In contrast, the vertical bruxer can accept a much steeper overbite because of the limited range of mandibular motion during bruxism. The occlusal goals in treating vertical bruxers are centric stops on the teeth and freedom surrounding these stops, which corresponds to the amount of mandibular movement during bruxism. This is determined by evaluating the existing wear on their natural teeth and monitoring the wear on the provisional restorations.

Once the type of parafunction has been identified, it is possible to begin designing the occlusion,

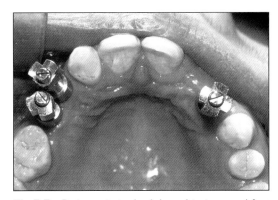

Fig 7-7a Patient missing both lateral incisors and first premolars. Note that the orthodontist moved one canine anteriorly next to the central incisor and the other canine posteriorly next to the second premolar, resulting in the occlusal guidance in both directions being on the implants.

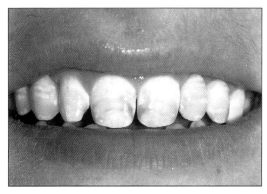

Fig 7-7b Although a low lip line made this patient's esthetics acceptable, moving the canines to their correct positions and using four single-tooth implants to replace the lateral incisors and first premolars would have provided a better result.

especially as it relates to the depth of the acceptable overbite. The next critical questions to consider for the implant restoration are:

1. Can any of the natural teeth guide the eccentric movements of the mandible, or will the implants be responsible for providing disclusion?
2. If there are not enough teeth in the correct positions for guidance, can the teeth be orthodontically repositioned to provide guidance? It will be necessary for the therapist to evaluate root length, diameter, and form to determine whether a single tooth will be adequate to provide guidance.
3. If not, can multiple teeth be used, as in group function, to provide guidance?

The importance of these questions can be exemplified by the patient in Fig 7-7, who presented after orthodontics and implant placement had been completed in the late 1980s. The patient had both maxillary canines, but the right canine had been moved mesially into the lateral incisor position, leaving two implants responsible for guiding the right eccentric movements. On the left side, the canine had been moved distally into the premolar position, again leaving an implant to guide the disclusion. A far better solution would have been to move both canines into their normal positions, leaving four single-tooth spaces that could each be

restored with an implant, none of which would have had to provide eccentric guidance. There are times when single canine implants are necessary. In these instances, using the central and lateral incisors and premolars for eccentric guidance is recommended (Fig 7-8).

Another challenge concerning natural tooth guidance is the type of bruxism. The patient in Fig 7-9 had natural anterior teeth for guidance and desired posterior implants. She also had a severe horizontal bruxing habit. When the restoration was completed in 1986, enough overbite was restored to disclude the fixed partial dentures on the posterior implants. But, due to the patient's pattern of bruxism, she could not tolerate the overbite provided, and within months she began fracturing the porcelain on the anterior teeth. After these restorations had undergone 18 months of repair, the maxillary incisors were finally shortened, thus reducing the overbite. This kept her from fracturing the porcelain for 6 more years. However, because the implant prostheses no longer had immediate disclusion, she subsequently started fracturing the implant components, both the retaining screws and the abutment screws, every 6 to 9 months. Ultimately, the restoration was redone in 1993 with a very shallow overbite and a removable partial denture on attachments to the implants. Therefore, the question is not simply if natural teeth are available to provide guidance, but rather if the

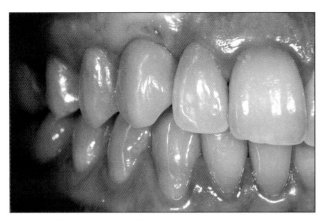

Fig 7-8a The missing maxillary canine was replaced with a single-tooth implant.

Fig 7-8b Note that eccentric guidance is provided by the lateral incisor and first premolar. The implant contacts in centric closure and is in light contact during forceful lateral movements. This greatly minimizes any risk of occlusal overload.

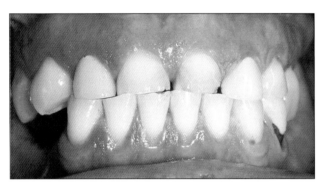

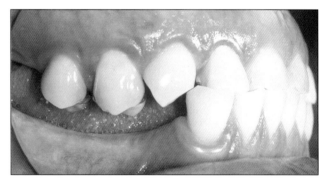

Figs 7-9a and 7-9b Classic appearance of a patient who had severe horizontal bruxism and who desired her posterior teeth be replaced with implants. Her anterior teeth were available to provide guidance but there was no overjet left.

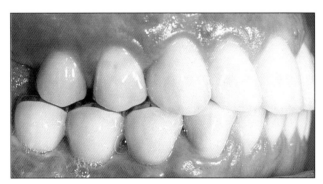

Fig 7-9c Following reconstruction in 1986. The anterior teeth were lengthened for better esthetics and to increase the overbite so as to provide disclusion to the posterior implant-supported restoration.

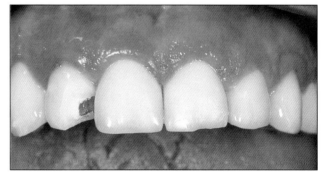

Fig 7-9d Because of the patient's horizontal bruxing habit, she fractured the porcelain on several of the anterior teeth in attempting to get them out of the way.

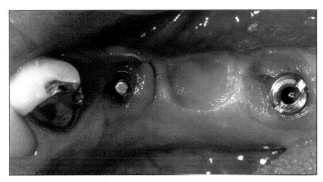 

Figs 7-9e and 7-9f In 1987, the anteriors were shortened to reduce the continued fracture of porcelain. However, this resulted in a lack of posterior disclusion for the implants and fracture of the abutment screws.

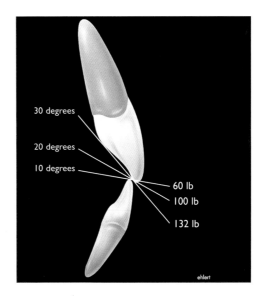

Fig 7-10 Diagram illustrating the relationship between the occlusal contact angle and torsional stress. When implants must guide the disclusion in a bruxer, the angle of guidance should be as shallow as possible.

patient can tolerate enough guidance on the natural teeth to immediately disclude the implants. In general, vertical bruxers tolerate implants very well because the remaining natural teeth accept a deep overbite, but horizontal bruxers are challenging implant patients because it is difficult for them to disclude the implants while maintaining a shallow overbite.

If implants are to provide eccentric guidance for the occlusion because there are no existing natural teeth to do so, it is critical to evaluate the angle of contact that will occur on the implants relative to the patient's parafunction. A patient having a deep overbite and evidence of horizontal bruxism who also needs multiple implants in the canine and premolar areas is almost always destined to have structural failures unless the deep overbite can first be

corrected with orthodontics, either alone or in concert with orthognathic surgery. Weinberg and Kruger[14] evaluated the impact of the occlusal contact angle on implants and discovered the following:

Starting with a 20-degree contact angle between the occluding surfaces, for every 10-degree change there is a 32% change in torsional stress at the abutment-to-implant connection.

Again, assuming a 20-degree contact angle, if there were 100 lb of torsional stress on an implant, changing the contact angle to 30 degrees would result in 132 lb of torsional stress, and changing it to 40 degrees would result in 174 lb of torsional stress. Decreasing the overbite to create a shallower contact angle would reduce the torsional stress to only 68 lb (Fig 7-10).

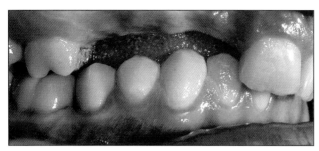

Fig 7-11a Patient who lost his maxillary right lateral incisor, canine, and premolars in an accident and wished to have them replaced with implants. Note the depth of the overbite and the fact that the implants will have to provide lateral occlusal guidance.

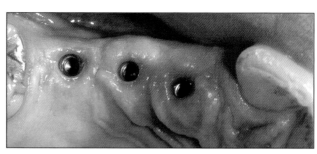

Fig 7-11b Three implants were placed in 1985. Note the wear facets extending across the edge of the patient's central incisor, indicating horizontal bruxism. At age 21, this patient has already worn all the enamel off the incisal edge of his central incisor.

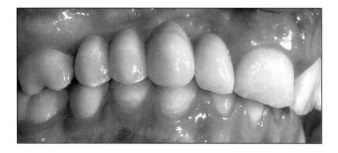

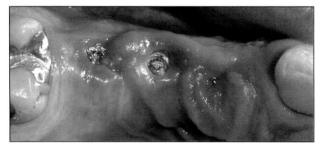

Fig 7-11c Implant-supported restoration replacing the four teeth in 1985.

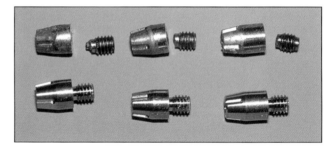

Figs 7-11d and 7-11e Within 1 year, all three abutment screws had fractured and the restoration had come off, while the abutment screws had remained in the implants. Given his bruxing habit, the only way this patient could have been successfully treated was with orthodontics and orthognathic surgery to decrease his overbite.

The contact angle is a function of two variables: (vertical) overbite and (horizontal) overjet. As the overbite is increased, the contact angle typically increases, or steepens. As the overbite is decreased, the contact angle also decreases, or becomes shallower. As the overjet is increased, the contact angle decreases, and as the overjet is decreased, the contact angle increases.

The patient shown in Fig 7-11 is a classic example of this relationship. In 1981, his maxillary right lateral incisor, canine, and premolars were avulsed in an accident, so he had no natural teeth in this area to provide the disclusion. In addition, he had a very deep overbite. A careful examination of his natural teeth revealed wear facets extending from centric across the incisal edges of the maxillary teeth, which is evidence of a horizontal pattern of bruxism. Note his centric contact in Fig 7-11a near the palatal aspect of the cingulum as compared to the facet in Fig 7-11b, indicating a wide range of mandibular movement during bruxism. Orthodontics and orthognathic surgery were recommended but the patient refused. Instead, he wanted his missing teeth replaced with implants. The restoration was completed in 1985 using a very steep contact angle and implants for lateral guidance. Within 1 year, he complained of the restoration loosening; he had in fact fractured all three abutment screws. They were replaced but were fractured again several times over the next few years, and the implants were ultimately lost. This case vividly illustrates that the inability to control the lateral loads on implants leads to almost certain structural failure, which could have been avoided by using orthodontics and orthognathic surgery to create a shallow overbite relationship. Otherwise, the patient would have been better served with a removable partial denture.

To summarize the orthodontist's role in improving the functional element of implant restorations:

1. Whenever possible, position the teeth and design an occlusion such that the natural teeth will guide the eccentric movements.
2. For any patients with evidence of parafunction, determine whether the parafunction is CNS or occlusally mediated and whether it is of a vertical or a horizontal nature.
3. If the parafunction is CNS mediated and horizontal in nature, alter the dental and skeletal relationships to provide a shallow overbite and overjet for the implants, minimizing the torsional stress.

Principles of Esthetics

The next element of implant treatment in which the orthodontist can influence the restorative result is esthetics, particularly in the gingival area around the implants.[15] To understand the orthodontist's role in the final gingival esthetic result, it is necessary to understand what effects the facial and interproximal tissue heights have on implants and teeth.

It is clear that the overlying gingival form reflects the underlying bone fairly accurately. Evaluating the differences between bony levels surrounding implants and those surrounding teeth provides a starting point for understanding the gingival differences. On natural teeth, there is a highly scalloped nature to alveolar bone from facial to interproximal to facial. This bony scallop essentially follows the rise and fall of the cementoenamel junction (CEJ), creating a dip of approximately 3 mm from facial to interproximal in the anterior

teeth and decreasing as the CEJ flattens out on the posterior teeth. In contrast, an implant has no bony scallop from facial to interproximal since the heads of the implant systems are flat rather than scalloped like a CEJ. Because of this, even if the bone were appropriately scalloped, placing the head of an implant flush with the interproximal bone would leave threads exposed on the facial of the implant that would not be covered by bone.

Conversely, if the implant were seated completely so that the facial bone covered the head of the implant, it would leave unsupported bone coronal to the head of the implant interproximally. This unsupported bone would resorb, removing the underlying support for what would have been the papilla. Because of these bony differences, it is extremely difficult to obtain a normal gingival scallop around multiple implants when compared with natural teeth. This difference is amplified by the differences in gingival height from facial to interproximal on natural teeth as compared with implants.

On natural teeth, a "biologic band" of connective tissue and epithelial attachment occupies an area on average 2 mm in height above the bone facially and interproximally.[16] Coronal to the attachment, the average sulcus depth on the facial surface is 1 mm, leaving 3 mm of total gingival height above bone on the facial surfaces. Interproximally, however, there is an average sulcus depth of 2.5 mm coronal to the attachment, resulting in a papilla height of 4.5 mm above bone. This 1.5 mm difference in gingival height above bone from facial to interproximal, when combined with the average 3-mm osseous scallop, results in an average gingival scallop of 4.5 mm from facial to interproximal. In other words, the tip of the papilla is located 4.5 mm more coronal than the facial free gingival margin (Fig 7-12). These numbers are of course averages that vary depending on the shape of the teeth and the nature of the periodontium, eg, flat and thick versus scalloped and thin.

The challenge in managing the esthetics between implants in the anterior is twofold. First, the bone between the implants is not as highly scalloped as it is around natural anterior teeth. This alone will result in a reduction in gingival scallop. In addition,

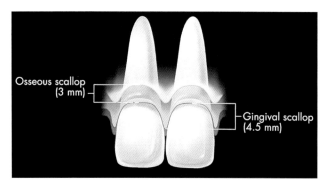

Fig 7-12 Diagram illustrating the osseous and gingival relationships that exist around natural anterior teeth. These relationships result in a papilla that is 4 to 5 mm more coronal than the free gingival margin.

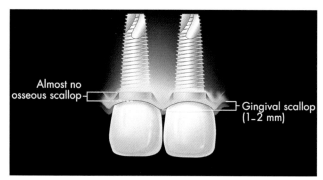

Fig 7-13 Relationship between side-by-side implants and the bone and gingiva surrounding them. Note reduction in osseous scallop from facial to interproximal and lack of a significant difference in gingival heights above bone from facial to interproximal compared with natural teeth. This combination of minimal osseous scallop and minimal change in gingival height leads to a flat gingival form.

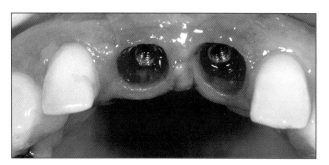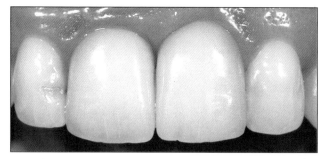

Figs 7-14a and 7-14b Clinical case illustrating the challenge of side-by-side implants. The final restorations have been in place for 5 years. Note how the height of the papilla between the implants is 1.5 mm to 2 mm more apical than that of the papilla between implants and adjacent lateral incisors.

the height differences (above bone) between facial and interproximal gingiva do not appear to be the same as that of natural teeth. As stated above, the average papilla on natural teeth is 4.5 mm above the bone compared with 3 mm for the facial gingiva.[17] The actual tissue height around implants appears to range from 2 mm to 4 mm depending on several factors, but with little difference between facial and interproximal (Fig 7-13). Therefore, for multiple implants side by side, the papilla is often only 1 mm to 2 mm more coronal than the facial free gingival margin, compared with 4.5 mm for natural teeth, so there can be almost no gingival scallop. This flat-looking gingival appearance is especially unesthetic in the anterior region (Fig 7-14).

Of the team members, the orthodontist is the one who can take a two-tooth pontic site and convert it into two single-tooth implant sites via tooth move-

ment. A common example is a patient missing maxillary lateral incisors and first premolars. Often the canine will erupt next to the central incisor, leaving a space for two pontics. If two side-by-side implants are used, the result is the esthetic problem discussed earlier, but in addition, these two implants would have to provide the occlusal guidance (see Fig 7-7a, patient's right). By orthodontically repositioning the canine into its correct location, the orthodontist can create four single-tooth implant sites. Functionally, this leaves the canine rather than the implants to guide the lateral excursions; in addition, the esthetic advantages of this type of alteration are remarkable. Rather than having two implants side by side with all the aforementioned bony and gingival difficulties in obtaining a papilla, the patient would have two implants separated from each other by a tooth and surrounded by teeth on ei-

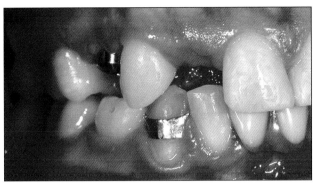
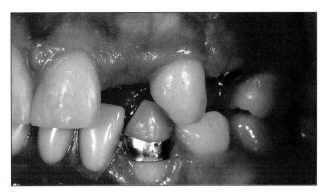

Figs 7-15a and 7-15b A young patient congenitally missing his maxillary lateral incisors and premolars. The canines had erupted next to the central incisors. One option was to place two adjacent implants on each side to restore the canines and premolars, then restore the natural canines to look like lateral incisors (since that is the position they were in). A far better option was the one chosen: the canines were moved into their correct positions, leaving four single-tooth implant sites.

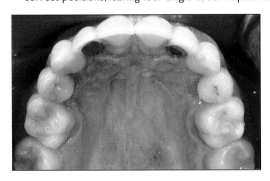

Fig 7-15c Completed restoration using four single-tooth implants to replace the lateral incisors and premolars.

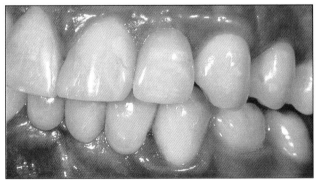
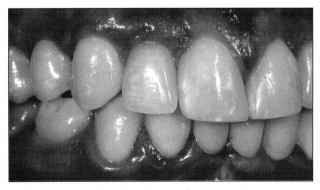

Figs 7-15d and 7-15e Left and right lateral views of the final restoration. Note the soft tissue form around the single-tooth implant and the occlusal guidance provided by the patient's natural canines.

ther side. These teeth would have highly scalloped CEJs, which the bone would follow from facial to interproximal. The bone around the teeth adjacent to the implant appears to be responsible for the height of the papilla. Thus, if the bone on the facial of the implant and the interproximal of the adjacent natural teeth is at the correct level, it is highly likely that an excellent esthetic result can be obtained gingivally, even if the bone on the interproximal of the implant is not at the same level as the bone on the

teeth. For the orthodontist, the question is simply this: Whenever there is a multiple-tooth pontic site, is it possible to move in an adjacent tooth to create two single-pontic sites?

Figure 7-15 illustrates this well. A male patient was congenitally missing multiple teeth, including the maxillary lateral incisors and premolars. The permanent canines had erupted next to the central incisors. One option would have been to leave the canines in this position and restore or reshape them to look like lateral incisors, then restore the canine and premolar areas with side-by-side implants. This would have been not only a functional compromise but an esthetic one as well. A much better choice would have been to move the canines back into their correct positions, leaving a site for a lateral incisor implant mesial to each canine and a premolar implant to the distal; thus the canine would be unrestored and in an ideal position for proper canine disclusion. As is almost always the case, the result was better and easier to achieve functionally and esthetically.

Summary

This chapter has identified the functional and esthetic principles of combined orthodontic-implant therapy and their biologic rationale. If these principles are followed, the likelihood of producing a functionally and esthetically favorable result will be greatly enhanced. Often, the orthodontist is the only member of the team who can create these possibilities through proper planning and tooth movement.

References

1. Jemt T, Linden B, Lekholm U. Failures and complications in 127 consecutively placed fixed partial prostheses supported by Brånemark implants: From prosthetic treatment to first annual checkup. Int J Oral Maxillofac Implants 1992;7:40–44.

2. Taylor TD. Prosthodontic problems and limitations associated with osseointegration. J Prosthet Dent 1998;79:74–78.

3. Skalek R. Biomechanical considerations in osseointegrated prostheses. J Prosthet Dent 1983;49:843–848.

4. Misch LE. Implant-protected occlusion: A biomechanical rationale. Compendium 1994;15:1330–1342.

5. Becker W, Becker BE, Newman M, Nyman S. Clinical and microbiologic findings that may contribute to dental implant failure. Int J Oral Maxillofac Implants 1990;5:31–38.

6. Katona TR, Goodacre CJ, Brown DT, Roberts WE. Force-moment systems on single anterior implants: Effects of incisal guidance, fixture orientation and loss of bone support. Int J Oral Maxillofac Implants 1993;8:512–522.

7. Weinberg LA. The biomechanics of force distribution in implant-supported prostheses. Int J Oral Maxillofac Implants 1993;8:19–31.

8. Dawson PK. Evaluation, Diagnosis and Treatment of Occlusal Problems, ed 2. St. Louis: Mosby, 1989.

9. Sheikholeslam A, Riise C. Influence of experimental interfering occlusal contacts on the activity of the temporal and masseter muscles during submaximal and maximal bite in the intercuspal position. J Oral Rehabil 1983;10:207–214.

10. Shape RJ. Effect of occlusal guidance on jaw muscle activity. J Prosthet Dent 1984;51:811–818.

11. Williamson EH, Lundquist DO. Anterior guidance: Its effect on electromyographic activity of the temporal and masseter muscles. J Prosthet Dent 1983;49:816–823.

12. Manns A, Chan C, Miralles R. Influence of group function and canine guidance on electromyographic activity of elevator muscles. J Prosthet Dent 1987;57:494–501.

13. Holmgren K, Sheikholeslam A, Riise C. The effect of a full arch maxillary occlusal splint on parafunctional activity during sleep in patients with nocturnal bruxism and signs and symptoms of craniomandibular disorders. J Prosthet Dent 1993;69:393–397.

14. Weinberg LA, Kruger B. A comparison of implant/prosthesis loading with four clinical variables. Int J Prosthodont 1995;8:421–433.

15. Gargiulo AW, Wentz FM, Orban R. Dimensions and relations of the dentogingival junction in humans. J Periodontol 1961;32:261–267.

16. Kokich VG, Spear FM, Mathews DM. Interdisciplinary treatment: Integrating orthodontics with periodontics, endodontics and restorative dentistry. Semin Orthod 1997;3:1–73.

17. Tarnow DP, Magner AW, Fletcher P. The effect of the distance from contact point to the crest of bone on the presence or absence of the interproximal papilla. J Periodontol 1992;63:995–996.

8 | Implant Considerations in the Growing Child

Larry J. Oesterle, DDS, MS

Implants are a popular and useful adjunct to the care of the partially or totally edentulous patient. The success of implants to restore function in edentulous patients is well documented; it has also become common to use implants to replace single or small numbers of teeth adjacent to natural teeth. Implants are generally not recommended in growing children because of the large changes that occur during growth that may decrease the useful life of the implant and require subsequent removal. In children with special problems or when implants can meet a unique need, such as for orthodontic anchorage, some consideration may be given to implant use; however, the provider must have a basic understanding of growth, growth timing, and implant response to growth. In this chapter a review of the need for implants in children and implant alternatives will be presented, followed by a review of implant behavior during growth, growth changes in the maxilla and mandible that affect implants, and, finally, recommendations for implant use.

Need for Implants in Children

Of the few legitimate indications for using endosseous implants in children, the most common is to support a prosthesis replacing congenitally absent or traumatically lost teeth. Another, less common, reason is for orthodontic anchorage, which is discussed elsewhere in this text. Congenital absence of teeth, excluding third molars, is reported to affect between 2% and 17.5% of the populations studied.[1] Most studies indicate an incidence in the United States of between 3.5% and 4.3%.[2,3] One study of children in New Orleans found an incidence of 7.44%.[4] However, samples from two black American samples found congenital absence of teeth to be as low as 2.57% compared with a Caucasian sample of 5.15%. The highest incidence of congenitally missing teeth has been reported in the Scandinavian countries, with rates as high as 10.1% in Norway[5] and 17.5% in Finnish Skolt-Lapps. Reports indicate that the incidence of missing teeth varies greatly depending on the population being studied; the highest incidence is found in the Scandinavian countries and the lowest is found among blacks and in some Asian countries.

The number of missing teeth is an important consideration; fortunately, most children are congenitally missing only one or two teeth. The mandibular second premolars are the most frequently absent, followed by the maxillary lateral incisors and second premolars. Less than 1% of children are missing more than two teeth and less than 0.1% are missing more than five teeth. The majority of children with large numbers of missing teeth are those with ectodermal dysplasia. Other congenital syndromes or anomalies associated with multiple missing teeth are clefts of the lip and/or palate and Down syndrome. However, the number of missing teeth is generally lower and the extent of the problem less severe in these syndromes than in ectodermal dysplasia. Thus, even in Sweden, which has a relatively high incidence of congenitally absent teeth, the number of children with more than eight congenitally missing teeth—who would therefore most benefit from early implant-assisted prostheses—is very low at 0.03%.

Trauma is the other main cause of missing teeth in children. Traumatic loss usually involves the maxillary central incisors and affects approximately 4 per 1,000.[6,7] Children with Class II malocclusions and incisor protrusion often suffer from traumatic incisor loss. Early orthodontic treatment in these children can decrease the effects of trauma,[8] which, fortunately, usually affects only one or two teeth.

In summary, missing teeth in children are caused by congenital absence, trauma, and to a lesser degree, caries. Congenital absence, trauma, and caries usually affect only one or two teeth, which can often be temporarily replaced with conventional prostheses. The most devastating condition is a large number of missing teeth. Fortunately, this affects a very small number of the child population, but these are the patients in whom implant-assisted orthodontic anchorage and prostheses are the most useful.

The presence and appearance of teeth are important in the development of a child's self-esteem and identity (Fig 8-1). Body perception and the ability to properly masticate food and interact socially with other children is important, as well. Language development and proper production of speech sounds also depend on a relatively intact dentition. These children may be the best candidates for the consideration of an implant-assisted prosthesis.

Behavior of Implants

When contemplating the use of implants in children, the clinician must consider how implants respond to growth. The intimate interlocking of bone into the microstructure of the endosseous implant, the mechanism which makes it so successful in adults, is the same mechanism that creates problems in children. Endosseous implant stability has been found to be closely related to the degree of bone-implant contact.[9,10] The stability of the endosseous implant is so great that it has been used successfully for orthopedic and orthodontic anchorage.[11–14] Natural teeth, in contrast, with their ligamentous attachment to bone, not only demonstrate some mobility during function but also move in response to forces placed on them and adapt to skeletal growth changes. The ankylosed primary tooth is poorly understood, but ankylosis appears to result from small, even microscopic areas of direct bone contact with the root.[15] This is analogous to the endosseous implant, except that the implant has a much larger area of bone-implant contact.

Since the number of long-term reports of endosseous implant use in children is limited, studying the ankylosed primary tooth is one way of predicting the fate of an endosseous implant during growth. Ankylosis of primary teeth most commonly occurs in molars and affects only 8% to 14% of children. Most ankylosed primary teeth cause few problems for the child. Although they appear below the level of occlusion of the adjacent teeth, most ankylosed primary teeth exfoliate nor-

Fig 8-1 A patient who benefited from a team approach to implant use. This 13-year-old girl had major esthetic and functional concerns because of large numbers of congenitally absent maxillary and mandibular teeth. She was missing all her permanent teeth except the maxillary and mandibular first molars, the maxillary central incisors, and the mandibular left canine. After orthodontic incisor intrusion and partial diastema closure, implants were placed and implant-supported maxillary and mandibular prostheses constructed. The mandibular left canine was removed as part of the prosthetic treatment plan to allow better positioning of implants, which were placed near the end of growth and away from the natural teeth. The treatment provided her with functional, esthetic, and stable rehabilitation that would have been difficult to duplicate by conventional means. (a) Pretreatment radiograph. (b-e) Facial and intraoral pretreatment photographs. (f-i) Facial and intraoral posttreatment photographs. (From Oesterle et al[17]; reprinted with permission.)

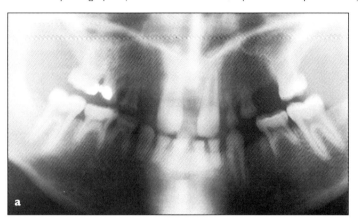

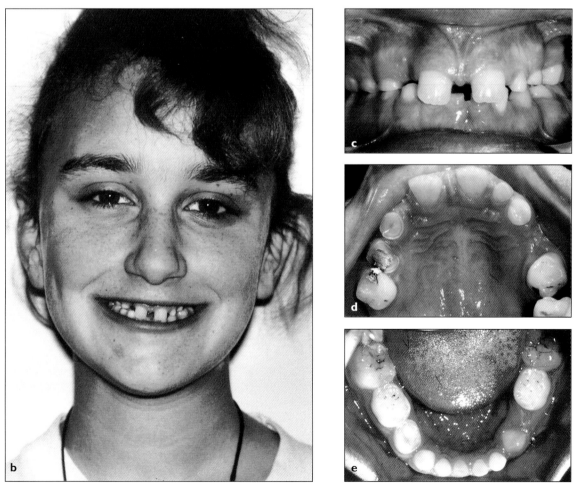

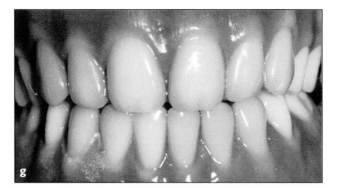

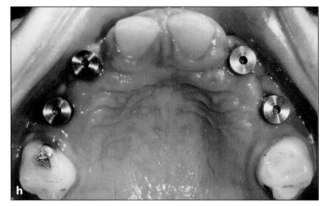

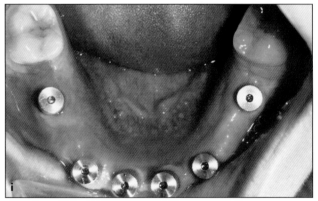

mally with the eruption of the succedaneous premolars.[16] However, those primary molars that are more severely ankylosed can create developmental problems. Case reports have demonstrated the devastating local developmental effects that can occur. One report provided examples of two 18-year-olds with ankylosed primary molars that were severely impacted in the maxilla, creating a localized area of malocclusion.[17] The primary teeth had once been in the oral cavity, as evidenced by their

restorations, but were shown nearly 1 cm above the plane of occlusion. This demonstrates not only the effects of ankylosis but also the large amount of vertical growth that occurs (Fig 8-2). As the maxilla and mandible grow anteroposteriorly, transversely, and vertically, the periodontal ligament allows the adjustment and eruption of the teeth to accommodate for jaw growth. The teeth erupt into the space created by the increasingly larger jaws, increasing the size of the alveolar bone that sup-

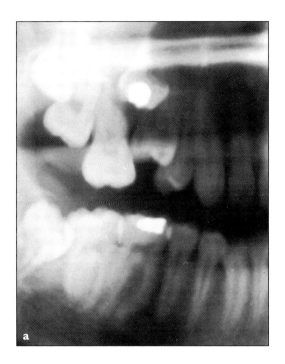

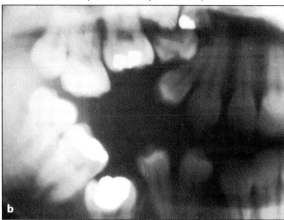

Fig 8-2 Ankylosed maxillary and mandibular teeth. These radiographs show the disruptive effects of large amounts of maxillary and mandibular growth on an ankylosed tooth. Ankylosis results in varying degrees of infraocclusion depending on the age at which it occurs and on the individual growth pattern. Endosseous implants placed at an early age would behave similarly to the ankylosed primary teeth. (From Oesterle et al[17]; reprinted with permission.)

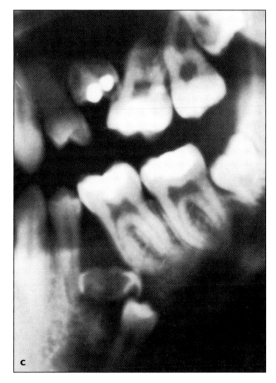

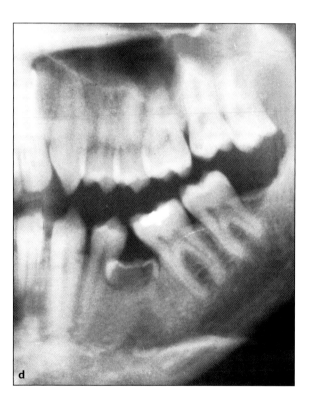

ports the erupting and adapting teeth. This adaptation and eruption does not occur with ankylosed teeth, often affecting adjacent normal teeth in their development. Endosseous implants, which likewise lack a periodontal ligament, can fail to adapt and erupt with the growing jaws and create a similar result, as has been demonstrated in both animal and human models.

Endosseous implants placed in 12-week-old pigs have clearly demonstrated the effects of ankylosed teeth.[18] Followed clinically and radiographically for only 165 days, and later by light microscopy in histologic ground sections, the pigs demonstrated the dramatic effects of the implants. Placed initially in alignment with adjacent mandibular teeth, after only 165 days the adjacent developing teeth had become positioned occlusally and angulated buccally to the implant. In the maxilla, the developing teeth were also occlusal to the implant. Tooth germs adjacent to the implant were displaced in their path of eruption. Those tooth germs in actual contact with the implant also demonstrated changes in their morphology. This study further confirmed the previous findings of both Ödman et al[19] and Thilander et al.[20] The clear conclusion from these animal studies is that implants do not accommodate growth and development of the jaws but remain fixed in their initial position. The behavior of endosseous implants during growth appears similar to that of severely ankylosed teeth.

Björk,[21,22] in his early classic studies of human growth, used small (0.5 × 1.5 mm) tantalum pins in the jaws of children to act as stable landmarks for his longitudinal cephalometric growth studies. These pins, like the endosseous implants in the pigs, were remarkably stable in the growing bone, but they were both too small and too far from the developing teeth to disturb dental development. Pins placed in areas of appositional bone growth gradually became embedded in bone. Pins placed in the paths of erupting teeth or on resorptive surfaces of bone were either displaced or lost. Pins placed on the anterior aspect of the maxilla and the anterior of the mandibular ramus were no longer found in bone as growth continued and bone resorption on those surfaces displaced the pins into

soft tissue. Attempts were made by Shaw[23] to use Björk's small implants to study the growth of infants with clefts of the lip and palate. Shaw had to abandon his study after losing one third of the implants he had placed shortly after birth. The extraordinary growth changes in infancy and early childhood were so dramatic, particularly in the lateral portions of the maxilla, that the use of even small study implants was impractical. These classic studies in humans support what is seen in animal studies with implants. Endosseous implants remain fixed in their initial position in bone and do not adapt to the often dramatic changes of skeletal and dental growth and development. Moreover, like ankylosed teeth, implants can create localized areas of malocclusion, lose their bony support and be lost, or become submerged in growing bone.

Maxillary Growth

Although growth of the dentition and jaws in relation to the cranium is in a generally downward and forward direction, it is not a simple additive process. There are several complex factors at work in facial growth that are not clearly understood. While the maxilla is thrust downward and forward under the influence of the soft tissues or perhaps the nasal septum, changes also take place on the surface of the maxilla itself. Enlow[24] has defined 10 concepts in his attempt to describe the ongoing processes involved in dentofacial growth. Two of these concepts are *displacement* and *drift*. Displacement is the physical movement of the entire bone or bony complex. The bone is displaced and carried by the expansive force of the soft tissues and then must remodel by resorption and deposition. Drift, a much simpler process, is the adding of new bone tissue on one side of a bony cortex and the removal or resorption on the other side. It may occur either as a result of a bone's displacement or as a distinct process. Thus, an implant can change its relative position by displacement, which generally is not a problem in implant procedures, since all adjacent dental structures are being displaced by an equal amount. However, the drift that occurs secondary to displacement can be

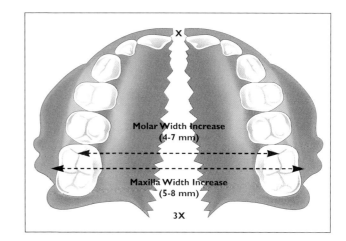

Fig 8-3 Transverse maxillary growth. The posterior portion of the midpalatal suture undergoes more growth than anteriorly by a factor of three. The increase in width is greatest in the posterior maxilla both dentally and skeletally, the dental increase being slightly greater. (Redrawn from Oesterle et al[17]; reprinted with permission.)

a problem for the implantologist because adjacent bone and dental tissues often must compensate for the change. Failure to compensate, as in the case of an implant, results in bone loss around the implant or submergence of the implant in bone. During early childhood, displacement is a major factor in maxillary growth, but its importance lessens as the anterior sutures of the cranial base (synchondroses) close. After the age of 7 years, only one third of all maxillary growth occurs by passive displacement, while the remaining growth occurs by drift (resorption and apposition of bone) in the maxilla itself.

For ease of understanding, growth of the jaws is commonly discussed according to its direction of manifestation: transverse, anteroposterior (sagittal), and vertical. In both the maxilla and the mandible, transverse growth is completed first, followed by growth in length, and finally vertical height growth. When describing growth, one must, of necessity, refer to the average or mean growth that occurs in a large sample of individuals. The confounding factor is that when these mean or average data are applied to the individual, they may miss the predictive mark considerably if the individual is at one end of the normal range.

Transverse maxillary growth

Tranverse growth, or growth in anterior width of both the maxilla and the mandible, is the dimension of jaw growth that is completed first. Although the width of the anterior portion of the arch is completed prior to the adolescent growth spurt, posterior width of the jaws is closely tied to increasing jaw length. Intercanine width changes very little after 12 years of age, but width across the second and third molar area continues to increase until these teeth are fully erupted.[25] The maxillary midline suture persists from prenatal development until late adolescence and is greatly influenced by width increases of structures superior to it, such as the cranial base and orbits. Starting at age 4 and continuing through adulthood, this suture contributes 5 to 6 mm of width to the maxilla. (Fig 8-3). Two millimeters of this increase occurs during the pubertal growth spurt, primarily at the posterior of the suture. If a central incisor was replaced with an implant shortly after eruption of the incisors, a diastema could develop between the implant and the adjacent natural central incisor, resulting in a subsequent shifting of the midline to the implant side. Replacement of both central incisors prior to the end of transverse anterior growth could result in increased bony width between the incisors and a diastema.

The midpalatal must be allowed to grow undisturbed and unrestricted for normal transverse growth to occur, as demostrated by both animal and human studies. In growing cats, Voss and Freng[26] surgically created submucous midpalatal clefts and found a resulting decrease in both maxillary and mandibular widths. Earlier, Freng[27] found that if he resected the posterior two thirds of the midpalatal suture in children having choanal atresia, their maxillas underwent a significant decrease. Of the 35 children that he treated, 52% had a posterior dental crossbite. Thus, limiting transverse growth by any transpalatal device is not indicated.

Dental arch width increases very little in the primary dentition but increases notably during the change to the permanent dentition. Most of the longitudinal studies demonstrate that succedaneous teeth erupt labial to the primary teeth they are replacing, resulting in a significant increase in arch width. Since girls' teeth generally erupt at an earlier age than boys', arch width increases occur earlier in girls. Boys have a longer growth period prior to eruption and prior to pubertal growth, in addition to having a longer growing period after maximum pubertal growth than do girls. All these factors result in greater width increases—consequently greater final arch widths—in boys than in girls, varying from 0.5 mm in the lateral incisor area to 3 mm in the molar area.[28] Although posterior width increases may be completed in females at 15 years, those in males continue until age 17 to 19.

For the implantologist, maxillary transverse growth prior to the cessation of growth and eruption of the permanent dentition has serious implications. Although transverse growth in the anterior maxilla is readily compensated by the ability of natural teeth to shift and anterior spaces to close, this is not true of implants. Anterior implants cannot compensate and will move apart during growth or, if fixed together, will restrict anterior growth. In case reports[29,30] of implants placed in the anterior maxilla as early as 9 years of age, no transverse problems have been reported; however, significant problems in the vertical dimension may overwhelm any transverse problem. Posterior growth restriction can occur and may be more significant, since posterior width change is greater than anterior change. Any transsutural appliance placed in the prepubertal, partially anodontic child may exaggerate whatever maxillary transverse deficiency was already present due to the original edentulous condition. Thus, the effects of transverse maxillary growth dictate great caution in implant use during growth.

Anteroposterior maxillary growth

Anteroposterior maxillary growth continues beyond the age at which transverse growth ceases, displacing the maxilla downward and forward relative to the cranial structures. However, not all the anterior displacement is manifest in forward change, but considerable drift occurs. The entire anterior surface of the maxilla is resorptive rather than depository. As the maxilla is displaced downward and forward, up to 25% of the displacement is lost to resorption. This could result in an endosseous implant gradually losing labial bone and possibly being lost due to lack of bone support. A case report of implants replacing a maxillary lateral incisor of a 13-year-old boy and an 11.5-year-old girl, respectively, noted problems with labial fenestrations as early as 11 months after placement in the girl and 19 months in the boy, increasing in severity with growth. Anteroposterior maxillary growth does not favor maxillary anterior implants. The response will be different in each individual due to differences in growth (Fig 8-4).

Growth in maxillary length usually continues throughout puberty and appears to be closely associated with growth in skeletal body height. Increases in length of the alveolar process are also associated with eruption of the second and third molars. In girls, anteroposterior growth is nearly completed by age 14 or 15, which is 2 to 3 years after menarche. Boys, on the other hand, grow in this dimension for a much greater period, often not reaching adult growth levels until the early 20s, or approximately 4 years after sexual maturation.

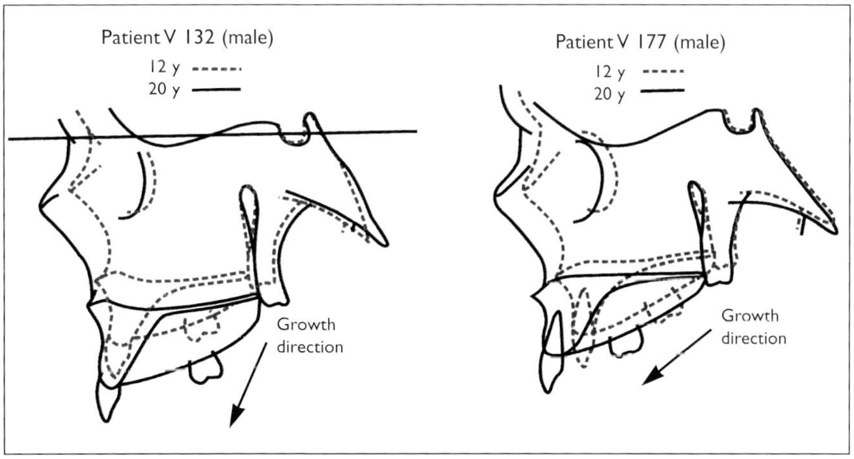

Fig 8-4 Maxillary growth direction, from early studies by Björk.[66] Because of dramatically varying growth directions, the fate of an implant fixed in bone would be much different in these patients. Differing amounts of bone drift would affect an implant placed during growth in different ways. Thus, an implant in one patient might be relatively successful while in another it could be lost or buried in bone. (Redrawn from Björk[66]; reprinted with permission.)

Vertical maxillary growth

Vertical growth in the maxilla continues beyond the age at which transverse and anteroposterior growth cease. Usually adult levels of vertical growth are reached at 17 or 18 years for girls and later for boys, continuing throughout resultant increases in face height and continued eruption of teeth, but at a much reduced level from that seen in children. However, over decades it can contribute to significant change.[31] Vertical maxillary growth is the most vexing for the implantologist because it has the greatest impact on the use of osseointegrated implants.

Skeletal maxillary vertical growth occurs by both displacement and drift. The maxilla is displaced downward away from the cranium by growth in the orbits as the eyes increase in size and by the nasal cavity and maxillary sinuses increasing in size by resorption on their nasal surface and by deposition of bone on their palatal and alveolar surfaces. The cartilaginous nasal septum may also play a part in pushing the maxilla downward and forward from the cranial base. Thus, as maxillary alveolar height increases by apposition of bone on its occlusal and incisal surfaces, it is simultaneously decreased by resorption of the nasal and maxillary sinus floor. One third of the total increase in alveolar height is lost by nasal resorption (Fig 8-5). This resorptive lowering of the nasal and sinus floor is uneven, occurring to a greater degree anteriorly than posteriorly; however, it is compensated for by the rotational displacement of the maxilla that occurs as a result of greater posterior than anterior alveolar growth. The resorptive nature of the superior (sinus and nasal) aspect of the maxilla is important in implant placement. An endosseous implant placed in an actively growing child or adolescent may become apically exposed in the maxillary sinus with only the thinnest of bone surrounding it, as in the case of the ankylosed teeth shown in Fig 8-2.

Vertical maxillary growth, combined with vertical alveolar development, exceeds growth in any other dimension. Between the ages of 9 and 25 years, vertical maxillary incisor changes are substantial, averaging 6 mm vertically and 2.5 mm anteriorly. Average eruption velocities are 1.2 to 1.5 mm per year during active growth and 0.1 to 0.2 mm per year even after age 17 or 18.[32] One author,[33] using two growth studies, calculated that if an implant were placed in the anterior maxilla at age 7, it would be a full centimeter shorter than a natural adjacent incisor at age 16. He also surmised that, at age 16, the apical end of the implant would be uncovered by resorption of bone on the floor of the nasal cavity. His analysis did not include the fact that the anterior maxilla is primarily resorptive in nature. Not only would the implant be significantly submerged, it would probably also be lost because of labial bone resorption.

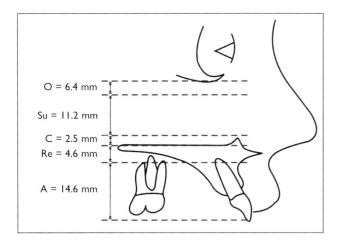

Fig 8-5 Vertical maxillary growth through displacement and cortical drift. Mean growth changes from age 4 to adulthood are contributed to by growth in a number of areas, as identified in Björk's[22] study: O = apposition at floor of orbit (drift); Su = sutural lowering of maxilla (displacement); C = apposition at the infrazygomatic crest (displacement); Re = resorptive lowering of the nasal floor (drift); A = appositional increase in alveolar height (drift). Displacement from growth at the sutures is a major contributor; however, the nearly 15 mm of alveolar vertical growth and the resorptive lowering of the nasal floor and expansion of the maxillary sinus with growth have the greatest effect on an implant placed during growth. (Redrawn from Björk[22]; printed with permission.)

O = 6.4 mm

Su = 11.2 mm

C = 2.5 mm
Re = 4.6 mm

A = 14.6 mm

Case reports in the literature support the assumptions drawn from the above empirical data. Ledermann et al[30] reported on the placement of 42 single-tooth replacement implants mostly in the maxillary anterior in 34 patients aged 9 to 18. They gauged the success of their implants primarily by their survival, which had a high success rate of 90%. Although these authors have shown that implants can be successfully placed in children, the question is the long-term survival. All the implants either had or were expected to have a shortening of the implant crown relative to the adjacent teeth. Brugnolo et al[29] provided better documentation of three patients 11.5 to 13 years of age with single-tooth implants, all of which were in infraocclusion at the 2.5- to 4.5-year follow-up, the most severely submerged 5 to 7 mm apical to the adjacent natural teeth. Two of these patients also had labial tissue fenestrations. All required lengthening of the crowns as the implants became progressively buried in the alveolus relative to the vertically developing adjacent teeth. Others have reported similar results.[34] Although the anterior maxilla is an area where an implant can be most readily placed, it is also one of the most hostile to long-term success.

The posterior portion of the maxilla offers no better prognosis. Not only is the maxilla resorbing on its nasal surface, but the eruption of teeth stimulates large amounts of alveolar growth (Fig 8-6).

From 9 to 25 years, the molars erupt more than 8 mm downward and 3 mm mesially, with maximum rate changes of 1.5 mm per year during peak growth. This alveolar change combined with skeletal changes in the maxilla results in over 1 cm of vertical change in the maxilla. An endosseous implant placed in the posterior maxilla of a 6- or 7-year-old with adjacent natural teeth could reasonably be in the same position as the ankylosed primary teeth shown in Fig 8-2. Clinical reports in the literature support this. Westwood and Duncan[35] reported placement of a single-tooth implant to replace a maxillary second premolar. After only 20 months, a posterior open bite was present in the implant area, affecting both the first molar and the first premolar. After 40 months, there was an even greater infraocclusion of the implant crown, as well as apparent mesial eruption of the first molar over the infraoccluded implant crown. Crater formation was present around the implant, and its apical end was within the maxillary sinus (Fig 8-7). These examples demonstrate that when an implant or an ankylosed tooth is placed in a dynamic growth environment, compensation for the change around them cannot occur, and they may become a nidus for a malocclusion.

The real question in the use of implants for single teeth or adjacent to natural teeth is not whether they can be done, but rather what their long-term success will be. There are some excellent reasons

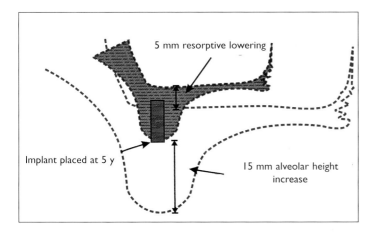

Fig 8-6 Vertical maxillary growth and its potential effects on an implant placed at age 4 or 5. In this hypothetical case, the implant would behave like the ankylosed teeth shown in Fig 8-2: the implant would be buried occlusally by appositional bone growth and exposed apically by resorptive nasal and sinus floor lowering.

Fig 8-7 Progressive infraocclusion of an implant replacing a second premolar placed in a boy at age 15 years 4 months. (a) Implant restoration at time of placement. (b) Infraocclusion of crown at 35-month follow-up. (c) Remake of implant crown to restore occlusion. (d) Radiograph at time of implant placement. (e) Radiograph 40 months after implant placement. Note difference in bone levels between the implant and the adjacent natural teeth and apparent mesial molar movement caused by adaptation of the teeth to growth. The long-term effects of a significant difference in bone level between the implant and adjacent teeth have not been determined. (From Westwood and Duncan[35]; reprinted with permission.)

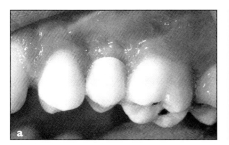
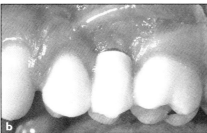
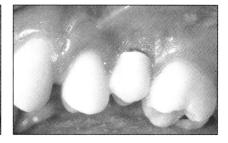

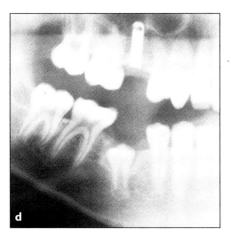
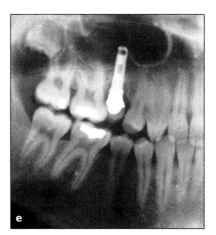

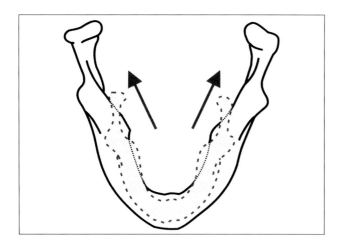

Fig 8-8 Mandibular anterior transverse width. This is established relatively early by only small amounts of skeletal widening. Large increases in transverse width occur as the mandible increases in length during growth. (Redrawn from Enlow[24]; printed with permission.)

for placing single-tooth replacement implants in children, particularly at the time of or soon after the loss of a tooth. The implants are successful because of good blood supply, positive immunobiologic resistance, and uncomplicated healing in children. Placement of an early implant can preserve alveolar bone that would otherwise atrophy. However, over the long term, the significant lack of alveolar development in the area of the implant and its effect on adjacent natural teeth could substantially overshadow any early benefit. The crown can be lengthened to compensate for progressive infraocclusion of the implant, but at the expense of a desirable crown-implant ratio. In addition, the vertical defect created by the submerged implant cannot be cleaned, resulting in infection, possible implant loss, and loss of adjacent supporting bone. The long-term risks to adjacent teeth over a 10- or 20-year period may prove to be much greater than any short-term benefit. Thus, the use of implants adjacent to natural teeth in the maxilla is contraindicated until early adulthood. Even maxillary implants in the anodontic child may not be indicated at an early age due to the nasal and anterior resorptive aspects of maxillary growth.

Mandibular Growth

The timing of mandibular growth is similar but not identical to that of maxillary growth. The former is more closely associated with growth in stature, whereas the latter is associated with growth of the cranial structures. This accounts for the greater amount of anteroposterior growth of the mandible than of the maxilla during adolescence. This "differential jaw growth" converts the more convex child profile to the straighter adult profile. In girls, mandibular growth is nearly completed 2 to 3 years after menarche, usually at age 14 or 15. In boys, growth can continue into the early 20s, but usually reaches adult levels by age 18. A longer, more robust pubertal growth period accounts for the larger size of males as well as the generally straighter profile that results from greater mandibular growth. Although major trends in a normal population are well known, how much and when an individual patient will grow can vary considerably.

Transverse mandibular growth

Transverse mandibular change is similar to that in the maxilla except to a smaller degree. Anterior mandibular and intercanine widths increase little or not at all after age 12. The width of the anterior mandible is established relatively early, increasing only slightly by appositional growth, with growth at the symphysis ceasing prior to eruption of the primary teeth. However, posterior mandibular width increases as the mandibular body lengthens due to its "V" shape. Increases in posterior mandibular and bicondylar width continue until the mandible ceases lengthening (Fig 8-8).

Dental transverse changes in the mandible occur with the eruption of teeth, as they do in the maxilla except to a lesser degree. Mandibular intercanine width begins to increase 1 year prior to eruption of the permanent lateral incisors and continues until eruption of the permanent canines. The initial increase in primary intercanine width occurs as the permanent lateral incisor erupts from the lingual toward the labial, pushing the primary canine both laterally and distally into the primate space. This width increase of 2 mm in females and 3 mm in males is completed after 2 years.[36] Once the mandibular lateral incisors are fully erupted, the intercanine width does not change significantly, even with the eruption of the permanent canine,[37] nor is the width maintained, decreasing slightly into and during adulthood.[38]

Posterior dental width increases along with tooth eruption. Interpremolar width increases 2 to 3 mm from primary intermolar width, as the premolars erupt somewhat to the buccal of the primary molars. After eruption and just prior to adulthood, an additional 1-mm increase in interpremolar width is seen in males, along with an average 1-mm decrease in females. In the mandibular first molar area, the greatest width increase occurs during eruption: 3 mm in males and 2 mm in females. In the mandibular second molar area, an increase of nearly 2 mm is seen in males and little or no change is seen in females between the ages of 12 and 18.

The degree of transverse change in the mandible is the least problematic to the implantologist. The problem lies in the extraordinary individual variability of the growth changes; some arch widths are no greater at age 8 than at 4, whereas others increase as much as 4 mm in the premolar area.[39] Predicting width change is difficult; little correlation is found between dental width[40] and body height (stature) or between dental width[40] at age 4 or 5 versus dental width at age 15.[41] Hence, although transverse dental changes are less problematic than vertical or anteroposterior changes, they are just as unpredictable relative to the use of single-tooth replacement implants. In the partially anodontic child who has no teeth to effect an alveolar change, the prognosis may be greatly increased;

however, no growth studies of width changes in the anodontic child are available.

Anteroposterior and vertical mandibular growth

Growth changes in the anteroposterior and vertical direction are intimately connected. Rotational growth of the mandible significantly affects the anteroposterior and vertical eruption patterns of the individual. The concept of rotational growth, which can be difficult to comprehend initially, is critical to understanding the variability found in individual patients.

The mandible is unlike the maxilla in that it is separated from the cranium by a movable joint, and its growth is not closely associated with the growth of the cranial base. When sequential cephalometric radiographs are superimposed on growing individuals, it appears as though the mandible is growing downward and forward from the cranium, but it is actually growing upward and backward, with little if any increase at the chin. Most of the anteroposterior growth occurs not only by vertical growth at the condyle but also by drift, that is, resorption on the anterior aspect of the ramus and deposition on its posterior aspect (Fig 8-9). The resulting increase in mandibular body length accommodates the eruption of the first, second, and third molars. Impacted third molars are therefore a direct consequence of a lack of mandibular anteroposterior body growth (Fig 8-10). Ramus height increases an average of 1 to 2 mm per year, while mandibular body length increases 2 to 3 mm per year. The increase in chin prominence during adolescence is due not so much to the small amount of bone apposition on the chin, but rather to the greater amount of mandibular anteroposterior versus maxillary growth. The infradental area above the chin is actually resorptive in nature, which increases chin definition but can result in labial bone loss for a prematurely placed dental implant (Fig 8-11).

Björk,[42] using small metallic implants, found that the mandible did not grow linearly. The inner core of the mandible (containing the neurovascular

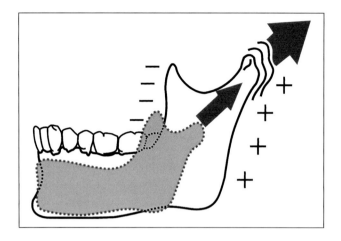

Fig 8-9 Anteroposterior and vertical mandibular growth. Although it appears that the mandible is growing downward and forward from the cranium, it actually grows in length by resorption on the anterior surface of the ramus and deposition on the posterior aspect. Vertical growth of the ramus and condyle add further to the increase in mandibular length. (Redrawn from Enlow[24]; reprinted with permission.)

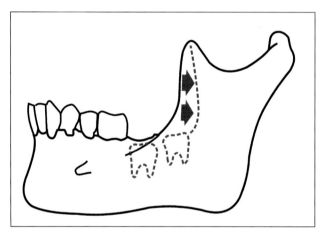

Fig 8-10 Anteroposterior and vertical mandibular growth. Teeth are accommodated by lengthening of the mandibular body through bone resorption on the anterior aspect of the ramus. An implant placed in the ramus for orthodontic anchorage during growth would need to be placed so as to avoid developing teeth; it would probably be lost to the soft tissue with increasing growth. (Redrawn from Enlow[24]; reprinted with permission.)

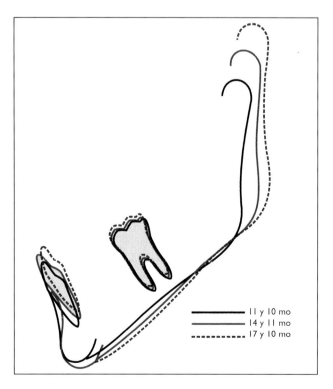

— 11 y 10 mo
— 14 y 11 mo
----- 17 y 10 mo

Fig 8-11 Anteroposterior and vertical mandibular growth. The mandibular incisor area undergoes dynamic change, with resorption in the infradental area and a small amount of deposition in the area of the chin. The mandible of this patient from Björk and Skieller's study[67] underwent dramatic changes in the anterior area but minimal changes in the molar area. Implants placed anteriorly before the end of growth near adjacent developing teeth would lose bone on their labial surface and be located apically and labially to adjacent teeth. (Redrawn from Björk and Skieller[67]; reprinted with permission.)

Fig 8-12 (a) Rotational effects of mandibular growth, resulting in changes in the lower border of the mandible and at the alveolar process. Teeth ankylosed or implants placed at an early age may by adulthood appear near the lower border of the mandible because of resorption. (b) Patients at the extremes of growth with different directions of condylar growth and mandibular rotation. The dental adaptations secondary to growth are dramatically different in each, as would be the effects of growth on any implants placed in these children. (Redrawn from Björk and Skieller[68]; reprinted with permission.)

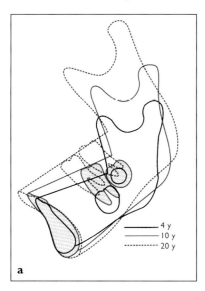
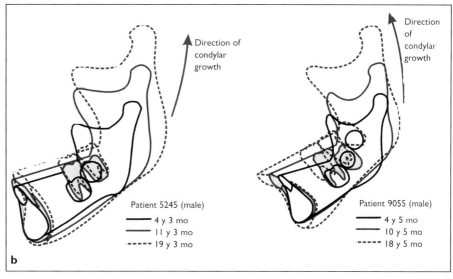

bundle) rotates downward at the gonial angle and upward at the chin. This rotation alone would otherwise result in a significant flattening of the angle of the lower mandibular border relative to the cranial base. However, the rotation is partially masked by changes in the alveolar and muscular processes of the mandible, ie, by resorption of the lower border of the mandible at the gonial angle and vertical alveolar growth (Fig 8-12).

Although this rotation represented the average degree of change, Björk found extraordinary differences in the directions of condylar growth, which affected the rotation of the mandible and how the teeth erupted (Fig 8-12b). In vertical condylar growth, he found a decrease in the gonial angle, having the center of the rotation near the incisor area. This resulted in a flattening of the angle between the lower border of the mandible and the cranium and in the incisors erupting more facially than vertically. The other end of the spectrum of rotation occurred when the condyle grew in a more

anteroposterior direction. In these patients, the gonial angle did not decrease and the center of rotation was located posterior to the mandible. With this type of rotation, the incisors erupted quite differently—lingually 2.5 mm and vertically 4 mm during the period of study. Children with average rotation had incisors that erupted 4 mm vertically but only 1 mm lingually. Rotation is important to the implantologist because variation in amount and direction of incisor eruption could dramatically affect the relationship of an implant to an adjacent tooth, since the implant cannot make compensatory dental changes either vertically or labiolingually. Whereas the average growing child maintained remarkably consistent incisor relationships during eruption, one of Björk's subjects exhibited extreme forward rotation of the mandible and vertical growth of the condyle. Because the incisors were unable to compensate for the rotation, the result was crowding and increased overbite.

The importance of Björk's studies is to highlight the high degree of variability in mandibular growth. When applied to the individual patient, a variety of growth and eruption effects can occur, many of them difficult to predict. Skieller et al[43] developed a method of predicting mandibular rotation that worked effectively within their sample. However, when others[44-46] attempted to apply their guidelines to other samples, the results were disappointing, demonstrating how inaccurate mandibular growth prediction in an individual can be.

Although mandibular growth rotation usually is not evident in routine serial cephalometric radiographs without Björk's markers, it can have dramatic effects on posterior as well as anterior dental development. The extraordinary variation in the behavior of ankylosed primary second molars can probably be best explained by variations in mandibular rotation. Although the ankylosed molars in some children appear minimally affected, the severe submergence in others is probably due to greater-than-average mandibular rotation. In this pattern, measurements of changes in molar height made from the lower border of the mandible do not reflect the total amount of vertical eruption because of concurrent resorption of the lower mandibular border (Fig 8-12). This would explain how an ankylosed primary or permanent molar could appear close to the lower border of the mandible, far from its normally erupting and adapting adjacent teeth. An implant placed under these conditions would meet the same fate. All implants placed in growing children would be submerged to some extent, but in those having this type of growth pattern, the amount would be significant and the chances of creating an area of malocclusion of adjacent teeth would be great.

Vertical mandibular alveolar increase accompanying tooth eruption is significant. When the mandibular primary incisors are lost, there is a transient period when anterior dental height actually decreases. However, when the permanent incisors erupt, dental height is reestablished, usually by age 9, and steadily increases until age 15. The increase is longer in males—continuing well beyond 15—whereas female anterior height increases very little after age 13 or 14. The amount of increase is significant, averaging 12 mm in males and 6 mm in females between the ages of 6 and 16. Just as significant are vertical increases in the first molar area, which average 10 mm in males and 7 mm in females between the ages of 6 and 16.[47] These measurements reflect a large amount of vertical growth but, because they were made from a resorbing mandibular lower border, they probably do not reflect the total amount of vertical increase. As the molars erupt vertically, they also erupt mesially, intruding on the leeway space and decreasing arch length, further confounding the effects on an implant.

The vertical and anteroposterior changes in the mandible are dramatic, and they would have an adverse effect on an implant placed either anteriorly or posteriorly in the mandible. This effect would be particularly striking if there were adjacent natural teeth, as in the case of a single-tooth implant. There are apparently no reports in the literature of single-tooth replacement implants placed at an early age. However, reports[35] of implants placed in a 16-year-old boy replacing both mandibular second premolars (14-month follow-up) and in a nearly 14-year-old girl replacing mandibular canines (56-month follow-up) indicate relative success. Follow-up examinations showed significant differences between the bone level of the implant and the adjacent teeth, some of which the authors postulate as being the result of continued vertical growth after implant placement. Implants placed in younger patients or in patients who undergo significant late growth would probably have less favorable results.

Measurable increases in mandibular height can continue until early adulthood in both males and females, with male increases extending into their 20s. As in the maxilla, vertical mandibular growth never really ends but continues during adulthood at levels that can be detected only if measured over decades.

Fig 8-13 Ectodermal dysplasia in 5-year-old patient missing all anterior permanent and primary teeth. Implants were placed on either side of the symphysis to support a prosthesis. The mandibular prosthesis, in combination with a conventional maxillary prosthesis, provided increased function, esthetics, lip support, and improved speech. Long-term results in patients without adjacent developing teeth may be better than in those with them. (From Cronin and Oesterle[52]; reprinted with permission.)

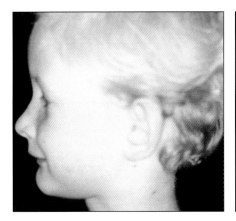
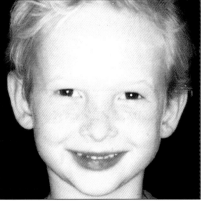
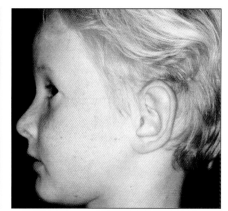

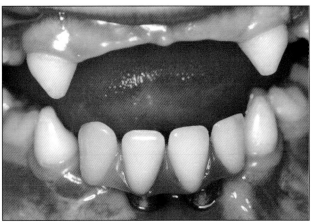
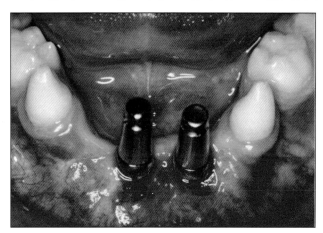

Mandibular growth and implants

The mandible, like the maxilla, is a dynamic, changing unit during growth. Transverse mandibular changes are not as dramatic as those in the maxillary arch either dentally or skeletally. Since the mandibular symphysis closes within months of birth, there is no concern, as in the maxilla, of limiting transverse growth. More encouraging is the use of implants in children who are missing large numbers of teeth and who do not have the alveolar change and compensation seen in dentulous children. Some of the growth changes that are of concern for implants close to natural teeth are probably not present in edentulous areas (Fig 8-13), but

the lack of alveolar bone in these patients presents a problem of sufficient bone for implant placement.[48] There are reports[49-53] of the use of endosseous implants in the mandibles of young, partially anodontic children (5 to 7 years of age), which can be useful in judging the advisability of implant use. Only two of these reports have any significant follow-up and three of the reports are of the same patient. All the patients reported were diagnosed with ectodermal dysplasia. The rareness of this condition (1 per 100,000 live births)[54] may explain why there are so few reports. The patient with the longest follow-up (11 years), having no natural teeth in the mandible, had mandibular implants placed at age 6. Both implants were placed

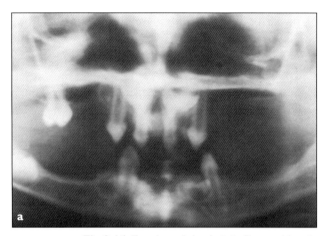 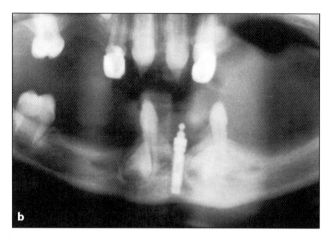

Fig 8-14 Ectodermal dysplasia in 5-year-old patient with only the right permanent molars and primary canines apparently present (a). A midline implant was placed at age 5 to support a prosthesis. A follow-up radiograph at age 10 (b) demonstrated infraocclusion of the implant with growth; however, adjacent developing teeth can now be observed, and these may increase alveolar development and contribute to implant infraocclusion. (From Smith and Vargervik[50]; reprinted with permission.)

in the anterior mandible and were reported to be functioning well at 17 years of age. Another author reported the placement of a single midline anterior mandibular implant in a 5-year-old boy.[50] Five years after placement, the implant became progressively submerged (Fig 8-14). The difference between the two patients was the presence of teeth. The second patient had primary canines present and permanent canines developing, which were visible radiographically. The implants adjacent to or near natural teeth appear to progressively submerge relative to natural teeth, while those implants not adjacent to or near natural teeth appear to be less significantly affected. The evidence is too scant to make a definitive assessment, but it confirms expectations.

In summary, the effects of mandibular growth on an endosseous implant appear to vary according to whether teeth are present. In the partially anodontic child without teeth near the implant, where the effects of growth appear to be limited, the limited evidence suggests that an anterior mandibular implant may be successful even in very young individuals. However, in the child with adjacent nat-

ural teeth, the effects of an implant on skeletal and alveolar growth appear to be much greater. Not only is the implant affected, but the distorting effects of the implant may also affect adjacent teeth. Unlike appliances in the maxilla, implants and prostheses that cross the mandibular midline do not pose a threat to transverse growth, but submergence of the implant by appositional vertical growth is a problem, both anteriorly and posteriorly, if there are adjacent natural teeth. In addition, an implant placed in the anterior mandible adjacent to natural teeth is at risk for exposure from labial resorption in the infradental fossa as the natural teeth erupt and adapt. Whether an implant will be submerged or labially exposed depends on the direction and amount of rotational growth of the individual mandible. Whereas natural teeth in the mandible are able to maintain a homeostatic relationship with both the mandible and the maxillary teeth, implants are unable to erupt, let alone change their eruption, in response to growth. The effects of an implant restricting the compensatory potential of the mandibular dentition are unknown at this time.

Factors in Growth

When considering the use of implants in any growing individual, it is important to understand the factors that influence the growth of that individual. Most of the information on growth applies to the average growth of a population, but there are individual factors that contribute to the extraordinary differences in growth between individual patients.

Timing and quantity of growth

The quantity of growth that an individual child will ultimately have is influenced by several factors. One major factor is the child's genetic potential. In general, children of tall parents will be tall and those of shorter parents shorter—likewise with jaw growth. However, over the past 300 to 400 years, a secular trend of increasing height has resulted in children often being slightly larger than their parents.[55] A common method of assessing growth is to compare the individual child's height and weight to a standardized growth chart. These charts give not only the mean height and weight but also standard deviations from the mean, which is more meaningful in evaluating children. Children can be normal in their growth even though they are not within the average range. Thus, a child may be on the small side in the range of the chart but nonetheless normal if, throughout growth, he or she remains consistently on the small side of the mean while otherwise showing progression along the charted growth curve. This child would not reach the average of height but would have met his or her genetic potential and still be normal in growth. Of concern would be a child who was in the average range of the growth chart, then fell to the lower area of the chart. Changes in growth pattern warrant investigation. However, an individual's growth pattern can change through normal variation, and this creates the greatest challenge in attempting to predict growth of that individual.

Timing of growth is also an important variable. Some children will mature at a relatively younger chronological age, while others will mature later, the quantity of growth being associated with the age of maturity. Those children maturing early do not have the same amount of prepubertal growth as later-maturing children and tend to be smaller. On the other hand, the late-maturing child grows for a longer period of time before puberty, grows during puberty, and ends up being taller. This is an important factor in implant use in children and adolescents. Although it may be safe to place an endosseous implant in an early-maturing girl of 14, it may be a disaster if placed in a 14-year-old late bloomer because of the large quantity of remaining alveolar growth.

Other factors can also have an effect on the quantity of growth of an individual. Adequate nutrition is necessary to reach one's growth potential. Whereas an excess of nutrition results only in excess fat storage, a nutritional deficiency can result in an individual not reaching his or her genetic growth potential. Illness, a psychologically traumatic event, or extreme emotional neglect can also decrease growth. Growth depends on the presence of an excess of energy above that required for survival. If illness or stress drains this excess away, then the individual will not grow normally. A common example of a growth disturbance is the neonatal line seen in primary teeth. This line demarcates the growth disturbance that occurs during the traumatic events surrounding birth. Though illnesses of short duration cause little or no disturbance, chronic and extended illnesses usually have a long-term effect on the quantity of growth. Thus the amount of growth can be reduced from its genetic potential.

Growth pattern

Björk was the first to recognize the importance of jaw rotation in his implant-marker studies. The differing patterns of rotation within the jaws, as mentioned earlier, have a marked effect on the amount and direction of dental change in the jaws. The dentition usually attempts to maintain as normal a dental relation as possible even in the face of skeletal jaw deficiency or excess. This compensation can result in dramatic differences in amount and direction of dental eruption.

These differences and compensations are commonly seen in individual patients. In the mandibular anteroposteriorly deficient patient, it is not uncommon to see the mandibular incisors proclined labially in an attempt to maintain contact with the maxillary incisors. In the long-faced, vertically growing patient, it is common for the incisors to attempt to maintain contact by alveolar vertical overdevelopment, resulting in excessive exposure of the maxillary incisors below the resting upper lip and in a long mandibular symphysis. In the patient with mandibular skeletal prognathism, the mandibular incisors tend to incline lingually while the maxillary incisors reach labially in an effort to maintain normal contact. Although these are extreme examples, individual patients with mild or moderate discrepancies also show compensations in the dentition, having an effect on the amount and direction of dental change during growth. These differences between individuals make the use of implants in the growing patient even more challenging.

Gender differences

There is much variation in growth between boys and girls. One need only observe the height differences and changes during the circumpubertal period. Girls enter puberty before boys, and consequently there is a period when girls may be taller than boys of the same chronological age. However, as time passes, boys not only catch up to but surpass girls in height. Not only do girls mature 2 years earlier than boys but their permanent teeth erupt earlier than boys'.[56] Usually a girl's growth is nearly complete at menarche, an important individual marker in evaluating the cessation of growth for girls. Whereas girls may have nearly completed their adolescent growth by 15 years of age, the same is not true for boys, who may grow well into their 20s. This difference in growth timing produces the differences in size between boys and girls. Not only do boys grow for a longer time than girls but the rate of growth during adolescence is greater. This greater amount and duration of male growth enhances the effects of adolescent differen-

tial jaw growth and results in the more prominent chin and straighter profile seen in males. These differences between boys and girls must be considered in implant use.

Determining growth cessation

Determining if growth has ceased is an important factor in planning and placing implants in adolescents or young adults. There is no reliable tool for judging when adult growth levels have been reached, but a workable approximation can be made. Although chronological age is a poor indicator of the cessation of growth, growth in stature is fairly well correlated with growth in the face and dentition. There are reliable indicators of the end of growth, but predicting growth direction and amount or when growth will end is not reliable. Growth prediction of more than 1 or 2 years has not proven to be successful. Therefore, observing by means of either serial cephalometric radiographs or serial measures of stature that growth has stopped is the best way of determining if implants can be safely placed.

The rate of growth in body height changes dramatically, being very high during infancy and decreasing during childhood (Fig 8-15). A small increase does occur during childhood but then decreases again as puberty approaches. A similar pattern of jaw growth is also seen, particularly in the mandible. A large increase in growth rate is seen during puberty, which then decreases until adult levels of growth are reached. The safest time to place implants is on the lower portion of the declining adolescent growth curve at or near adulthood. Monitoring changes in statural height is one way of determining growth status. The only completely accurate way of determining that the jaws are not growing is by superimposing tracings of serial cephalometric radiographs taken at least 6 months apart. If, after a period of 1 year, no growth change is seen, the implantologist can be reasonably certain that growth has ended. Unfortunately, this method, while reliable, requires a great deal of time and may unnecessarily delay implant use.

Fig 8-15 Hand-wrist radiograph indicators used to place a patient in the general area of the growth curve. The chart shows a decelerating rate of growth from birth into childhood; a small increase in growth rate during childhood; a large increase during adolescence; and a decreased rate until adulthood. The ulnar sesamoid of the thumb usually begins to calcify during the accelerating phase of the pubertal growth spurt. Capping of the middle phalanges of the third finger usually occurs after the maximum growth velocity has passed and indicates a deceleration of the pubertal growth spurt. When the epiphysis of the radius fuses, growth is considered to be at adult levels.(From Cronin and Oesterle[48]; reprinted with permission.)

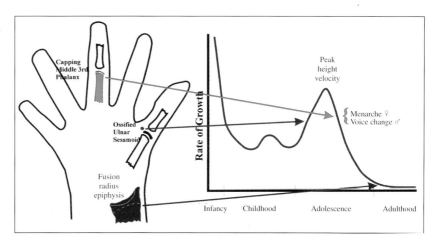

Since there is an association between jaw growth and statural growth, another means is available. Though serial cephalometric radiographs remain the most reliable indicator, evaluating the growth of long bones, especially the hand and wrist, can provide an educated guess of individual growth status. A conventional radiograph of the hand and wrist can be made and compared against a standardized atlas[57] of hand and wrist bone development to appraise skeletal growth status fairly accurately. A faster—though less accurate—assessment of a hand-wrist film will place the individual patient on his or her growth curve and give the clinician a better idea of growth status than will chronological age.[58] The following quick indicators can serve as a useful adjunct at the initial appointment (Fig 8-15).

Adductor sesamoid of the thumb. This bone first appears as a small, roundish center of ossification medial to the junction of the epiphysis and diaphysis of the proximal phalanx of the thumb. As ossification continues, it becomes progressively larger and denser. As an indicator, the appearance of the adductor sesamoid signals that the adolescent growth spurt has begun and places the individual on the accelerating portion of the adolescent growth curve. Since a substantial amount of growth is ahead, this is an inappropriate time to place an implant.

Epiphysis capping of the third finger's middle phalanx. Capping of the epiphysis of the middle phalanx of the third finger occurs during the transition to closure of the epiphysis. The rounded lateral margins of the epiphysis start to flatten and form projections that point toward the diaphysis at an acute angle. As an indicator, capping places the individual beyond the peak of the growth curve, headed down the decelerating slope toward adulthood. This correlates with the approximate onset of menstruation in girls and deepening of the voice in boys. Since most pubertal growth has been completed, consideration of implant placement can begin. However, since the exact length and rate of growth are still unknown, some risks still exist.

Epiphyseal fusion of radius. When the epiphyseal plate fuses and forms a bony union with the diaphysis, adult levels of skeletal growth have been attained and no further increase in statural height can be expected. The safest time to place an implant is when this indicator of skeletal maturity is present. Little or no growth above low adult levels is expected.

Using these growth indicators allows the clinician to estimate growth status in an individual patient. This allows more precise determination of the appropriate time for implant placement, particularly for the single-tooth replacement adjacent to teeth that will be developing and compensating for jaw growth. For the fully or partially anodontic patient with natural teeth far from the implant site, consideration of skeletal maturity may not be as important since there are no erupting, compensating adjacent teeth. The best and safest time to place the single-tooth implant adjacent to natural teeth is when the final indicator, radial epiphyseal closure, has occurred. This indicates that skeletal growth is complete and facial growth is either complete or so close as not to be a factor.

The question remains: How well do these indicators work in real patient care? A study of Thilander et al[59] supports the effectiveness of using skeletal and statural indicators for implant placement. Although the sample was relatively small (8 boys, 7 girls; 19 maxillary and 8 mandibular implants), this study supports the use of skeletal indicators. The study patients ranged in age from 13 years 2 months to 19 years 4 months (mean age 15 years 4 months), and all had fully erupted permanent dentitions. The researchers measured body height and assessed skeletal maturity from hand-wrist radiographs. Changes were seen in all the growing patients, who had progressive implant infraocclusion that varied between 0.8 and 1.6 mm over the 3-year observation period. Superimposed tracings of serial cephalometric radiographs showed that the subjects demonstrating the most craniofacial growth also exhibited the greatest increase in body height. This increase was closely correlated with the amount of infraocclusion of the implant. The subjects having the greatest increase in stature showed the greatest amount of infraocclusion and those with less increase in stature demonstrated less implant infraocclusion. A boy with no increase in stature had no infraocclusion of the implant. This study by Thilander et al confirms the validity of using skeletal assessment of long bones to determine implant suitability.

Adult growth

Just when the patient has completed growth and the implantologist begins to hope for implant stability, along come reports[60-62] of adult growth. Conventional theory held that, once adulthood is reached, growth of the jaws is no longer a factor.

Unfortunately, long-term cephalometric studies have proven that theory wrong. The face, jaws, and teeth change in many ways as we age; some of these changes are not consistent with sagging and wrinkling of the visible face but rather are closer to the growth seen in adolescents. However, whereas the growth in adolescents is measured in millimeters per year, the growth in adults is measured in millimeters over decades of life. Growth direction also appears to vary between men and women; men grow in a more horizontal direction and women grow more vertically. There is also a suggestion that women who bear children show some effect of the growth hormones of pregnancy by increased growth during the childbearing years. The amount of change over 2 or 3 decades is small, probably amounting to only 1 or 2 mm of vertical increase, with extremes of 2 to 3 mm possible. When added to the remaining adolescent growth that leads to infraocclusion of an implant, these small changes may be enough to cause implant failure. Endosseous implants have a nearly 30-year history of success; however, the majority were used in edentulous individuals with no adjacent natural teeth. In patients having adjacent natural teeth, long-term infraocclusion of the implant prosthesis would be noticeable but may not be apparent in patients with significant occlusal wear of their natural dentition. Single-tooth replacement implants have a much shorter history than implants in edentulous patients, perhaps too short to show evidence of the effects of adult growth.

Recommendations for Implant Use in Growing Individuals

Endosseous implant-supported prostheses can be an extraordinarily beneficial means of replacing missing teeth. In the partially anodontic child, implants placed in mandibular edentulous areas away from natural teeth appear to be successful even when placed at an early age and offer the child a stable mandibular prosthesis that may not be obtainable in other ways. Implants placed at an early age in the edentulous maxilla may not be so successful, but there are as yet no reported cases. The need for implants in the maxilla may not be as great since the maxilla is not as frequently affected by anodontia, and there is usually sufficient retention available for a removable temporary prosthesis. The potential problems from endosseous implants stem not from their use in the edentulous, but in the dentulous child, particularly adjacent to natural teeth that are erupting and compensating for growth of the jaws.

Even when placed during adolescence, the long-term effects of the single-tooth implant on adjacent teeth have yet to be determined. Certainly 1 or 2 mm of infraocclusion can be overcome by lengthening the prosthetic crown on the implant. But what about the differences in bone level between the adjacent natural teeth and the infraoccluded endosseous implant? In the natural dentition we would be concerned about the inability to clean that particular area and the potential insult to the periodontal ligament. Peri-implantitis, or infection around an implant, is a serious complication that is difficult to treat and would in most cases result in implant failure.

Also, what is the effect of this large difference in bone level on adjacent teeth? In the Thilander et al study, an average loss of marginal bone level on teeth adjacent to the single-tooth implant was 1.3 mm during the 3-year study period. There was, however, a large variation in individual response; some patients showed a 3-mm decrease and one patient a 9-mm bone level decrease between the cementoenamel junction and the marginal bone. Certainly this amount of bone loss has a high potential for failure. Case reports in the literature have emphasized the infraocclusion of the implant prosthesis and the ability to increase prosthesis height. However, a greater problem may be the inability to clean the area and the subsequent infections and bone loss around not only the infraoccluded implant but also the adjacent teeth. The advantages of placing implants early to avoid bone atrophy and to increase function and esthetics may be overshadowed by the potential to harm or even lose adjacent natural teeth.

Team Approach

It is clear that the use of implants in children, particularly the prepubertal partially anodontic child, must be a team effort. In order to provide the patient the best result as an adult, the team should consist of a surgeon, who places the implant; an orthodontist; a prosthodontist; and a periodontist. In younger children the care of a pediatric dentist is also required. The surgical placement of the implant must be secondary to the needs of both the prosthodontist and the orthodontist. If other teeth are present, the orthodontist must place the remaining teeth in the most optimal position for long-term success. This may require using the implant as an orthodontic anchor to obtain the most ideal tooth positioning. The prosthodontist must provide interim tooth replacement for esthetics and function, as well as for long-term planning. Both orthodontic treatment and implant placement must consider the final adult restoration of the patient. Because the final prosthetic rehabilitation of the child is paramount to success, the prosthodontist must take a lead in determining where the orthodontist should place the teeth and, secondarily, where the surgeon should place the implant for the best results.

General Recommendations

The foregoing discussion of the growth and development of the maxilla, the mandible, and the dentition must be the basis for any recommendations regarding implant use. The greatest difficulty in making recommendations is the extraordinary variation in growth amount and direction between individual children. For the individual child, the general growth trends may be far from accurate. Another unknown is how the child with large numbers of missing teeth will grow. The lack of alveolar development and the small size of the jaws in the anodontic child appear to indicate that many of the growth changes seen in the dentulous child may not occur in the edentulous child. Placement of implants in a child as early as 5 or 6 years of age has been done with apparently some success when the implants are far from natural teeth and in the anterior mandible. The number of children with large numbers of missing teeth is small, which makes it difficult to gather a sufficient sample size for study.

The most conservative approach is to provide the implant portion of treatment only after completion of both skeletal and dental growth and development. Often there are strong psychological, physiological, and social factors that pressure the clinician to consider earlier treatment[63]; however, a prudent clinician should always attempt to use a conventional prosthesis, which, while lacking the comfort and function of an implant-assisted prosthesis, does not invite implant loss, malocclusion, or bone loss around adjacent teeth. An interim conventional prosthesis can be used to gather functional and esthetic information to aid in the design of the final prosthesis and to allow as much growth as possible before initiating the implant-assisted phase of treatment. During this period, the team of caregivers can develop and implement the most optimal treatment plan for the patient while observing growth and facial change. Treatment must often include extractions staged at the appropriate time and orthodontic treatment to place the teeth in their most optimal positions. The use of implants in the partially anodontic child may be indicated for appropriate orthodontic anchorage because they can enable orthodontic movements that would otherwise be impossible. However, if the implants are in areas affected by growth, they may be used only as temporary anchorage devices and then removed. Conventional prostheses, often combined with orthodontic appliances, can be used throughout this preparatory period to maintain esthetics and function, allowing for continual reevaluation of the final treatment plan, alveolar bone loss, and skeletal maturation.

There are obvious short-term benefits of early implant use in preserving alveolar bone and improved esthetics and function, as well as patient comfort. In treating patients with traumatically lost or congenitally absent maxillary anterior teeth, there is a great deal of pressure to provide an early "permanent" solution, but placing an implant prior to 13 to 16 years of age is not recommended in the literature.[64,65]

Recommendations by Area

Anterior maxilla

As noted above, the anterior maxilla is an important area because of the pressures for early resolution of the sequelae of traumatic tooth loss or congenital absence. However, due to the amount, the direction, and the unpredictability of growth in this area, it may be one of the most risky in which to place an implant, particularly in the presence of adjacent natural teeth. When growth-related problems are considered along with the esthetic demands of tooth exposure and gingival contours, the use of early implants in this area is probably not warranted. Vertical growth in this area exceeds growth in other dimensions and continues to a later age. Premature implant placement can result in the need to repeatedly lengthen the transmucosal implant connection, as well as poor implant-prosthesis ratios and adverse load magnification. Since the midpalatal suture remains open into puberty, maxillary transverse skeletal growth can also have an adverse effect on implants placed too early. On a long-term basis, early placement can adversely affect adjacent natural teeth. Implants in the maxillary anterior area should be delayed until after growth is completed. Although chronological ages of 15 for girls and 17 for boys have been assigned as safe, the best strategy is to place implants only after skeletal growth is completed. If implants are placed prior to this time, the patient and his or her parents must be informed of the risks involved.

Posterior maxilla

The maxillary posterior area presents the same problems as the anterior area. Large variations exist in the amount and direction of both anteroposterior and vertical growth, and the unpredictability of the growth pattern only adds to the difficulty. Vertical growth occurs in quantities approaching 1 cm. Growth occurs not only by apposition on the alveolar aspect but also by resorption on the nasal or maxillary sinus area of the maxilla. This can result in an early implant being submerged occlusally and exposed apically because of resorption of bone in the maxillary sinus. Worsening the situation is the increase in transverse dimension of the maxilla. Certainly any prosthetic transpalatal connector that would limit transverse growth must be avoided at an early age, a conclusion supported in the literature. Vertical growth and the compensatory anteroposterior changes in the dentition remain the major factors.

The use of implants adjacent to natural teeth would present the worst prognosis due to progressive implant infraocclusion and its long-term effects on both the implant and the adjacent teeth. Implants in the anodontic child may also be problematic because of the appositional and resorptive pattern of the posterior maxilla. Because of the superior retention of conventional prostheses and the absence of supporting bone in this area, reports of the early use of implants have not surfaced. The recommendation for use of implants in the posterior maxilla is to place them only after cessation of growth.

Anterior mandible

The mandibular anterior area is the one area where early placement of dental implants is indicated in the anodontic child. Although this area has as dynamic a growth pattern as other areas, alveolar growth appears minimal when no teeth are present. The anterior mandible offers the advantage of completing the majority of its transverse and anteroposterior growth relatively early. The mandibular symphysis is not of concern because it closes in early childhood. Anteroposterior growth occurs mainly at the posterior of the mandible. Reports in the literature describe placement of implants as early as 5 years of age with short-term success. Though long-term treatment results are lacking, this area seems to hold the greatest potential for early use of an implant-supported prosthesis. This is also an area in which it is more difficult to gain adequate retention and support for conventional prostheses.

The use of implants in this area to replace single teeth is, however, not advisable. The significant compensatory change in the dentition in this area during growth, combined with the small space available and the lack of sufficient bone volume, demands that the mandibular anterior area be avoided when natural teeth are present near the implant site. Case report evidence supports this contention.

Posterior mandible

Unlike the anterior mandible, growth changes in the posterior mandible occur relatively late. Large amounts of anteroposterior, transverse, and vertical growth occur in this area. As the mandible undergoes rotational growth, significant changes occur in both the alveolus and the lower border. When teeth are present, vertical growth is a major factor in dental height increase and results in anteroposterior compensatory changes in the dentition. In the edentulous mandible, such changes are not so clear, but an implant could be affected adversely. A lack of reports of early implant use in the edentulous posterior mandible further decreases the advisability of implant use.

Although the advisability of placing implants in the edentulous posterior mandible is not clear, the placing of implants adjacent to natural teeth has been documented. Progressive infraocclusion and risk of harm to the supporting tissues of adjacent teeth preclude the early placement of implants in these areas. A conservative approach in the posterior mandible dictates that implants not be placed until skeletal growth is completed.

References

1. Koch G, Bergendal T, Kvint S, Johansson U. Consensus Conference on Oral Implants in Young Patients. Stockholm: Förlagshuset Gothia, 1996.

2. Muller TP, Hill IN, Peterson AC, Blayney JR. A survey of congenitally missing permanent teeth. J Am Dent Assoc 1970;81:101–107.

3. Silverman NE, Ackerman JL. Oligodontia: A study of its prevalence and variation in 4,032 children. J Dent Child 1979;46:470–477.

4. Maklin M, Dummett CO Jr, Weinberg R. A study of oligodontia in a sample of New Orleans children. J Dent Child 1979;46:478–482.

5. Hunstadbraten K. Hypodontia in the permanent dentition. J Dent Child 1973;40:115–117.

6. Todd JE. Children's Dental Health in England and Wales. London: Social Survey Division and Her Majesty's Stationery Office, 1983.

7. Holland T, Mullane DO, Clarksson J, et al. Trauma to permanent teeth of children, aged 8, 12, and 15 years, in Ireland. J Paediatr Dent 1988;4:13–16.

8. King GJ. Results of the Florida Class II Study. Guest presentation, "Quick Scan Reviews in Orthodontics." Birmingham, AL: Educational Reviews. Sept 1998.

9. Wennerberg A, Albrektsson T, Andersson B. Design and surface characteristics of 13 commercially available oral implant systems. Int J Oral Maxillofac Implants 1993;8:622–633.

10. Johansson C, Albrektsson T. Integration of screw implants in the rabbit: A 1-year follow-up of removal torque of titanium implants. Int J Oral Maxillofac Implants 1987;2:69–75.

11. Roberts WE, Marshall KJ, Mozsary PG. Rigid endosseous implants utilized as anchorage to protract molars and close an atrophic extraction site. Angle Orthod 1990;60:135–152.

12. Higuchi KW, Slack JM. The use of titanium fixtures for intraoral anchorage to facilitate orthodontic tooth movement. Int J Oral Maxillofac Implants 1991;6:338–344.

13. Smalley WM, Shapiro PA, Hohl T, et al. Osseointegrated titanium implants for maxillofacial protraction in monkeys. Am J Orthod Dentofac Orthop 1988;94:285–295.

14. Turley PK, Kean C, Shur J, et al. Orthodontic force application to titanium endosseous implants. Angle Orthod 1988;58:151–162.

15. Rubin PH, Weisman EJ, Bisk F. Experimental tooth ankylosis in the monkey. Angle Orthod 1984;54:61–72.

16. Kurol J, Kock G. The effects of extraction of infraoccluded deciduous molars: A longitudinal study. Am J Orthod 1985;87:46–55.

17. Oesterle LJ, Cronin RJ, Ranly DM. Maxillary implants and the growing patient. Int J Oral Maxillofac Implants 1993;8:377–387.

18. Sennerby L, Ödman J, Lekholm U, Thilander B. Tissue reactions towards titanium implants inserted in growing jaws: A histological study in the pig. Clin Oral Implants Res 1993;4:65–75.

19. Ödman J, Gröndahl K, Lekholm U, et al. The effect of osseointegrated implants on the dentoalveolar development: A clinical and radiographic study in growing pigs. Eur J Orthod 1991;13:279–286.

20. Thilander B, Ödman J, Gröndahl K, Lekholm U. Aspects on osseointegrated implants inserted in growing jaws: A biometric and radiographic study in the young pig. Eur J Orthod 1992;14:99–109.

21. Björk A. Variations in the growth pattern of the human mandible: A longitudinal radiographic study by the implant method. J Dent Res 1963;42:400–411.

22. Björk A. Growth of the maxilla in three dimensions as revealed radiographically by the implant method. Br J Orthod 1977;4:53–64.

23. Shaw WC. Problems of accuracy and reliability in cephalometric studies with implants in infants with cleft lip and palate. Br J Orthod 1977;4:93–100.

24. Enlow DH. Facial Growth, ed 3. Philadelphia: Saunders, 1990.

25. Moyers RE. Standards of Human Occlusal Development. Ann Arbor, MI: Univ of Michigan Center for Human Growth and Development, 1976.

26. Voss R, Freng A. Growth of dental arches after ablation of midpalatal suture: A study in domestic cats. J Maxillofac Surg 1982;10:259–263.

27. Freng A. Growth in width of the dental arches after partial extirpation of midpalatal suture in man. Scand J Plast Reconstr Surg 1978;12:267–272.

28. Knott V. Longitudinal study of dental arch widths at four stages of the dentition. Angle Orthod 1972;42:387–394.

29. Brugnolo E, Mazzocco C, Cordiolo G, Majzoub Z. Clinical and radiographic findings following placement of single-tooth implants in young patients: Case reports. Int J Periodont Rest Dent 1996;16:421–433.

30. Ledermann PD, Hassell TM, Hefti AF. Osseointegrated dental implants as alternative therapy to bridge construction or orthodontics in young patients: Seven years of clinical experience. Pediatr Dent 1993;15:327–333.

31. Behrents RG. Growth in the aging craniofacial skeleton, monograph 17 and 18, Craniofacial Growth Series. Ann Arbor, MI: Univ of Michigan Center for Human Growth and Development, 1985.

32. Iseri H, Solow B. Continued eruption of maxillary incisors and first molars in girls from 9 to 25 years, studied by the implant method. Eur J Orthod 1996;18:245–256.

33. Ranly DM. Implants in the circumpubertal patient: Growth considerations. Am J Dent 1998;11:86–92.

34. Johansson G, Palmqvist S, Svenson B. Effects of early placement of a single tooth implant. A case report. Clin Oral Implants Research 1994;5:48–51.

35. Westwood RM, Duncan JM. Implants in adolescents: A literature review and case reports. Int J Oral Maxillofac Implants 1996;11:750–755.

36. Moyers RE, Van der Linden FP, Riolo ML, et al. Standards of human occlusal development, monograph 5, Craniofacial Growth Series. Ann Arbor, MI: Univ of Michigan Center for Human Growth and Development, 1976.

37. Holcomb AE, Meredith HV. Width of the dental arches at the deciduous canines in white children 4 to 8 years of age. Growth 1956;20:159–177.

38. Knott V. Longitudinal study of dental arch widths at four stages of dentition. Angle Orthod 1972;42:387–394.

39. Meredith HV, Hopp WM. A longitudinal study of dental arch width at the deciduous second molars on children 4-8 years of age. J Dent Res 1956;35:879–889.

40. Lavelle CL. A study of dental arch and body growth. Angle Orthod 1976;46:361–364.

41. Jones B, Meredith H. Vertical change in osseous and odontic portions of the human face between the ages of 5 and 15 years. Am J Orthod 1966;52:902–921.

42. Björk A. Variations in the growth pattern of the human mandible: A longitudinal radiographic study by the implant method. J Dental Res 1963;42:400–411.

43. Skieller V, Björk A, Linde-Hansen T. Prediction of mandibular growth rotation evaluated from a longitudinal implant sample. Am J Orthod 1984;86:359–70.

44. Baumrind S, Korn E, West E. Prediction of mandibular rotation: An empirical test of clinician performance. Am J Orthod 1984;86:371–385.

45. Ari-Viro A, Wisth PJ. An evaluation of the method of structural growth prediction. Eur J Orthod 1983;5:199–207.

46. Lee RS, Daniel FJ, Swartz M, et al. Assessment of a method for the prediction of mandibular rotation. Am J Orthod Dentofac Orthop 1987;91:395–402.

47. Riolo ML, Moyers RE, McNamara JA, et al. An Atlas of Craniofacial Growth, monograph 2, Craniofacial Growth Series. Ann Arbor, MI: Univ of Michigan Center for Human Growth and Development, 1979.

48. Cronin RJ, Oesterle LJ. Implant use in growing patients: Treatment planning concerns. Dent Clin North Am 1998; 42:1–34.

49. Bergendal T, Eckerdal O, Hallonsten L, et al. Osseointegrated implants in the oral habilitation of a boy with ectodermal dysplasia: A case report. Int Dent J 1991;41:149–156.

50. Smith RA, Vargervik K. Placement of an endosseous implant in a growing child with ectodermal dysplasia. Oral Surg Oral Med Oral Pathol 1993;75:669–673.

51. Kraut RA. The role of a hospital-based dental implant center. Implant Dent 1993;2:31–35.

52. Cronin RJ, Oesterle LJ. Mandibular implants in the growing patient. Int J Oral Maxillofac Implants 1994;9:55–62.

53. Bergendal B, Bergendal T, Hallonsten A, et al. A multidisciplinary approach to oral rehabilitation with osseointegrated implants in children and adolescents with multiple aplasia. Eur J Orthod 1996;18:119–129.

54. Clark A. Hypohidrotic ectodermal dysplasia. J Med Genet 1987;4:339–52.

55. Van Wieringen JC. Secular growth changes. In: Falkner F, Tanner JM (eds). Human Growth, ed 2. New York: Plenum Press, 1986.

56. Marshall WA, Tanner JM. Puberty. In: Falkner F, Tanner JM (eds). Human Growth, ed 2. New York: Plenum Press, 1986.

57. Pyle SI, Waterhouse AM, Greulich WW. A Radiographic Standard of Reference for the Growing Hand and Wrist. Cleveland: Case Western Reserve University Press, 1971.

58. Hägg U, Taranger J. Maturation indicators and the pubertal growth spurt. Am J Orthod 1982;82:299–309.

59. Thilander B, Ödman J, Gröndahl K, et al. Osseointegrated implants in adolescents: An alternative in replacing missing teeth? Eur J Orthod 1994;16:84–95.

60. Bishara SE, Treder JE, Jakobsen JR. Facial and dental changes in adulthood. Am J Orthod Dentofac Orthop 1994;106:175–186.

61. Forsberg CM. Facial morphology and ageing: A longitudinal cephalometric investigation of young adults. Eur J Orthod 1979;1:15–23.

62. Formby WA, Nanda RS, Currier GF. Longitudinal changes in the adult facial profile. Am J Orthod Dentofac Orthop 1994;105:464–476.

63. Boj JR, Von Arx JD, Cortada M, et al. Dentures for a 3-year-old child with ectodermal dysplasia: Case report. Am J Dent 1993;6:165–167.

64. Guckes AD, Brahim JS, McCarthy GR, et al. Using endosseous dental implants for patients with ectodermal dysplasia. J Am Dent Assoc 1991;122:59–62.

65. Hancock RR, Nimmo A, Walchak PA. Full arch dental reconstruction in an adolescent patient: Clinical report. Implant Dent 1993;2:179–181.

66. Björk A. Cranial base development: A follow-up x-ray study of the individual variation in growth occurring between the ages of 12 and 20 years and its relation to brain case and face development. Am J Orthod 1955;41:198–225.

67. Björk A, Skieller V. Facial development and tooth eruption. Am J Orthod 1972;62:339–383.

68. Björk A, Skieller V. Normal and abnormal growth of the mandible: A synthesis of longitudinal cephalometric implant studies over a period of 25 years. Eur J Orthod 1983;5:1–46.

9 | Orthodontic Anchorage with Osseointegrated Implants: Bone Physiology, Metabolism, and Biomechanics

W. Eugene Roberts, DDS, PhD

The predictable use of implants as a source of orthodontic and dentofacial orthopedic anchorage requires a practical understanding of the fundamental principles of bone physiology and biomechanics. Implants can be used as supplemental anchorage for closing spaces, retracting anchorage segments, generating new periodontium, or for preprosthetic alignment.[1-3] However, a careful evaluation of prospective patients is indicated because many candidates for implant-anchored orthodontics are affected by osteopenia, osteoporosis, or other medical problems. Optimal use of osseointegrated implants requires a thorough knowledge of bone biomechanics, particularly when the patient is skeletally and/or periodontally compromised. This chapter will review the basic science principles and related clinical considerations for implant-anchored orthodontics.

Bone Tissue

Three distinct types of bone (woven, lamellar, and composite) are involved in postoperative healing and maturation of the osseous tissue supporting an implant (Figs 9-1 and 9-2). Woven bone has high cellularity, a rapid formation rate (30 µm/day or more), relatively low mineral density, high random fiber orientation, and poor strength. Since woven bone is more compliant than mature osseous tissue, it serves an important stabilization role in postoperative healing of endosseous implants (Fig 9-3). During the initial healing process, woven bone fills all spaces at the bone-implant interface. Although capable of stabilizing an unloaded implant, woven bone lacks the strength to resist masticatory function. Lamellar bone is the principal load-bearing tissue of the adult skeleton. It is the predominant component of a mature bone-implant interface (Fig 9-4). Lamellar bone is formed relatively slowly (less than 1.0 µm/day), has a highly organized matrix, and is densely mineralized. Composite bone is a combi-

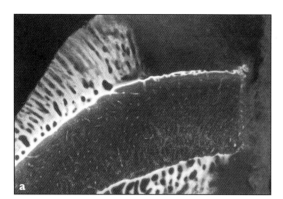
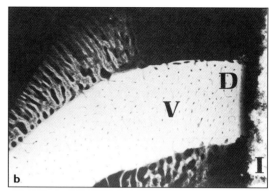

Fig 9-1 (a) Cylindrical titanium, HA-coated implant placed in the femur of a rabbit. Tetracycline was administered for 3 days. One week postoperatively, fluorescent microscopy shows that the mineralization of the new callus emerges from undamaged periosteum peripheral to the wound (original magnification ×10). (From Roberts[4]; reprinted with permission.) (b) Microradiographic image of the same section showing dead bone (D) adjacent to the wound. The devitalized bone is slightly demineralized (more radiolucent) compared with adjacent vital bone (V). The callus is composed primarily of woven bone (original magnification ×10). (From Roberts[4]; reprinted with permission.)

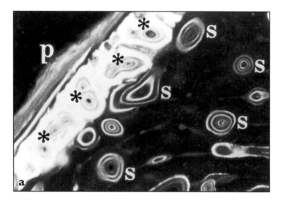
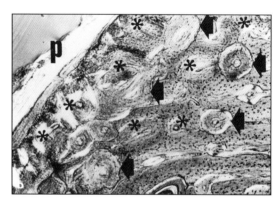

Fig 9-2 (a) Modeling and remodeling aspects of cortical bone growth as demonstrated by fluorescent bone labels administered at weekly intervals. Bright, diffuse labels mark new primary osteons at the periosteal (p) surface. The advancing front of primary cortical bone is remodeled by secondary osteons (s). More distinct labels mark the lamellar bone formed in secondary osteons (s) and the internal portion of primary osteons (*) (original magnification ×25). (From Roberts[50]; reprinted with permission.) (b) Polarized light illumination of the same section illustrating the characteristic lamellar patterns of primary (*) and secondary (arrows) osteons associated with cortical bone apposition at the periosteal (p) surface. (From Roberts[50]; reprinted with permission.)

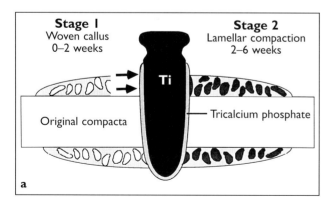
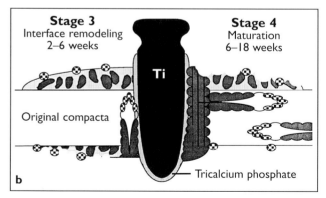

Fig 9-3 Modeling and remodeling aspects of postoperative implant healing in rabbits (divided into four stages). (a) Woven bone formation in the initial generation of the callus (left) and lamellar bone compaction of the callus (right). (b) Once the implant is stabilized by the periosteal and endosteal calli, remodeling of the nonvital interface is accomplished by cutting-filling cones (left). The entire interface is eventually remodeled (right), as is a substantial portion of the supporting cortex. Once the implant is rigidly integrated with lamellar bone, the endosteal and periosteal calli resorb. (From Roberts[4]; reprinted with permission.)

Fig 9-4 (a) Bright-field photomicrograph of a 100-μm-thick section through a titanium implant placed in a dog mandible for 6 months. Note osseointegration of the interface (original magnification ×10). **(b)** Polarized light illumination of the same section, illustrating a predominantly lamellar bone pattern (original magnification ×10). (c) Fluorescent microscopy of the section showing intense label uptake at and near the implant interface. Multiple fluorochrome labels were administered every 2 weeks (original magnification ×10). (d) Microradiographic image of the section showing a layer of cortical bone *(c)* supported by trabeculae *(t)*. The mineralization pattern is consistent with a high rate of remodeling for bone at and near the implant interface. (From Roberts[52]; reprinted with permission.)

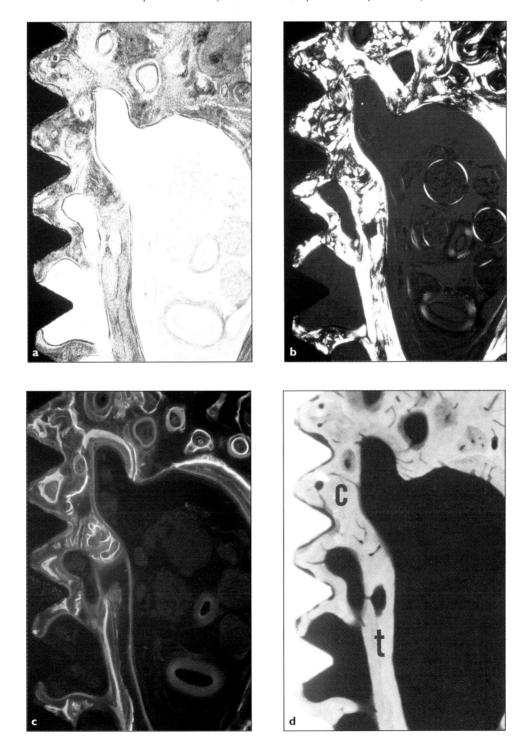

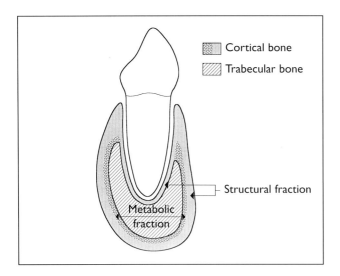

Cortical bone
Trabecular bone

Structural fraction

Metabolic fraction

Fig 9-5 Metabolic and structural fractions of alveolar and basilar bone. The structural fraction is controlled by biomechanical factors (eg, functional loads). The metabolic fraction is a reservoir of calcium to meet metabolic needs. (From Roberts[38]; reprinted with permission.)

nation of paravascular lamellar bone deposited on a woven bone matrix. During the initial wound-healing phase, a highly porous, woven bone lattice (callus) emanates from intact (unstripped) periosteum at the periphery of the wound (Fig 9-1). The highly vascular callus grows toward the implant on both the endosteal and periosteal surfaces. The paravascular cavities then fill with high-quality lamellae, achieving adequate strength for load bearing (Fig 9-2).[4] Formation of composite bone is an important step in achieving stabilization of an implant during the rigid integration process (Fig 9-3).

Bone Physiology

Bone provides the structural support for the stomatognathic system and its physiology is an important consideration. Modern principles of bone physiology are essential for diagnosis, treatment planning, and effective delivery of bone manipulative therapy. Most candidates for implant-anchored orthodontics have lost teeth and experienced some degree of skeletal atrophy. Bone pathophysiology should be carefully considered as part of the diagnostic workup. Implant-anchored orthodontics usually involves extensive bone manipulation over an extended period of time. Progressive metabolic bone disease is a contraindication for bone manipulative therapy.

The strength of a bone (quantity, quality, and geometric distribution) is directly related to its loading history.[5] Bone that is not adequately loaded is preferentially resorbed. The skeletal system continuously adapts to achieve optimal strength with minimal mass. This delicate balance is challenged by the essential life-support function of bone, ie, serving as the metabolic reservoir of calcium.[6] An adequate reserve of osseous tissue must be maintained to provide a continuous stream of ionic calcium without compromising skeletal integrity. To provide structural support while simultaneously serving as a source of ionic calcium, the skeleton has evolved a unique compartmental organization system. The peripheral aspects of the skeleton provide the principal structural support, while the internal osseous tissue turns over more rapidly to provide a continuous source of metabolic calcium. This skeletal organization is referred to as the structural and metabolic fractions (Fig 9-5).

Osteopenia (inadequate bone mass) may reflect functional atrophy and/or negative calcium balance. Prospective dental implant patients present a particularly high risk for both localized and systemic skeletal deficiencies because *(1)* edentulous areas of the jaws are usually atrophic, *(2)* metabolic bone disease and negative calcium balance are more prevalent in middle-aged and older adults, *(3)* loss of teeth per se is a risk factor for osteoporosis, and *(4)* integrated implants are often indicated for patients with a history of localized bone loss.[7,8]

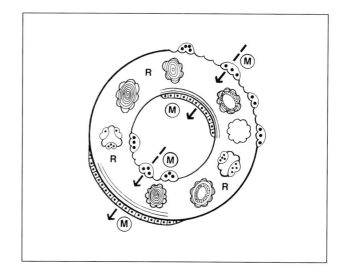

Fig 9-6 Modeling (M) is a series of uncoupled formation and resorption events that change the size, shape, or position of a bone. Remodeling (R) is turnover of previously existing bone. Modeling is largely controlled by functional loading, whereas remodeling responds primarily to demand for metabolic (ionic) calcium. (From Roberts et al[23]; reprinted with permission.)

Modeling and Remodeling

Unique mechanisms of bone adaptation maintain skeletal integrity, repair fatigue damage, and provide a continuous stream of metabolic calcium (Fig 9-6). Modeling involves individual (uncoupled) sites of bone formation or resorption that change the shape or form of a bone. This is the principal mechanism for adapting osseous structure to functional loading. Remodeling is the mechanism of bone turnover. It involves coupled sequences of cell activation (A), bone resorption (R), and bone formation (F). The duration of the ARF remodeling cycle (sigma[9]) for humans is about 4 months for trabecular bone[9] and approximately 6 months for cortical bone.[10,11]

Modeling is the principal means of skeletal adaptation to functional and therapeutic loads. Relatively modest changes in the distribution of osseous tissue along cortical bone surfaces dramatically affect the overall load-bearing capability. Similar to other structural materials, the stiffness of a long bone, such as the body of the mandible, is related to the fourth power of the diameter, eg, doubling the diameter of a bone increases its stiffness 16 times. Thus, even modest layers of mineralized tissue deposited on the outer surface of a bone can substantially increase its stiffness and strength.[5] Skeletally atrophic patients may experience a substantial increase in skeletal mass of the mandible following a functional restoration of occlusion with

implants. This is an example of the hypertrophic mechanism for increasing bone strength by adding osseous tissue at the periosteal surface.

All bones are able to adapt by modeling mechanisms. Focused bone resorption and formation events are the means of trabecular "micromodeling" to optimally resist functional loads.[9] A good example of this process is the network of secondary trusses that forms in the marrow cavity to support an integrated implant (Fig 9-7).[12] The internal loading of the maxilla and mandible via osseointegrated implants can produce marked changes in external and internal skeletal architecture. Bone mass and geometry reflect the distribution of stress associated with dynamic loading.

Cortical bone remodeling (internal turnover) is accomplished by paravascular cutting-filling cones. The latter is a functional unit of osteoclasts and osteoblasts organized around a proliferating, dedicated blood vessel (Fig 9-8). Trabecular bone (spongiosa) remodels in a similar manner via "hemicutting-filling cones" that selectively remove and replace a set volume of bone at a specific site (Fig 9-9). The principal difference in trabecular remodeling is the lack of an internal, dedicated blood supply. The hemicutting-filling cone depends on the vascularity of the marrow.

Trabecular bone remodels at about 20% to 30% per year. From a metabolic perspective, the spongiosa is the most important calcium reservoir in the body.[13] Virtually all trabecular bone is within

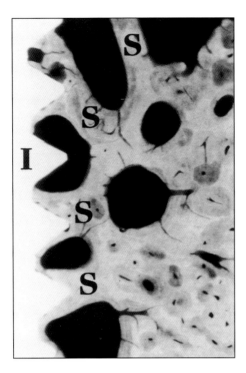

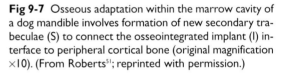

Fig 9-7 Osseous adaptation within the marrow cavity of a dog mandible involves formation of new secondary trabeculae (S) to connect the osseointegrated implant (I) interface to peripheral cortical bone (original magnification ×10). (From Roberts[51]; reprinted with permission.)

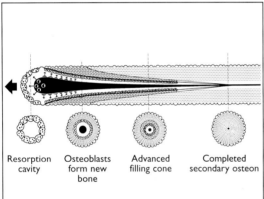

Fig 9-8 The cutting-filling cone is the mechanism of cortical bone remodeling (turnover). The cutting head of osteoclasts, derived from circulating precursor cells, removes old bone. The trailing filling cone of osteoblasts, derived from paravascular cells, forms a new secondary osteon. (From Roberts[38]; reprinted with permission.)

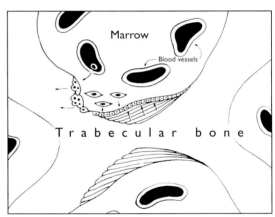

Fig 9-9 The hemicutting-filling cone is the mechanism of trabecular bone remodeling. It is similar to the cutting-filling cone of cortical bone except that it has no internal vascularity and must depend on the blood supply of the adjacent marrow. (From Roberts[51]; reprinted with permission.)

the metabolic fraction. Remodeling can be accomplished without compromising skeletal integrity because *(1)* only a small portion of the supporting osseous tissue is turning over at any time, and *(2)* the remodeling process preferentially attacks the metabolic fraction. The latter is the least structurally important aspect of the bone.[14]

Under most circumstances, cortical bone remodels at about 2% to 10% per year. Since only a portion of the cortex is in the metabolic fraction, the remodeling rate for cortical bone is usually 3 to 10 times less than for adjacent trabecular bone. Because all of it is in the metabolic fraction, trabecular bone usually has a remodeling rate of 20% to 30% per year.[13]

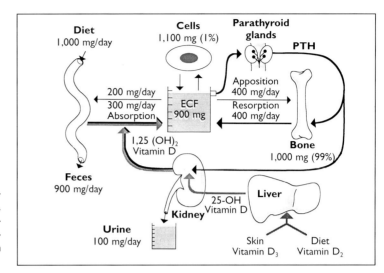

Fig 9-10 Schematic drawing depicting ideal calcium metabolism to maintain bone mass (zero calcium balance). Inadequate absorption and/or excessive excretion of calcium drains the calcium reservoir (bone) to maintain adequate ionic calcium in the extracellular fluid (ECF). (From Roberts[38]; reprinted with permission.)

Calcium Metabolism

Calcium metabolism is a primal, life-support function. About 99% of body calcium is in bone; in effect, the skeletal system serves as a metabolic reservoir (Fig 9-10). When challenged by sustained negative calcium balance such as low-calcium diet, estrogen deficiency, or long-term corticosteroid treatment, the least mechanically protected portions of the skeleton are preferentially resorbed.[15] Metabolically compromised edentulous and partially edentulous patients are particularly susceptible to loss of jaw structure. Not only is the alveolar process exposed to disuse atrophy because of tooth loss, but there is also extensive loss of bone from the metabolic fraction, ie, trabecular bone and the inner (endosteal) portion of the cortex. In individuals with optimal oral function, metabolic demand for calcium tends to spare the jaws and preferentially mobilizes calcium from other parts of the body (Fig 9-11). Thus, normal functional loading can help protect bone-supporting teeth and implants.

Metabolic Bone Disease

An evaluation of bone metabolism is a key element of the diagnostic workup. The minimal screening procedure involves a careful medical history, evaluation of signs and symptoms of skeletal disease, and an assessment of risk factors associated with negative calcium balance.[7] The most prevalent metabolic bone diseases in middle-aged and older patients are:

- Renal osteodystrophy—poor bone quality (fibrous dysplasia) that is secondary to inadequate kidney function
- Hyperparathyroidism—elevated serum calcium is often associated with high-turnover osteopenia (low bone mass) secondary to a parathyroid adenoma
- Thyrotoxicosis—high bone turnover leading to osteopenia, associated with hyperthyroidism or overtreatment of hypothyroidism
- Osteomalacia—poor mineralization of osteoid due to a deficiency of the active metabolite of vitamin D (1, 25-dihydroxycholecalciferol)
- Osteoporosis—usually defined as symptomatic osteopenia; most common fractures are of the spine, wrist, and/or hip. Fragility of other weight-bearing joints such as the knee and ankle are also common problems.

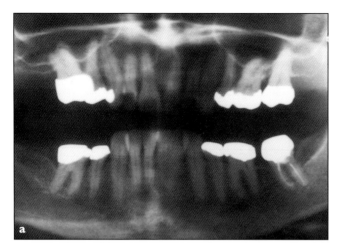

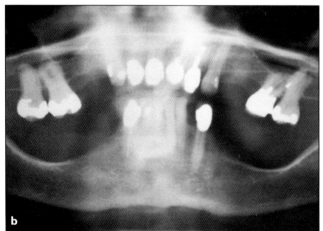

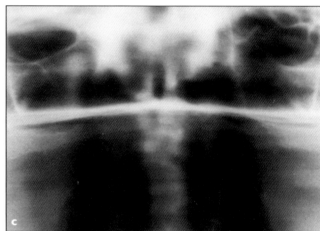

Fig 9-11 Panoramic radiographs of three postmenopausal women with various expressions of osteopenia. (a) When key teeth are preserved in all four quadrants, functional loads protect the bone from metabolic resorption. (b) Loss of mandibular posterior teeth results in disuse atrophy of the alveolar process. (c) Severe resorption is due to edentulousness (poor mechanical loading) and negative calcium balance secondary to long-term, low-dose corticosteroid therapy. (From Roberts[51]; reprinted with permission.)

Osteoporotic Dental Patients

Osteoporosis can result in a severe loss of bone structure. If there is enough residual bone for adequate postoperative stabilization of an implant, bone healing is usually normal. For instance, osteoporotics have normal bone, just not enough of it. If mechanical and metabolic deficits are not corrected, the pathophysiological environment persists after the healing response subsides. This scenario is clearly detrimental to the patient's health and may negatively affect the longevity of implant-supported prostheses.

Although loss of teeth is an established risk factor for osteoporosis, the symptoms and fracture profiles of osteoporotic dental patients is unknown. In a sample of 16 osteoporotic dental patients over the age of 50,[3,16,17] fractures and bone fragility in

joints were more common than the classic fractures of the hip, wrist, and spine. Two of the 16 osteoporotic patients who were receiving orthodontic and implant therapy experienced fractures or joint failure of the knee and ankle. It is not known if this pattern of orthopedic symptoms is a trend for osteoporotic dental patients, but clinicians should be aware of it.

Osteopenic Risk Factors

Patients in negative calcium balance are poor risks for dental implants because of progressive skeletal atrophy. Becker et al[16] have recently reviewed the risk factors for low skeletal mass (osteopenia or "osteoporosis") for a sample of dental patients. The most well-established risk factors are:

- Age—progressive incidence in older patients
- Race—Caucasians, as well as Asians from industrialized countries, are preferentially affected
- Sex—about 50% of females and 20% of males are at risk
- Heredity—strong familial tendency, almost an 80% chance if a first-order relative (parent or sibling) is affected
- Slight stature—particularly when maintained by habitual dieting
- Loss of teeth—strongly associated with systemic osteopenia
- Diet—calcium deficiency and/or excessively high protein consumption (metabolic acidosis is associated with a high meat diet)
- Exercise—lack of consistent, weight-bearing activity
- Tobacco—osteopenia is directly related to the amount of nicotine consumed (pack years = number of packs smoked per day times years)
- Alcohol—related to excessive consumption, usually defined as more than two alcoholic beverages per day; moderate alcohol consumption is healthful
- Drug therapy—corticosteroids, lithium, anticonvulsants (such as Dilantin), thyroid hormone, and a number of other long-term drug regimens are associated with osteopenia.

As the numbers and ages of partially edentulous adults increase, orthodontists will treat larger numbers of patients at high risk for osteopenia and osteoporosis. A careful assessment of osteoporosis risk factors is particularly important for partially edentulous patients having substantially compensated malocclusions. The latter often require preprosthetic alignment with implant-anchored orthodontics and may be a subgroup of patients that requires special consideration.[3,8,17]

Therapeutic Measures

Although remodeling is an essential physiological mechanism for repairing fatigue damage and providing metabolic calcium, the rate of turnover must be controlled. Under steady-state conditions, skeletal remodeling is accomplished at a structural cost. Each ARF cycle results in a slight negative calcium balance, ie, not quite as much bone is replaced as was removed. A normal rate of remodeling results in a slow, age-related loss of bone. Within limits, this physiological loss of bone is not a problem because structural demands diminish with age. However, an excessive rate of bone remodeling, such as occurs in postmenopausal women or in thyrotoxicosis, may result in high-turnover osteopenia or osteoporosis.[13]

From a metabolic perspective, the remodeling frequency (number of ARF events/unit time) is enhanced by both parathyroid (PTH) hormone and thyroid (TH) hormone. Parathyroid hormone is a specific hormone for mobilizing and conserving calcium primarily within the metabolic fraction (Fig 9-5). Thyroid hormone increases remodeling by elevating the metabolic rate of the entire body. Estrogen suppresses the remodeling frequency, so estrogen replacement therapy (ERT) is effective in preventing the high-turnover osteopenia that begins at menopause. Growth hormone (GH) and anabolic steroids (AS) also tend to build skeletal mass but by a different mechanism. They enhance muscle mass, which stimulates periosteal bone formation (modeling) to build the structural fraction of bone. Despite well-established anabolic effects, neither GH nor AS is commonly used to treat osteoporosis because of a propensity for side effects like cardiac hypertrophy and other acromegalic signs.[7]

Metabolic bone disease is a complex medical problem best treated by specifically trained physicians with access to appropriate diagnostic and treatment-monitoring equipment. Such facilities are available in most major medical centers, usually associated with the endocrinology section of a department of medicine. Depending on etiology, osteopenia or osteoporosis may be treated with exercise, dietary supplements (calcium and/or vitamin D), hormones, and/or specific drugs. Bone loss may be suppressed by decreasing the remodeling frequency with estrogen replacement therapy (ERT) or by directly inhibiting resorption with calcitonin or bisphosphonates. Estrogen replacement

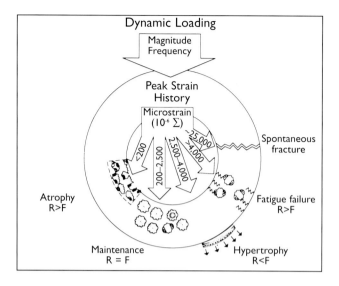

Fig 9-12 Biomechanical control of osseous adaptation (bone modeling and remodeling) is related to the magnitude and frequency of dynamic (intermittent) loads. The peak strain history (bone deformation over time) dictates the osseous response. Bone deformation (strain) is expressed as microstrain (μE), which is strain × 10^{-6}. Since percent strain is 10^{-2}, 1,000 μE is the same as 0.1% strain. Repetitive loading at more than 4,000 μm results in pathological overload and eventual fatigue failure of bone. Compared with the ultimate strength of cortical bone (25,000 μE), repetitive loading at as little as 16% of that level can result in a stress fracture. (From Roberts[38]; reprinted with permission.)

therapy is usually considered to be the most effective long-term therapy for women. At present there is no equivalent hormonal therapy for men.[7]

Estrogen treatment is no problem for prospective dental implant patients. However, calcitonin, bisphosphonates, and other antiresorptive agents are a concern because bone resorption is an essential element for postoperative healing and long-term maintenance of integrated implants. Devitalized, immature, and fatigued bone can be removed only by osteoclastic activity. Tamoxifen and raloxifene are selective estrogen receptors that suppress the rate of turnover. They are both effective in preserving the skeleton and protecting the hearts of postmenopausal women without increasing the risk of breast cancer.[18] Raloxifene is recommended for female patients with an intact uterus because it does not stimulate the endometrium. Estrogen, tamoxifen, and raloxifene are currently the therapies of choice for treating or preventing osteoporosis during active bone manipulative therapy.

Biomechanics

In addition to its metabolic calcium role, bone remodeling is also driven by mechanical stress and strain (Fig 9-12). This is the body's mechanism for preventing excessive accumulation of microdamage.[19,20] At a few highly stressed sites, like the alveolar process and mandibular condyle, bone

turnover may be 30% per year or higher.[1] This elevated remodeling rate is probably related to the high strain and subsequent fatigue damage that results from masticatory function. Thus, the most critical bone in the dental apparatus (alveolar bone and TMJ) is highly labile, turns over very rapidly, and may be susceptible to mechanical overload. The unique nature of bone in the stomatognathic system is an important consideration in diagnosis and treatment planning of functionally compromised patients. Preprosthetic alignment of the residual dentition with implant-anchored orthodontics is a major advantage in accomplishing an optimal load distribution for the restored occlusion.

Bone cells are sensitive to strains (deformation). The peak strain history of dynamic (normal cyclic) loading is related to magnitude and frequency of functional loads. As the peak strain of cyclic loads increases, the physiological hierarchy responds as follows: *(1)* prevention of bone atrophy, *(2)* maintenance of osseous mass, *(3)* bone hypertrophy, and *(4)* pathological overload (fatigue failure) (Fig 9-12). This stepwise relation of the strain-related effects is well accepted, but the actual strains controlling these events may be site and species specific.

Bone is a composite biomaterial that structurally adapts to its mechanical environment. It is well suited for long-term function when optimally loaded in the physiological range. Suboptimal loading results in atrophy of both bone mass and structural orientation. Bone deformation of about

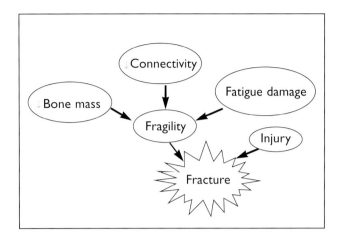

Fig 9-13 An injury that abruptly loads a bone beyond its inherent strength results in a fracture. However, when the bone is weakened by a significant decrease in bone mass, loss of connectivity (optimal geometric distribution of osseous tissue), and an accumulation of fatigue damage, it may be fractured by normal functional loads. (From Roberts[38]; reprinted with permission.)

2.5% (25,000 µE) results in a spontaneous fracture. Relative to its maximal strength, the upper limit of the physiological loading range for steady-state maintenance (2,500 µE) is only about 10% of the ultimate strength of the bone (2,500/25,000 microstrain, µE).

Moderate overloading (from about 10% to 15% of ultimate strength) induces a hypertrophic response to suppress remodeling and increase the bone diameter. Pathological overload (over 16% of ultimate strength) is defined as repeated (cyclic) loads exceeding the usual adaptive capacity of the bone. Accumulation of fatigue damage, in the presence of low bone mass and poor connectivity, may result in a spontaneous fracture (Fig 9-13). Localized areas of fatigue failure may contribute to a loss of osseous support (eg, bone recession, craters). Repeated dynamic loading exceeding the body's range to adapt may result in a stress fracture.[21]

Implant-Supported Prostheses

Mechanical loading optimizes mineralized tissue mass, quality, and orientation. An extensive alveolar process supports the teeth in both jaws. Because the maxilla is loaded primarily in compression, its osseous structure is similar to the body of a vertebra, ie, predominantly trabecular bone with thin cortical plates. In the maxilla, the palatal plate is generally thicker than the labial plate. The mandible has much thicker cortices than

the maxilla because it is a cantilever that is subjected to substantial torsion[22] (Fig 9-14a).

Alveolar bone, the specialized osseous tissue that is formed to support teeth, probably requires a higher strain to avoid atrophy than does the basilar bone of the jaws. When teeth are lost, the alveolar process often resorbs until only the basilar mandible and maxilla remain. At the original vertical dimension of occlusion (VDO), there is a large intermaxillary space (Fig 9-14b). Rigidly fixed ("osseointegrated") implants restore atrophic bone to masticatory function (Fig 9-14c). Prostheses supported by osseointegrated implants present unique biomechanical challenges because *(1)* restoring the VDO often requires an unfavorable crown-root ratio for the suprastructure, *(2)* there is a lack of a cushioning periodontal ligament (PDL), and *(3)* there are compromised neurological feedback mechanisms for controlling occlusal force. All these factors tend to concentrate the occlusal load at the periosteal margin of supporting bone (Fig 9-14c).

Heavy functional loads and/or poor prosthetic load distribution can contribute to fatigue failure of the implant, its suprastructure, and/or the adjacent bone. Clinicians must be particularly vigilant to avoid mechanical overloading during the first year of function. The osseous support is fragile because of the high rate of turnover and lack of mineral maturation.[23] The high sustained rate of remodeling within 1 mm of the implant surface results in a layer of less mineralized, more compliant bone at the bone-implant interface (Fig 9-4c).[24]

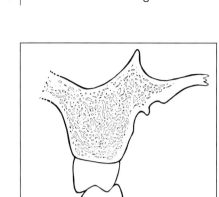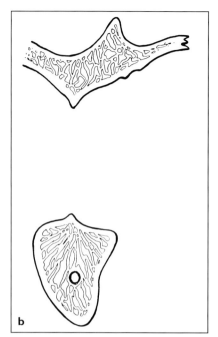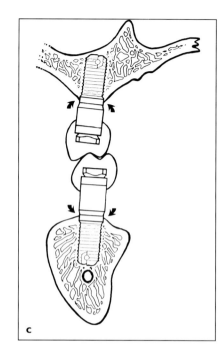

Fig 9-14 (a) When natural teeth have normal bone support, there is a relatively short lever arm from occlusion to the level of alveolar bone. (b) Resorption of the edentulous alveolar process increases the vertical dimension between the maxilla and mandible. (c) Implant-supported prostheses constitute a long lever arm from occlusal contact to the level of bone support. Thus, lateral forces in occlusion place a heavy load on bone where the alveolar crest contacts the implant *(arrows)*. (From Roberts[51]; reprinted with permission.)

Attaching orthodontic brackets to implant-supported prostheses is often a problem. Banding the prosthesis is difficult if not impossible. Bonding brackets to gold or porcelain surfaces is challenging and rarely satisfactory, particularly in the mandibular arch. Since a bracket bonded to an implant-supported prosthesis is usually the principal source of anchorage, bonding failures are serious problems. It is recommended that the prosthesis be a cast gold restoration with a bondable stainless steel bracket attached prior to casting. The bracket is warmed and attached directly to the wax pattern (Fig 9-15) so that it can be carefully aligned in three dimensions. Because stainless steel melts at a higher temperature than gold, the wax pattern with the bracket attached is drawn and invested. Following burnout, molten gold is cast to the back of the bondable bracket base. When the orthodontic attachment is no longer needed, the prosthesis is removed and the orthodontic bracket is ground off. Thus, the permanent gold prosthesis serves temporarily as an orthodontic anchorage abutment. Avoiding the construction of a provisional prosthesis is less expensive for the patient and less problematic for the orthodontist.

Healing and Integration

A wide variety of bone-compatible materials, which can achieve osseointegration, are used to construct implants. The most common materials interfacing with bone are titanium, titanium alloy, and hydroxyapatite (HA). The first osseointegrated implants, for which the modeling and remodeling sequence of postoperative bone healing was described, were coated with tricalcium phosphate (TCP) and sterilized in an autoclave[25] (Fig 9-1). When similar implants were sterilized with radiation, they had a high failure rate because the TCP coating was too soluble. It was later found that autoclaving implants converts the TCP to HA and other less soluble calcium phosphates. Historically, TCP (really HA)-coated implants are important in the development of osseointegrated anchorage because they were the first implants used to define the histological mecha-

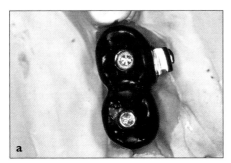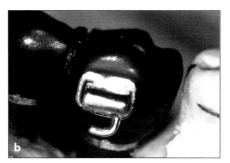

Fig 9-15 (a) Occlusal view of wax pattern for an implant-supported prosthesis showing the direct attachment of an orthodontic bracket. (b) Lateral view of the orthodontic bracket demonstrates adjustment of the height angulation to achieve an ideal relationship with adjacent natural teeth. (From Roberts et al[52]; reprinted with permission.)

nism of osseointegration.[4] It was subsequently found that a variation of the same modeling and remodeling sequence is the healing mechanism for all endosseous implants.[2,25–29]

Prior to placing implants, most edentulous sites are atrophic as a result of pathological bone loss and/or inadequate mechanical loading. Placing a dental implant overrides the steady-state physiologic mechanisms. A time-dependent, localized healing response (Fig 9-1), controlled primarily by local cytokines from the blood clot and adjacent injured tissue, is elicited. Once the healing reaction subsides, systemic metabolic and localized mechanical factors determine the form and function of bone at the site of implantation (Figs 9-4 and 9-7) and throughout the stomatognathic complex.

The postoperative acceleration of bone remodeling (regional acceleratory phenomenon [RAP]) lasts for about 1 year (2 to 3 sigma). During the first 4 months (1 sigma), the major events are *(1)* resolution of the acute postoperative inflammation, *(2)* callus formation and maturation, and *(3)* initiation of bone remodeling at the interface and within supporting bone.[4,7,14,30,31] Depending on the quality of supporting bone, defined as quantity and distribution of cortical bone directly contacting the implant surface, an implant can be loaded immediately or may require up to 6 months of unloaded healing. Traditionally, a 4-month closed healing phase is recommended for implants placed in cortical bone (such as the mandible). Six months is

usually required if an implant is placed in trabecular bone (such as the maxilla) (Fig 9-14).

The healing potential for an implant is determined by three factors: *(1)* quality of bone at the site of implantation, *(2)* postoperative stability of the implant, and *(3)* degree of integration of the interface. If there is good postoperative stability of the implant in cortical bone, the healing response involves six physiological stages:

1. Callus formation (0.5 month)—initial, cytokine-driven response to stabilize the implant (Fig 9-1)
2. Callus maturation (0.5 to 1.5 months)—lamellar compaction, remodeling, and reduction of the callus (Fig 9-2)
3. Regional acceleratory phenomenon (RAP) (1.5 to 12 months)—remodeling of the nonvital interface and supporting bone (Fig 9-16)
4. Osseous integration of the interface (1.5 to 12 months)—completion of the RAP, increased direct contact of living bone at the interface (Fig 9-17)
5. Maturation of supporting bone (4 to 12 months)—completion of the RAP, secondary mineralization of new bone (Fig 9-18a) and increased direct contact of living bone at the interface (Fig 9-18b)
6. Long-term maintenance of osseointegration (from 1 year on)—continuous, localized remodeling within 1 mm of the implant surface maintaining a less mineralized, more compliant layer (Fig 9-19).

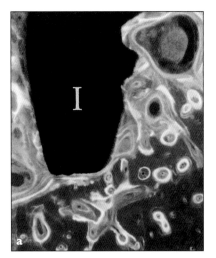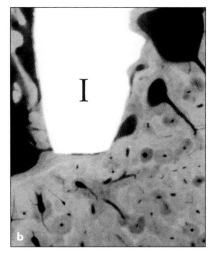

Fig 9-16 (a) Fluorescent microscopy of a section through the base of a titanium implant left in the mandible of a dog for 6 months, showing a decreasing gradient of remodeling from the implant into the cortical bone. This is a postoperative regional acceleratory phenomenon (RAP) associated with bone healing. Bone labels were administered at 2-week intervals (original magnification ×10). (b) Microradiograph of same section demonstrating that newly remodeled secondary osteons are more radiolucent than adjacent bone (original magnification ×10). (From Roberts[38]; reprinted with permission.)

Immediate Loading

For good-quality postoperative support, presently defined as a cortical thickness greater than 2.5 mm and/or bicortical stabilization of the implant, there is a trend toward loading implant-supported prostheses immediately. Under optimal circumstances, there is adequate (albeit dead) bone at the interface to stabilize the implant while it is remodeled into a vital interface. Small foci are remodeled individually and vital integration (apposition of living bone on the implant surface) is achieved in a stepwise manner. Thus, an immediately loaded implant can achieve osseointegration without loss of endosseous stabilization. Implants placed in good-quality bone can be loaded immediately and can maintain stability as the interface heals. Although immediate loading is an option, an unloaded healing phase of 4 to 6 months is often preferable because the latter is the only proven method having favorable long-term follow-up.

The endosteal and periosteal calluses are another important factor in postoperative stabilization of the implant (Figs 9-1 and 9-4). As the healing response subsides, mechanical and metabolic factors reestablish control of osseous form. Bone generated by the cytokine-driven healing response is retained only if it is adequately loaded.[14] Despite the trend toward immediate masticatory function, the effect of superimposing an orthodontic load on an implant-supported prosthesis is unknown.

If the bone quality of the implantation site and the healing callus are adequate to achieve stability, the implant can be used immediately after surgery as a source of anchorage. Immediate loading of anchorage implants, which are out of occlusion (Fig 9-20), is supported by stress analysis at the bone-implant interface and within the supporting bone. Chen et al[32] used finite element modeling to show that orthodontically loading the retromolar anchorage mechanism has only a slight effect on the stress at the implant interface. Apparently, most of

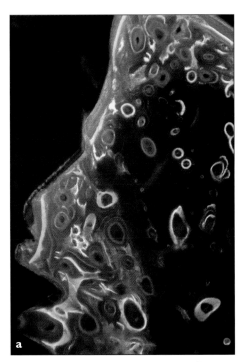

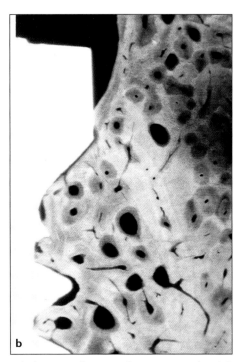

Fig 9-17 (a) Fluorescent microscopy of a section through the cervical region of a titanium implant left in a dog mandible for 6 months showing more intense uptake of bone labels (administered at 2-week intervals) near the implant surface (original magnification ×10). (From Roberts et al[52]; reprinted with permission.) (b) Microradiograph of same section demonstrating the intense remodeling of primary bone near the implant surface (original magnification ×10). (From Roberts et al[52]; reprinted with permission.)

Fig 9-18 (a) Primary (p) and secondary (*) mineralization illustrated in a rapidly remodeling area of dog cortical bone. Note that primary (p) mineralized osteons and new circumferential lamellae (c) are more radiolucent than older adjacent bone (original magnification ×25). (From Roberts[51]; reprinted with permission.) (b) Six months after implant placement in dog mandible, microradiography reveals woven bone (w) of the periosteal callus as well as surgically devitalized (D) areas augmented by periosteal apposition of vital (V) bone and remodeling to secondary osteons (*). Microradiography provides a valuable historical record of the complex bone physiology associated with implant healing and adaptation to applied loads (original magnification ×10). (From Roberts[23]; reprinted with permission.)

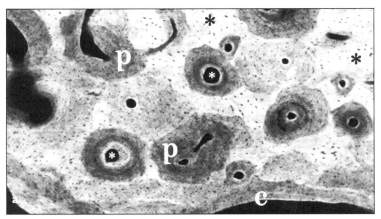

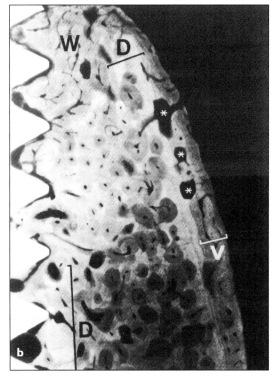

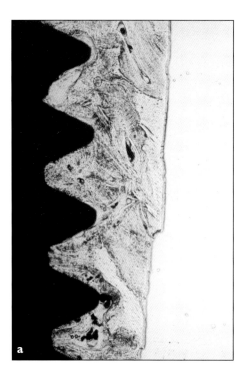

Fig 9-19 (a) A 10-mm Brånemark implant (Nobel Biocare) was recovered from an adult man after serving as a source of orthodontic anchorage in the mandibular retromolar area. This bright-field photomicrograph demonstrates the architecture of the bone supporting the implant (original magnification ×10). (b) Two tetracycline labels were administered 1 week apart prior to surgical recovery. Intense uptake of the label is noted within 1 mm of the implant surface (original magnification ×10). (From Roberts[33]; reprinted with permission.) (c) Microradiograph of the same section showing more radiolucent bone corresponding to the areas of label uptake. Collectively, these data indicate that cortical bone integrating an implant is remodeled indefinitely at a very high rate (original magnification ×10). (From Roberts[33]; reprinted with permission.)

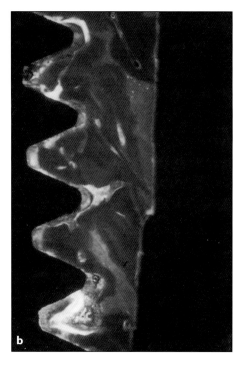

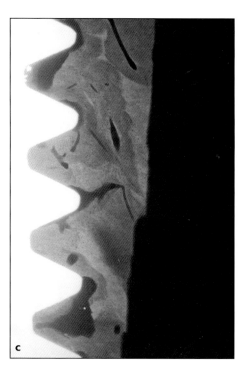

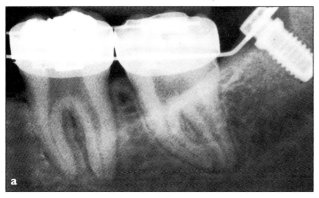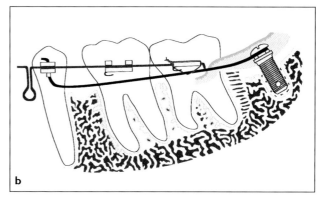

Fig 9-20 (a) A 4-mm Brånemark flanged implant was placed in the mandibular retromolar area to serve as a source of orthodontic anchorage. (From Hohlt and Roberts[34]; reprinted with permission.) (b) Internal abutment concept, demonstrating a titanium alloy wire attached to the implant with a standard surgical healing screw. The anchorage wire passes into the oral cavity through an incision in the depth of the buccal fold. (From Roberts et al[23]; reprinted with permission.)

the stress at the interface is related to the mismatch in the modulus of elasticity between titanium and cortical bone. As the living mandible functions, a surface shear is generated at the interface that greatly exceeds the stress due to the indirect orthodontic loading. Based on this research, the unloaded healing phase was eliminated for retromolar anchorage implants (Fig 9-20). Over a 10-year period, 30 immediately loaded retromolar implants have provided effective orthodontic anchorage[2,3,17,33–35] with no failures. It is concluded that implants for retromolar implant anchorage can be loaded immediately if *(1)* there is adequate thread engagement of cortical bone postoperatively (Fig 9-20a) and *(2)* the implant is not in occlusal function (Fig 9-20b).[2,3,17,33–35] However, it is important to remember that if an implant-supported prosthesis is in occlusion, a 4- to 6-month unloaded healing protocol is recommended before exposing it to masticatory function or orthodontic loading.

Maturation of Supporting Bone

As previously described, placing an endosseous implant results in an intense bone modeling and remodeling response that lasts for about a year (Figs 9-16 to 9-18). Callus formation at the periosteal and endosteal surfaces is a form of anabolic modeling that decreases the flexure of the operated segment. Although the bone at the interface is devitalized postoperatively, it still maintains the structural strength to support the implant. Assuming optimal surgical technique and an appropriate osseous site, the implant will be well stabilized and have adequate osseous support. During the remodeling cycle, bone is removed and replaced in localized sites (foci) along the interface. As resorptive cavities form, localized support is lost until bone refills the resorption cavity several months later. Although the entire devitalized interface is remodeled eventually, only about one third of the osseous interface is uncovered by resorption at any time (Figs 9-16 to 9-19). The uncovered areas of the implant surface are equivalent to resorption cavities in cortical bone and are referred to as *remodeling space*. It is concluded that *(1)* bone integrating the implant surface can be continuously remodeled without the loss of structural integrity, and *(2)* an implant interface integrated with rapidly remodeling cortical bone cannot be 100% integrated because bone turnover requires remodeling space. For example, assume a steady state of remodeling, a 6-week interval from the start of bone resorption to the start of bone formation, and a 24-week remodeling cycle. Under these conditions, 25% of an osseointegrated interface will not be in contact with mineralized tissue at any given time (Fig 9-19).

The healing and maturation phases of implant integration are modeling and remodeling dependent. Maturation of the mineralized interface and supporting bone is a critical step in the integration process. There is a direct relationship between the age of bone tissue and its mineral density (Fig 9-18a). Following a maturation phase of about 1 week, newly formed osteoid is mineralized by a large number of small hydroxyapatite crystals. During this period of primary mineralization, osteoblasts deposit about 70% of the mineral found in mature vital bone. Secondary mineralization (remaining 30%) is a noncellular crystal growth phenomenon that occurs over a period of about 8 months. Mineral maturation is important to integrated implant support because stiffness and strength of lamellar bone is directly related to its mineral content.[5]

Long-term Maintenance of Osseointegration

Occasionally, well-integrated prosthetic implants are removed when they are damaged or no longer needed. Orthodontic anchorage implants are commonly removed at the end of treatment. Prior to removing an osseointegrated implant, administration of two doses of tetracycline (7 to 10 days apart), followed by a postlabeling period of 3 to 7 days before biopsy, provides important dynamic information on steady-state remodeling of supporting bone. A series of 20 well-integrated titanium implants was removed for prosthetic or orthodontic reasons. All had been in service from 2 to 5 years and were double labeled with tetracycline before removal. Despite a variety of intraoral locations and loading conditions, all specimens demonstrated a high rate of bone remodeling within 1 mm of the implant surface (Fig 9-19). It was concluded that bone within 1 mm of the bone-implant interface remodels continuously at a rate of about 500% turnover per year.[36] This intense remodeling process is apparently the mechanism of sustained osseointegration. Inhibiting the remodeling process by a blockade of resorption with a powerful bisphosphonate was associated with the loss of an entire implant-supported prosthesis.[37]

Biodynamics of Tooth Movement

The stomatognathic apparatus is probably the most adaptive musculoskeletal complex in the body. Maintaining optimal occlusal function over a lifetime requires a physiological mechanism for differential movement of dentition within its supporting bone. Tooth movement is mediated by the periodontal ligament (PDL), an adaptive interface between the root of a tooth and its supporting bone. Periodontal ligament is a specialized layer of osteogenic tissue that is more of a vascularized, collagenous membrane than a true ligament. Ligaments restrain the mobility of joints, whereas the PDL is an adaptive connection between the root of a tooth and its adjacent alveolar bone. It is a physiologically "dynamic" tissue because of its differential response to applied loads. High-magnitude, cyclic loads of short duration, ie, mastication, do not move teeth. However, light continuous forces (postural or therapeutic) elicit an adaptive response that changes the position of a tooth relative to its alveolar support (Fig 9-21).[38]

The positions of the teeth within the alveolar processes are controlled by the posture of the oral soft tissues.[39,40] Tooth position is dictated by the equilibrium of forces acting on it: soft tissue posture, occlusion, parafunction, and habits. In effecting tooth movement, the duration of the load is more important than its magnitude. Constant or long-duration intermittent loads move teeth. Orthodontic therapy with fixed appliances is accomplished by applying static loads (forces and moments) to teeth. The static therapeutic load is superimposed on the cyclic loading of normal masticatory function. The overall change in dynamic loading disturbs the equilibrium maintaining tooth position. The affected teeth move, via PDL modeling and alveolar remodeling responses, until a new equilibrium position is established. Relating orthodontics to the dynamic principles of orthopedic biomechanics (Fig 9-12), therapeutic bone formation probably occurs in the hypertrophic range (2,500 to 4,000 µE), whereas resorption is favored with localized areas of alveolar bone that are exposed to dynamic loading in the fatigue failure range (over 4,000 µE). The advantage of osseointe-

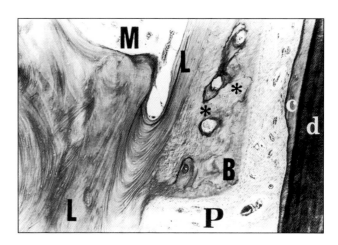

Fig 9-21 Osteogenic mechanism of orthodontic movement demonstrated by a demineralized histological section through the periodontium of a tooth being moved to the right. Cementum (c) covers dentin (d) of the root. The periodontal ligament (P) separates the tooth from alveolar bone. Lamellar (L), woven (*), and bundle (B) bone are shown (hematoxylin-eosin stain; original magnification ×10). (From Roberts et al[50]; reprinted with permission.)

grated implants for orthodontic anchorage is that they do not move relative to basilar bone. However, the energy transferred via the implant to the bone may elicit an osseous response of the periosteum.[12,14] In effect, the bone responds to the applied load even though the implant does not move relative to its supporting bone.

Periodontal Ligament, Ankylosis, and Osseointegration

The principal challenge in orthodontic therapy is to achieve the desired movement of malaligned teeth without detrimental changes in the position of the anchorage segments. Osseointegrated implants are a source of rigid orthodontic and orthopedic anchorage (Fig 9-22a). Teeth with an intact PDL can continue to move relative to basilar bone, but the implant is rigidly fixed within the bone (Fig 9-22b). Rigidly integrated implants have redefined the scope of orthodontic therapy, particularly in partially edentulous patients. With respect to endosseous implants, the term *integration* is defined as direct osseous apposition onto the surface of an implant or tooth, rigidly fixing it within adjacent supporting bone (Fig 9-23). Thus, an osseointegrated implant is physiologically equivalent to an ankylosed tooth. Rigidly integrated abutments (implants or ankylosed teeth) are not moved by typical orthodontic loads because there is no continuous adaptive interface (PDL) (Figs 9-24a to 9-24c).

Despite having only 1 to 2 mm^2 of actual bone integration, ankylosed teeth are not moved with typical orthodontic mechanics. In comparison, endosseous implants typically have only about 60% of the interface integrated with vital bone. As little as 10% integration has proved successful for rigid orthodontic/orthopedic anchorage (Fig 9-25).[12] It is clear that small amounts of osseous bridging across the PDL is adequate to prevent tooth movement.

The PDL allows the dentition to adapt to changes in the size of jaws and the intermaxillary relationship. Physiologic tooth movement is guided by the inclined planes of the occluding dentition. Optimal masticatory function is maintained despite differential growth of the jaws, loss of teeth, or traumatic injury. If arch integrity and/or centric stops of occlusion are lost, the continuing extrusion and drift of teeth can produce decreased facial height and substantially compensated malocclusions.[3,17]

Implant Anchorage

Integrated bone modeling and remodeling activity is the mechanism of tooth movement (Fig 9-24a). When the periodontium is healthy, orthodontic loading moves the tooth with its supporting tissues. On the other hand, osseointegrated implants do not move in response to orthodontic loads (Fig 9-24c). Although there is intense remodeling activity within 1 mm of the implant surface, resorption

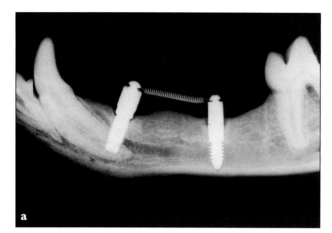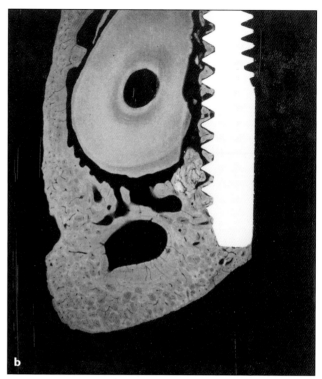

Fig 9-22 (a) Titanium implants that were placed in the mandible of a dog and allowed to heal for 12 weeks. They were reciprocally loaded with up to 5 N continuous force superimposed on function. The implants did not move relative to the basilar bone. (From Roberts et al[12]; reprinted with permission.) (b) Frontal section through the most anterior implant showing that the root of the canine was inadvertently cut when the implant was placed. Note that integration proceeded normally and a new periodontal ligament formed (original magnification ×2.5). (From Roberts et al[23]; reprinted with permission.)

cavities at the interface (remodeling space) uncover only about 35% to 40% of the surface at any time. The remaining 60% to 65% of the interface is rigidly integrated, preventing movement of the implant relative to its supporting bone (Figs 9-16, 9-17, 9-18b, 9-19, and 9-23).

Implants are ideal anchorage units because they do not move in response to applied force within the orthodontic range (less than 5 N).[12] On the other hand, implants placed within the arches can be a problem because they may block the desired path of tooth movement. It is often wise to place anchorage implants in retromolar areas of the mandible and the tuberosity region of the maxilla.

Then the residual teeth can be moved to ideal positions without interference of the rigid anchorage abutments.

Moving Ankylosed Teeth with Implant Anchorage

Although fatigue failure is usually detrimental, the fundamental principles of biomechanics (Fig 9-12) can be used for the nonsurgical movement of ankylosed teeth. In effect, the anchorage value of ankylosis versus osseointegration is tested by using well-integrated implants as anchorage to "move"

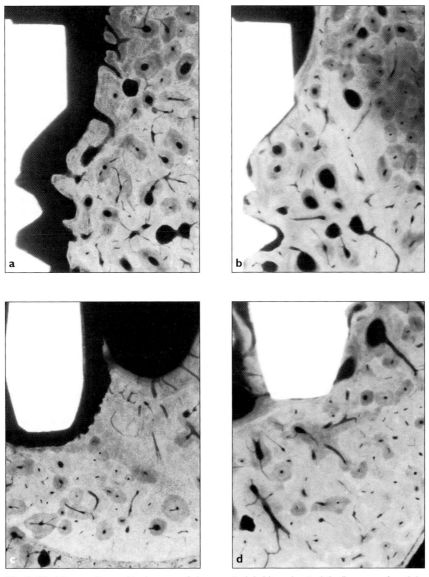

Fig 9-23 Microradiographic images of the cervical (a,b) and apical (c,d) areas of mobile (a,c) and rigid (b,d) implants illustrating the mineralization patterns of supporting bone. Note that the osseointegrated implant (right) was not moved by up to 5 N continuous loading (original magnification ×10). (From Roberts et al[12]; reprinted with permission.)

an ankylosed tooth. A heavy force with a short range of activation is superimposed on normal functional loading to produce a dynamic load that concentrates in the area of ankylosis. The purpose is to produce a localized fatigue failure of the osseous bridge so that the ankylosed tooth can be moved without surgical luxation.

A clinical case demonstrating dynamic fatigue mechanics to move an ankylosed tooth is shown in Fig 9-26. The patient had a history of severe maxillary anterior trauma associated with an automobile accident during the juvenile years (Fig 9-26a). The maxillary left first premolar erupted normally but became ankylosed and could not be moved with

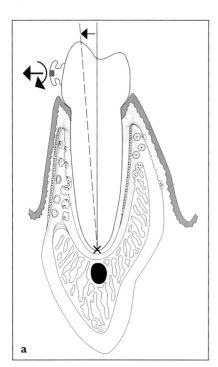 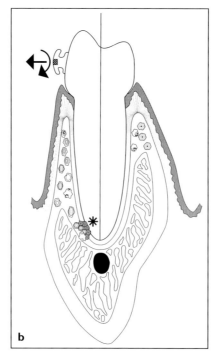 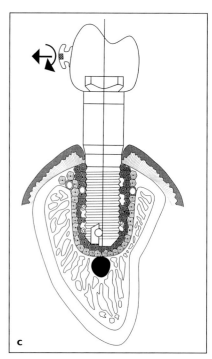

Fig 9-24 (a) A force and a moment are used to move a mandibular premolar buccally. A continuous periodontal ligament allows the tooth to move relative to basilar bone. (b) Similar force applied to an ankylosed tooth will not move it. Although the area of ankylosis (*) is typically small (1 to 2 mm²), the lack of a continuous periodontal ligament prevents tooth movement. (c) An endosseous implant in the same site maintains an intense bone remodeling response at and near the interface. Since there is no continuous periodontal ligament separating the implant from the bone, the implant does not move and is a source of rigid orthodontic anchorage. (From Roberts[52]; reprinted with permission.)

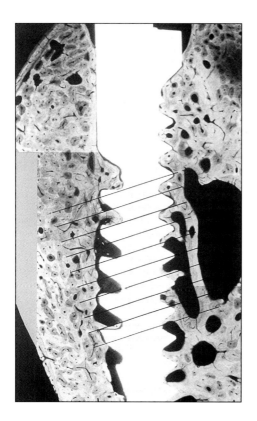

Fig 9-25 Composite microradiographic image from two titanium implants with different surface configurations showing that the implant with the symmetrical threaded surface *(left)* achieves a higher degree of interface contact with bone compared with that achieved by the asymmetric design *(right)*. (From Roberts[52]; reprinted with permission.)

Fig 9-26 (a) Patient with a history of trauma to the maxillary anterior region, with implant-supported prostheses placed during the late mixed dentition to replace the segment from the maxillary right canine to the left lateral incisor. The maxillary right first premolar erupted normally. (b) During the early permanent dentition, this maxillary right first premolar became ankylosed, was displaced palatally, and was not moved with routine orthodontic mechanics. (c) A .019 × .025-inch wire was used to construct a spring that delivered a heavy torsional load to the ankylosed tooth. The implant-supported prosthesis was used as anchorage. (d) The heavy force apparently fatigued the ankylosed attachment, breaking the rigid attachment to bone. Frequent reactivation of the spring resulted in stepwise movement of the ankylosed tooth into near ideal alignment. (From Roberts[52]; reprinted with permission.)

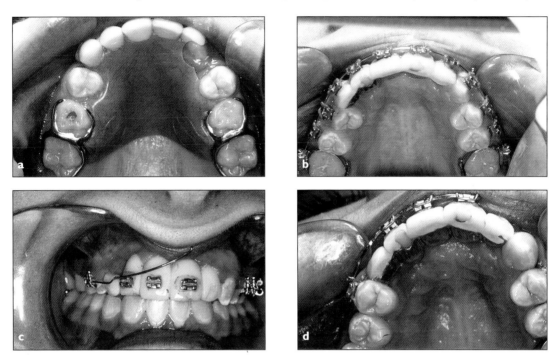

conventional orthodontic mechanics (Fig 9-26b). Utilizing the maxillary anterior, implant-supported fixed prosthesis, a torsional load of about 3,000 gm-mm was applied to the ankylosed premolar (Fig 9-26c). About 3 weeks after activation, the patient reported that the tooth moved "all of a sudden and stopped." Although she could feel pressure when the spring was activated, there was no appreciable pain associated with the tooth movement. With each activation, the ankylosed tooth moved 1 to 2 mm and reintegrated in the new position. Following three activations at monthly intervals, a suitable alignment of the ankylosed tooth was achieved (Fig 9-26d). The clinical course following each activation was similar to the initial separation of a midpalatal suture with a jackscrew appliance.

The theoretical basis of the implant-anchored approach is that the heavy orthodontic load is con-

centrated in the area of ankylosis (Fig 9-24b). In effect, the osseous bridge across the PDL is prestressed into the fatigue failure range (Fig 9-12). Superimposing the normal cyclic loading of occlusion provides repeated strains that produce microdamage in the osseous bridge. Fatigue damage accumulates faster than it can be repaired by remodeling, so the area of ankylosis fractures. Then the tooth moves within the range of activation of the appliance, as restrained by the mechanical resistance of the attached tissues. After an abrupt movement of 1 to 2 mm, the tooth root rapidly reintegrates in the new position via the bone wound-healing mechanism. Assuming adequate implant anchorage, repeated reactivation of an implant-anchored mechanism can be used to orthodontically move an ankylosed tooth a substantial distance.

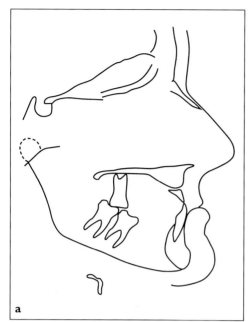

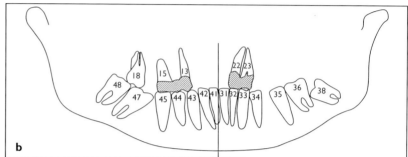

Fig 9-27 (a) Cephalometric tracing of a partially edentulous adult woman showing a concave profile, deep curve of Spee, and closed VDO associated with a mutilated Class III malocclusion. (b) Tracing of the panoramic radiograph revealing the probable etiology of this complex compensated malocclusion. The patient reported losing all four first permanent molars and multiple primary teeth during the mixed dentition, resulting in overclosure of the mandible that produced a Class III intermaxillary relationship. Additional loss of maxillary incisors, premolars, and molars in the permanent dentition contributed to the Class III overclosed malocclusion. Restoration of occlusion with a maxillary partial denture was uncomfortable and unesthetic because of the excessive mandibular curve of Spee, decreased maxillary incisor exposure, and anterior crossbite. (From Roberts[52]; reprinted with permission.)

Compensated Partially Edentulous Malocclusions

When antagonists or adjacent teeth are lost, the extrusion and drift of residual dentition can result in severe malocclusions (Fig 9-27). Compensated malocclusion in a partially edentulous adult often requires orthodontic alignment to achieve an optimal restoration of esthetics and function.[3,17]

Osseointegrated implants have revolutionized the treatment of partially edentulous adults, especially those with severe occlusal compensation resulting from a lack of bilateral posterior occlusion. Particularly when the VDO is altered, the intermaxillary relationship may change substantially due to *(1)* rotation of the mandible, *(2)* repositioning of the condyle within the fossa, and *(3)* adult condylar growth.[41–43]

The objectives of orthodontic treatment are to *(1)* establish the desired intermaxillary relationship as planned on the visual treatment objective (Fig 9-28) and *(2)* optimally align the residual dentition consistent with the preprosthetic objectives for each arch. Once the orthodontic goals are realized, an optimal restoration of occlusion and esthetics can be achieved with routine prosthodontic treatment (Fig 9-29).

Applying the fundamental principles of bone physiology, implant-supported prostheses restore normal masticatory function and the VDO. Opening the bite is strongly resisted by most restorative dentists because it is considered to be unstable. However, there is an important distinction in patients with no posterior occlusal stops. The VDO has been compromised by overclosure of the mandible (Fig 9-27a). Thus, when lower facial height is increased during treatment (Fig 9-28), the VDO is "restored" and not "opened."

Tissue Engineering with Orthodontics

Orthodontic loading will not move an implant relative to its basilar bone because there is no reactive PDL at the bone-implant interface (Fig 9-24c). However, the static load superimposed on function may generate an osseous hypertrophic response in the supporting bone.[12,14] Hypertrophic responses of bone (Fig 9-12) and its associated attached tissues

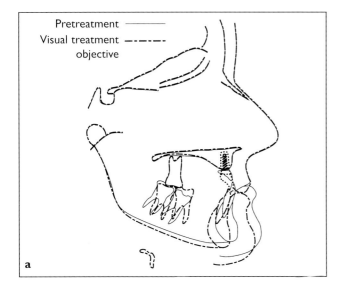

Pretreatment ———
Visual treatment – – – – –
    objective

a

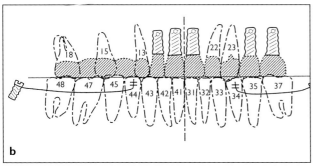

b

Fig 9-28 (a) Sagittal visual treatment objective (VTO) corrects the etiology of the problem by: *(1)* opening the VDO to achieve an optimal profile and interlabial relationship, *(2)* correcting the axial inclination of the molars, *(3)* flattening the curve of Spee, and *(4)* closing the mandibular edentulous spaces by protracting the molars. (b) Panoramic VTO defines the implants, relative tooth movement, and prostheses necessary to achieve the facial and functional goals projected in (a). (c) Horizontal VTO (occlusograms) showing the relative tooth movement and prostheses needed to achieve goals projected in (b). (From Roberts[52]; reprinted with permission.)

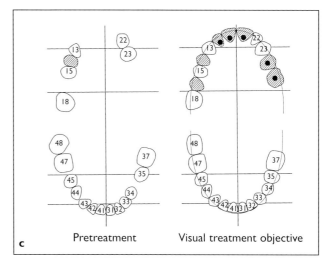

c   Pretreatment   Visual treatment objective

are the physiologic basis of tissue engineering with orthodontics.

Orthodontic loads superimposed on function disturb the biomechanical equilibrium, eliciting a modeling and remodeling response that changes the relationship of the dentition within its supporting bone. The stable position of the orthodontically aligned dentition is dictated by the new dynamic equilibrium. Assuming that the residual dentition has a healthy periodontium, teeth can be moved into atrophic edentulous areas.[1,2,44] In effect, implant-anchored orthodontics is a means of tissue engineering for producing new bone and attached gingiva (Figs 9-29a to 9-29d).

When severely compromised partially edentulous patients are treated, it is usually necessary to restore the VDO with implant-supported prostheses and/or interocclusal orthotics (splints). Once stable bilateral occlusal function is achieved and occlusal interferences are relieved, the teeth can be orthodontically aligned. In asymmetric partially edentulous patients, it may be necessary to wear a splint throughout treatment. An interocclusal space thus created allows for the substantial tissue engineering associated with alignment and extrusion of the residual dentition (Fig 9-28).

Within the alveolar processes, a healthy tooth takes the periodontium with it, whether it is intruded, extruded, tipped, or translated. Atrophic extraction sites can be closed, third molars can be moved mesially into edentulous areas, and incisors can be moved labially or lingually. Within physiological limits, teeth with a healthy periodontium can be moved throughout the alveolar process. Limitations on the envelope of tooth movement are imposed by the drape of soft tissue and basilar bone.

Fig 9-29 (a) Cephalometric tracings of the mandible documenting about 1 cm mesial movement of a mandibular molar, using a retromolar implant for anchorage. As the occlusion with the maxillary molar improved, the mandible spontaneously postured more mesially about 2 mm. (b) Pretreatment view of a partially edentulous buccal segment showing a mandibular molar occluding distally to the terminal maxillary molar. Note the severely atrophic alveolar ridge mesial to the mandibular molar. (c) The mandibular molar was moved mesially about 10 mm into the atrophic site, generating new bone and attached gingiva. In effect, implant-anchored orthodontics is tissue engineering. (d) Orthodontically aligned molar serving as abutment for a fixed prosthesis. (From Roberts et al[52]; reprinted with permission.)

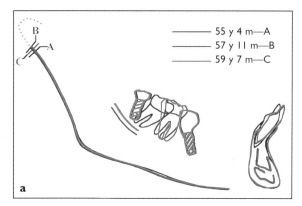

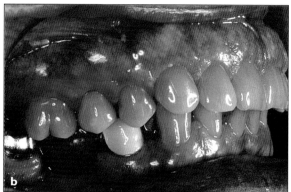

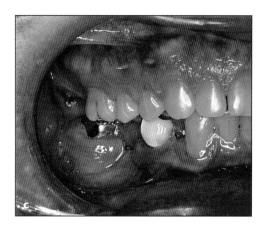

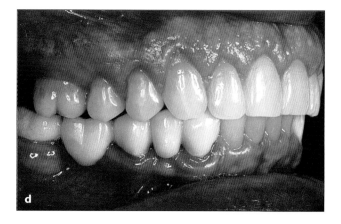

Complications

Placing an implant in an atrophic mandible may result in operative or postoperative fracture.[45–47] Bones are weakened by drilling holes and screwing in implants. The fracture may occur during surgery or within 3 to 4 weeks postoperatively. The fractures during the postoperative healing period are probably due to functional propagation of cracks (stress risers) generated during surgery.[14] Implant-anchored orthodontics may pose a special risk for stress fractures and other orthopedic complications in functionally compromised patients because static loads superimposed on function can strain atrophic bones.

To test the biodynamics of applied static loads, titanium implants were placed in the femora of rabbits and loaded with a 1 N compressive force. All bones spontaneously fractured within 1 week postoperatively.[14] When the implants were allowed to heal (adapt) for 6 weeks prior to applying the 1 N compressive load, no fractures occurred and all bones showed a hypertrophic osteogenic response. In effect, this animal experiment tested two fundamental premises of orthodontics and dentofacial orthopedics: (1) titanium implants can be used as a source of rigid anchorage, and (2) static forces and moments superimposed on function create a new set of dynamic loading conditions that change the functional equilibrium of the stomatognathic system.

No reports of spontaneous fracture of the jaws or alveolar process due to orthodontic therapy have been published. Even immediate loading of retromolar anchorage implants has been uneventful, probably because the retromolar region is a highly stressed area owing to the cantilever nature of the mandible.[48] Finite element modeling of the retromolar area, with and without an anchorage implant, has revealed that orthodontic loads are very small compared with the stress of mastication.[49] These favorable results with immediate loading probably extend to other sites in the mandible where there is adequate cortical bone. However, the trabecular bone of the maxilla is another matter. There are no reports of immediate loading of anchorage implants in the maxilla. It is currently recommended that implants in the trabecular bone of the maxilla be allowed to heal for 4 to 6 months before serving as orthodontic anchors.

Stress fractures are relatively common in highly stressed bones, particularly when they are loaded in tension. However, the trend toward treating more complex problems with implant anchorage presents new risks for stress fractures because of the potential for abnormal dynamic loads associated with compromised occlusion.

Case report

A 55-year-old female presented with a mutilated malocclusion, a closed VDO, and a failing fixed partial denture (FPD) supported by a severely tipped mandibular third molar. The principal concern was an alveolar defect distal to the maxillary right central incisor (Fig 9-30a). Bone and attached gingiva had been lost when an onlay bone graft failed. The treatment plan was to achieve prepros-

thetic alignment using multiple endosseous implants for orthodontic anchorage (Figs 9-30b to 9-30f). The three maxillary incisors were moved into the defect to generate new periodontal tissue. A space was opened distal to the maxillary left lateral incisor with a coil spring (Fig 9-30c). The patient wore a removable maxillary orthotic device (occlusal splint) to permit occlusal function (Fig 9-30b). As the incisors were translated to the right, a premature contact developed between the maxillary lateral incisor and the occlusal splint. Instead of presenting to have the appliance adjusted, the patient continued to force the splint into place and function on it. Thus, in addition to the tensile load separating the maxillary left lateral incisor and canine, there was an additional cyclic load associated with occlusion on the poorly fitting occlusal splint. The patient reported that after about 2 to 3 weeks of this abnormal dynamic loading pattern, pain was evident in the space between the lateral incisor and canine. A radiograph revealed a linear radiolucency that was consistent with a stress fracture in the space being opened with the coil spring (Figs 9-30g and 9-30h). The following emergency treatment was rendered: (1) the occlusal splint was adjusted to relieve the abnormal force on the incisors; (2) active maxillary mechanics were terminated and a passive arch wire was used to stabilize the teeth; (3) pain was treated with ibuprofen as needed; and (4) the patient was placed on a soft diet. Pain resolved in about 10 days, and implant-anchored orthodontic therapy was reinstituted in about 6 weeks. The fracture healed uneventfully and orthodontic treatment was completed with no further problems.

To the author's knowledge, this was the first stress fracture associated with orthodontic therapy to be reported.[52] Although a stress fracture is exceedingly unlikely during routine orthodontic therapy in a patient with a full complement of teeth, it is a risk for complex malocclusions with compromised function. This case underscores the importance of a thorough understanding of basic science when managing complex mutilated malocclusions with implant-anchored orthodontics.

Fig 9-30 (a) Failure of a bone graft in the maxillary right anterior region, resulting in a large unesthetic defect with no keratinized tissue. The adjacent maxillary incisors were periodontally healthy. (b) Interocclusal orthotic device constructed to the desired VDO. The device was periodically adjusted to control occlusal interferences during orthodontic treatment. (c) Opening a space distal to the maxillary lateral allowed the three-tooth incisor segment to be translated laterally into the atrophic defect. (d) Occlusal view of the surgical defect and the adjacent three-tooth incisor segment. (e) Implant-supported provisional prostheses constructed to replace the maxillary canine and premolars. An anchorage implant was placed in the tuberosity area on the opposite side. (f) Bilateral implant anchorage enabled the three-incisor segment to be translated around the arch and into the defect. The second premolar on the opposite side was moved distally to create a pontic space between the premolars. (g) Patient complained of pain in the space that was opened mesial to the canine. A radiolucent line is noted in the orthodontically opened site. (h) Periapical radiograph confirms what appears to be a stress fracture in the space that was opened. (From Roberts[52]; reprinted with permission.)

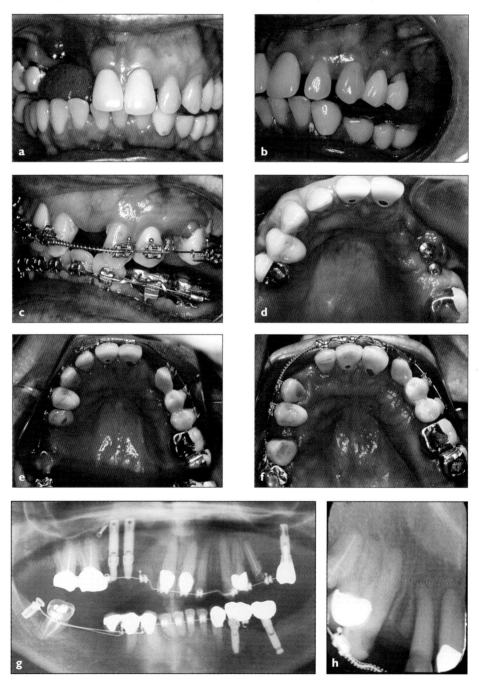

Summary and Conclusions

Localized and systemic skeletal compromise is common for partially edentulous patients. Use of rigid integrated implants opens a new range of treatment possibilities, assuming the clinician appreciates the complexity of the integration process with respect to host compatibility. Routine clinical success with rigid (osseointegrated) bone implants demands a firm grasp of the modern concepts of bone physiology, metabolism, and biomechanics. Anchorage implants, placed in good quality cortical bone (mandible) and not in occlusion, can be orthodontically loaded immediately. If the implant is placed in trabecular bone (maxilla) or is in occlusal function, it is wise to follow a routine unloaded healing protocol. Implant anchorage is rapidly expanding the scope of orthodontic therapy, but patients with severe functional deficits and localized atrophy present special therapeutic problems. Every case must be carefully evaluated and frequently reassessed during treatment.

References

1. Roberts WE, Marshall KJ, Mozsary PG. Rigid endosseous implant utilized as anchorage to protract molars and close an atrophic extraction site. Angle Orthod 1990;60:135–152.

2. Roberts WE, Nelson CL, Goodacre CJ. Rigid implant anchorage to close a mandibular first molar extraction site. J Clin Orthod 1994;28:693–704.

3. Roberts WE, Hartsfield JK Jr. Multidisciplinary management of congenital and acquired compensated malocclusions. J Indiana Dent Assoc 1997;76:42–51.

4. Roberts WE. Bone tissue interface. J Dent Educ 1988;52:804–809.

5. Currey JD. The Mechanical Adaptations of Bones. Princeton: Princeton University Press, 1984:1.

6. Roberts WE, Garetto LP, Arbuckle GR, et al. What are the risk factors of osteoporosis? J Am Dent Assoc 1991;122:59–61.

7. Roberts WE, Simmons KE, Garetto LP, DeCastro RA. Bone physiology and metabolism in dental implantology: Risk factors for osteoporosis and other metabolic bone diseases. Implant Dent 1992;1:11–21.

8. Becker AR, Handick KE, Roberts WE, Garetto LP. Osteoporosis risk factors in female dental patients. J Indiana Dent Assoc 1997;76:15–18.

9. Frost HM. Intermediary Organization of the Skeleton, vol I. Boca Raton, FL: CRC Press, 1986:1.

10. Brockstedt H, Christiansen P, Mosekilde L, Melsen F. Reconstruction of cortical bone remodeling in untreated primary hyperparathyroidism and following surgery. Bone 1995;16:109–117.

11. Brockstedt H, Kassem M, Eriksen EF, et al. Age- and sex-related changes in iliac cortical bone mass and remodeling. Bone 1993;14:681–691.

12. Roberts WE, Helm FR, Marshall KJ, Gongloff RK. Rigid endosseous implants for orthodontic and orthopedic anchorage. Angle Orthod 1989;59:247–256.

13. Parfitt AM. The physiological and clinical significance of bone histomorphometric data. In: Recker RR (ed). Bone Histomorphometry: Techniques and Interpretation. Boca Raton, FL: CRC Press, 1983:143–223.

14. Roberts WE, Smith RK, Zilberman Y, Mozsary PG, Smith RS. Osseous adaptation to continuous loading of rigid endosseous implants. Am J Orthod 1984;86:95–111.

15. Midgett RJ, Shaye R, Fruge JF. The effect of altered bone metabolism on orthodontic tooth movement. Am J Orthod 1981;80:256–262.

16. Becker AR, Handick KE, Roberts WE, Garetto LP. Osteoporosis risk factors in female dental patients: A preliminary report. J Indiana Dent Assoc 1997;76:15–19.

17. Roberts WE. Adjunctive orthodontic therapy in adults over 50 years of age. J Indiana Dent Assoc 1997;76:33–40.

18. Eastell R. Treatment of postmenopausal osteoporosis. N Engl J Med 1998;338:736–746.

19. Burr DB, Martin RB, Schaffler MB, Radin EL. Bone remodeling in response to in vivo fatigue microdamage. J Biomech 1985;18:189–200.

20. Schaffler MB, Radin EL, Burr DB. Mechanical and morphological effects of strain rate on fatigue of compact bone. Bone 1989;10:207–214.

21. Martin RB, Burr DB. Structure, Function, and Adaptation of Compact Bone. New York: Raven Press, 1989:1.

22. Hylander WL. Patterns of stress and strain in the macaque mandible. In: Carlson DS (ed). Craniofacial Biology. Ann Arbor, MI: Center for Human Growth and Development, 1981:1–35.

23. Roberts WE, Garetto LP, DeCastro RA. Remodeling of devitalized bone threatens periosteal margin integrity of endosseous titanium implants with threaded or smooth surfaces: Indications for provisional loading and axially directed occlusion. J Indiana Dent Assoc 1989;68:19–24.

24. Huja SS, Katona TR, Moore BK, Roberts WE. Microhardness and anisotropy of the vital osseous interface and endosseous implant supporting bone. J Orthop Res 1998;16:54–60.

25. Roberts WE. Rigid endosseous anchorage and tricalcium phosphate (tcp)-coated implants. Calif Dent Assoc J 1984;12(7):158–161.

26. Van Roekel NB. The use of Brånemark system implants for orthodontic anchorage: Report of a case. Int J Oral Maxillofac Implants 1989;4:341–344.

27. Higuchi KW, Slack JM. The use of titanium fixtures for intraoral anchorage to facilitate orthodontic tooth movement. Int J Oral Maxillofac Implants 1991;6:338–344.

28. Turley PK, Gray JW, Kean CJ, Roberts WE. Titanium endosseous and vitallium subperiosteal implants as orthodontic anchors for tooth movement in dogs [abstract]. J Dent Res 1984;63:344.

29. Valeron JF, Valazquez JF. Implants in the orthodontic and prosthetic rehabilitation of an adult patient: A case report. Int J Oral Maxillofac Implants 1996;11:534–538.

30. Roberts WE, Poon LC, Smith RK. Interface histology of rigid endosseous implants. J Oral Implantol 1986;12:406–416.

31. Roberts WE, Garetto LP, Simmons KE. Endosseous implants for rigid orthodontic anchorage. In: Bell WH (ed). Surgical Correction of Dentofacial Deformities, vol 4. Philadelphia: Saunders, 1992:1230–1236.

32. Chen J, Chen K, Garetto LP, Roberts WE. Mechanical response to functional and therapeutic loading of a retromolar endosseous implant used for orthodontic anchorage to mesially translate mandibular molars. Implant Dent 1995;4:246–258.

33. Roberts WE. The use of dental implants in orthodontic therapy. In: Davidovitch Z (ed). Biological Mechanisms of Tooth Eruption Resorption and Replacement by Implants. Birmingham, AL: Harvard Society for the Advancement of Orthodontics, 1994:631–642.

34. Hohlt WF, Roberts WE. Rigid implants for orthodontic anchorage. In: Davidovitch Z (ed). Biological Mechanisms of Tooth Eruption Resorption and Replacement by Implants. Birmingham, AL: Harvard Society for the Advancement of Orthodontics, 1994:661–666.

35. Roberts WE. Dental implant anchorage for cost-effective management of dental and skeletal malocclusion. In: Epker BN, Stella JP, Fish LC (eds). Dentofacial Deformities: Integrated Orthodontic and Surgical Correction, ed 2, vol 4. St. Louis: Mosby, 1999:2375–2408.

36. Garetto LP, Chen J, Parr JA, Roberts WE. Remodeling dynamics of bone supporting rigidly fixed titanium implants: A histomorphometric comparison in four species including humans. Implant Dent 1995;4:235–243.

37. Starck WJ, Epker BN. Failure of osseointegrated dental implants after bisphosphonate therapy for osteoporosis: A case report. Int J Oral Maxillofac Implants 1995;10:74–78.

38. Roberts WE. Bone physiology, metabolism, and biomechanics in orthodontic practice. In: Graber TM, Vanarsdall RL Jr (eds). Orthodontics: Current Principles and Techniques. St. Louis: Mosby–Year Book, 1994:193–234.

39. Weinstein S, Haack DC, Morris LY, Snyder BB, Attaway HE. On an equilibrium theory of tooth position. Angle Orthod 1963;33:1–26.

40. Weinstein S. Minimal forces in tooth movement. Am J Orthod 1967;53:881–903.

41. Behrents RG. Growth in the Aging Craniofacial Skeleton. Ann Arbor, MI: Center for Human Growth and Development, 1985:1.

42. Behrents RG. The consequences of adult craniofacial growth. In: Carlson DS, Ferrara A (eds). Orthodontics in an Aging Society. Ann Arbor, MI: Center for Human Growth and Development, 1988:53–99.

43. Behrents RG. Adult facial growth. In: Enlow DH (ed). Facial Growth. Philadelphia: Saunders, 1990:423–443.

44. Roberts WE, Arbuckle GR, Analoui M. Rate of mesial translation of mandibular molars utilizing implant-anchored mechanics. Angle Orthod 1996;66:331–337.

45. Tolman DE, Keller EE. Management of mandibular fractures in patients with endosseous implants. Int J Oral Maxillofac Implants 1991;6:427–436.

46. Mason ME, Triplett RG, Van Sickels JE, Parel SM. Mandibular fractures through endosseous cylinder implants: Report of cases and review. J Oral Maxillofac Surg 1990;48:311–317.

47. Rothman SLG, Schwarz MS, Chafetz NI. High-resolution computerized tomography and nuclear bone scanning in the diagnosis of postoperative stress fractures of the mandible: A clinical report. Int J Oral Maxillofac Implants 1995;10:765–768.

48. Chen J, Chen K, Roberts WE. The effects of occlusion and orthodontic force on the stresses around an endosseous implant. Adv Bioeng 1993;26:431–434.

49. Chen J, Lu X, Paydar N, Akay HU, Roberts WE. Mechanical simulation of the human mandible with and without an endosseous implant. Med Eng Phys 1994;16:53–61.

50. Roberts WE, Turley PK, Brezniak N, Fielder PJ. Bone physiology and metabolism. Calif Dent Assoc J 1987;15:54–61.

51. Roberts WE. Fundamental principles of bone physiology, metabolism and loading. In: Naert I, van Steenberghe D, Worthington P (eds). Osseointegration in Oral Rehabilitation: An Introductory Textbook. London: Quintessence, 1993:157–169.

52. Roberts WE. Bone dynamics of osseointegration ankylosis and tooth movement. J Indiana Dent Assoc 1999;78(3):24–32.

10 | Application of the Principles of Distraction Osteogenesis Using Osseointegrated Implants

Minoru Ueda, DDS, PhD

Distraction osteogenesis is the technique of bone generation and osteosynthesis by the stretching of native preexisting bone. The history of bone lengthening is long, starting in 1905 with the first report by Codivilla[1] on lengthening the legs. Later, this technique was widely developed by G. A. Ilizarov,[2,3] a Russian orthopedic surgeon who used new approaches to treat thousands of patients with various orthopedic disorders. He detailed the many uses of distraction in general orthopedic reconstruction, as well as the experimental basis for such techniques. Of particular relevance to a surgeon interested in distraction is the distinction between the following types of distraction osteogenesis: *(1)* monofocal, *(2)* bifocal, and *(3)* trifocal[4] (Fig 10-1). Understanding the requirements of the various types of distraction and their physiological bases will allow the surgeon to apply distraction successfully.

The application of this method to structurally complex maxillofacial bone is different from its application to tubular bone such as that found in the limbs and fingers, and its history is short. The first report on this technique was done by Snyder et al,[5] who used monofocal distraction to lengthen the canine mandible. Based on the experimental results of Snyder and colleagues, distraction osteogenesis was first applied to the maxillofacial region by McCarthy and associates,[6] who were successful in improving the shape of the hypoplastic mandible in young children with hemifacial microsomia. The first successful case of segmental mandibular reconstruction was reported by our research group,[7,8] which used trifocal distraction to regenerate a 6.0-cm defect in the human mandible.

The long-term histology and biomechanical properties of experimentally regenerated maxillae and mandibles is now better understood, allowing for more effective transfer to clinical practice.[9] When applying this method to the maxillofacial region, however, there is a difficult set of problems not encountered when applied to limbs and

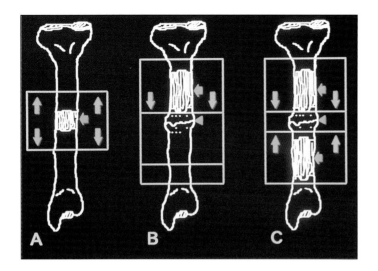

Fig 10-1 Three types of distraction osteogenesis: (A) monofocal, (B) bifocal, and (C) trifocal. Blue arrows indicate the direction of distraction; green arrows indicate the distraction area; green arrowheads indicate the area of compression osteosynthesis. (From Costantino et al[36]; reprinted with permission.)

other types of orthopedic surgery. One of these problems concerns fixation of the distraction device. Most facial bone is not tubular like limbs but is made up of thin, tabular bone of a complex structure, making it impossible to transmit sufficient external force to fix the device with an external pin. External distraction fixators can also have potentially negative effects on the psychological well-being of patients and their ability to comply with therapy because they cause visible external scarring. A new method of fixation and a new distraction device is therefore needed.

Our experimental studies indicate that it is feasible to apply distraction osteogenesis to maxillofacial bone advancement using osseointegrated implants. We have successfully combined the use of a subperiosteal osteotomy, an intraoral distraction device, and intraorally placed osseointegrated titanium implants to anchor the fixation-distraction device. In these experiments, we used canine bone as a tabular bone model and conducted experiments to clarify the following points: *(1)* the possibility of horizontal and vertical bone distraction in the maxilla and mandible and its healing process, *(2)* the usefulness of osseointegrated implants as sources of anchorage for a distraction device in maxillofacial bone, and *(3)* the loading force on pure titanium implants placed in thin bone. As for the loading force on the implant, Higuchi and Slack[10] reported that implants could withstand orthodontic forces of approximately 300 g. However, the exact

distraction force loaded on the implants was not determined. To address these problems, the bone-healing process at the interface between implant and surrounding bone should be studied. Fundamental to solving these problems is the explication from the clinical standpoint of distraction osteogenesis applied to the maxillofacial region.

General Concepts of the Healing Process in Distracted Bone

Common methods of bone lengthening are osteotomy and slow progressive movement by a distraction device.[11] The type of osteotomy, the timing and rate of distraction, and the apparatus have varied considerably.[12] It has been established that slow distraction does not break the bony callus but actually stimulates osteogenesis and the growth of surrounding soft tissues. This principle has been termed the *law of tension-stress*, but the exact mechanism is not understood. Ossification is generally classified into two types: intramembranous (direct) and endochondral (indirect). Intramembranous ossification is typically seen during embryonic development of the cranial vault, but at numerous other sites where there is no preexisting cartilaginous model, new bone is formed directly by differentiated osteoblasts. Typical endochondral ossification is seen during embryonic development of long bones. New bone formation

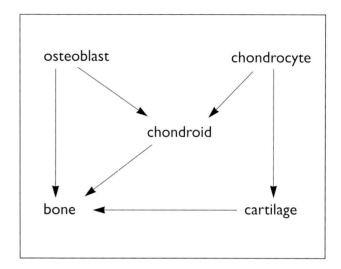

Fig 10-2 Types of bone formation in distracted area.

may be regarded as endochondral when cartilage is formed first and later replaced by new bone. In the physeal growth plate, for example, a highly ordered structure of resting, proliferating, hypertrophic, and calcifying cartilage is first established by differentiating chondrocytes.[13] The calcified cartilage matrix is then invaded by capillaries, and new bone is laid down by osteoblasts in the space previously occupied by hypertrophic chondrocytes. The fate of hypertrophic chondrocytes in calcifying cartilage remains controversial. Some authors believe that all the cells degenerate[14] or are programmed to die,[15] while others believe that they survive to become osteoblasts under the influence of vascularization.[16]

Kojimoto and coworkers[17] previously reported their histological findings in lengthened segments in rabbits and concluded that new bone is formed predominantly by endochondral (indirect) ossification. Other reports[18] of canine experiments have established that intramembranous (direct) bone formation is the main mechanism of ossification during distraction osteogenesis. Factors such as the stability of fixation, the timing and rate of distraction, and species-related differences may determine the relative share of endochondral and intramembranous bone formation.

It was thought that endochondral ossification was predominant during the early stages of distraction osteogenesis, especially in the circumferential region where cartilaginous callus had been formed during the 7 days between osteotomy and distraction. This cartilaginous callus appeared to grow to some extent in the initial stage of distraction but was eventually totally replaced by bone, leaving intramembranous ossification as the main mechanism of new bone formation. In addition to various growth factors and cytokines released from broken bone matrix, appropriate strain may contribute to the stimulation of bone formation during the distraction phase.

The third ossification mechanism produces chondroid bone. This has not attracted much attention, although it was identified some time ago as an intermediate tissue between cartilage and bone.[19] More recently it has been suggested that some hypertrophic chondrocytes undergo further differentiation into osteoblastlike cells and participate in initial bone formation.[20] If this is the case, a compound tissue of bone and cartilage should be produced unless chondrocytes turn into osteoblasts very rapidly. Many researchers[21] have found that chondrocytelike and osteocytelike cells coexisted in chondroid bone with no clearly distinguishable boundary. The columnar arrangement of these cells suggests that they were derived from a common mesenchymal cell, and careful observation of sequential histological sections has confirmed the gradual transition from cartilage to bone via chondroid bone (Fig 10-2).

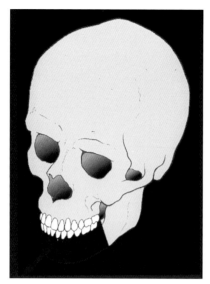

Fig 10-3 Schematic drawing of mandibular lengthening.

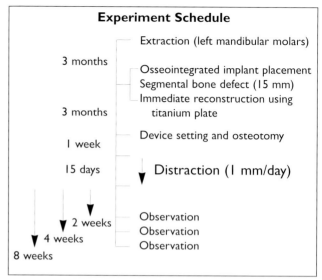

Fig 10-4 Experiment schedule of mandibular lengthening using osseointegrated implants in dog.

Mandibular Lengthening Using Osseointegrated Implants

Snyder et al[5] published the first report on using distraction osteogenesis to lengthen the canine mandible. Michieli and Miotti[22] lengthened a dog mandible using an intraoral distraction device attached to the mandibular dentition. Other investigators[23,24] have also reported successful experimental studies of mandibular lengthening by distraction osteogenesis (Fig 10-3). In most of these reports, extraoral transcutaneous pins were used to anchor the distraction device. The disadvantages of an extraoral device include extraoral nerve injury and conspicuousness. The study described below[25] was designed to evaluate mandibular distraction osteogenesis using an intraoral device and osseointegrated implants.

Experimental mandibular lengthening in an animal

Healthy adult male mongrel dogs, each weighing 20 to 25 kg, served as the experimental subjects. The protocol and guidelines for our series of studies were approved by the Institutional Animal Care and Use Review Committee of Nagoya University School of Medicine. The animals were procured by the Nagoya University Experimental Animal Center. The pre- and postoperative care of these animals was overseen by university veterinarians to ensure proper and humane treatment. The procedure involved five steps: *(1)* tooth extraction, *(2)* implant placement, *(3)* corticotomy and device setting, *(4)* distraction, and *(5)* fixation (Fig 10-4). The left mandibular premolars were extracted 2 months before implant placement. Two endosseous titanium implants were placed 30 mm apart in the left mandible of each dog. The implants were cylindrical, threaded, 10 mm long, and 3.75 mm in diameter. The relationship of the implants to each other was transferred by implant mounts and stainless bars; acrylic resin was used for making the superstructure.

The implants were surgically exposed after 3 months. Standard abutments, 5.5 mm in length, were connected to the osseointegrated implants with abutment screws. After the device was adjusted, a subperiosteal corticotomy around the mandible using a fissure bur in an electrical handpiece created an artificial fracture between the implants to give mobility to the segments. Finally, the distraction device was connected to abutments so that the proximal and distal bone fragments could be fixed.

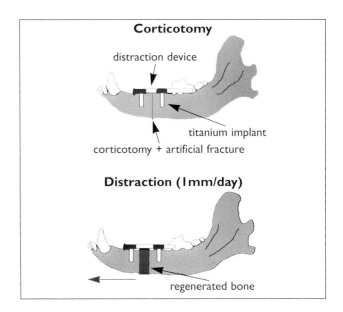

Fig 10-5 Monofocal distraction osteogenesis in the dog mandible using osseointegrated implants and an intraoral device.

After a 10-day healing of the periosteum, the distraction was performed at the rate of 1 mm per day, in accordance with Ilizarov,[2] for 10 consecutive days to elongate the bone by 10 mm. Then the device was stabilized with acrylic resin (Fig 10-5). Radiographs were obtained before and after corticotomy, immediately before initial distraction, at days 5 and 10 during distraction, and at 1-week intervals after completion of distraction.

At 2, 4, 6, and 8 weeks after completion of the distraction, the subjects were placed under general anesthesia with pentobarbital sodium. Perfusion with saline solution cleared the blood from the carotid artery to the neck veins, then the tissues were fixed with a freshly depolymerized solution of 4% paraformaldehyde and 0.5% glutaraldehyde in phosphate buffered at pH 7.35. The entire mandible was harvested and the distraction device removed. After a soft-ray radiograph was taken, the mandibular specimen involving the newly formed bone was sectioned and, except for a section taken 8 weeks after distraction, decalcified. Histological observation was carried out using hematoxylin-eosin and azan stains. The section prepared 8 weeks after completion of distraction underwent nondecalcified staining (toluidine blue) for observation of tissue surrounding the titanium implant. Histomorphometric quantitative analysis

was done with a computer-based system (NIH Image) by measuring bone-implant contact.

Bone healing of mandible after distraction

During the experimental period, there were no problems with the host or the device. All the animals tolerated the operation and distraction well. Furthermore, the distraction device remained stable.

Morphological findings demonstrated definite elongation of the mandible, a resulting shift of the mandible to the right, and a severe crossbite (Fig 10-6). The distance between the two abutments was found to be 10 mm greater than preoperatively (Fig 10-7). The soft tissues were intact and normal in appearance. The gingiva around the abutments and wounds from incision and suturing showed normal healing. None of the implants had lost osseointegration. Bimanual palpation showed that the elongated site had elastic hardness and mobility 2 weeks after completion of distraction and gradually became firm by 6 weeks. No abnormal healing of fracture, such as fibrous union or pseudoarthrosis, was found in any cases.

The axial radiograph of the mandible initially showed a line of radiolucency corresponding to the corticotomy. The width of the line began to de-

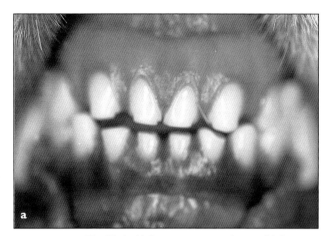
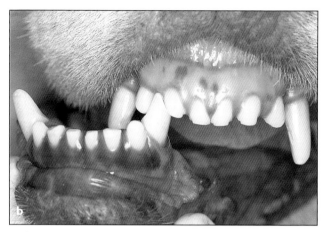

Fig 10-6 (a) Pretreatment occlusion. (b) Posttreatment occlusion showing severe crossbite after mandibular lengthening.

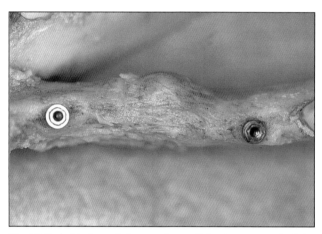

Fig 10-7 Axial view of distracted mandible after removal of the distraction device. The left side of the mandible was clearly elongated. Titanium implants are presently immobile.

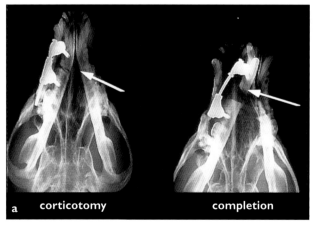
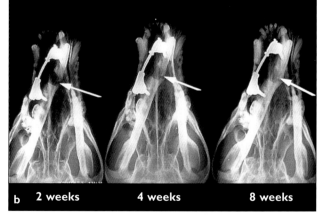

Fig 10-8 Axial radiographs of the mandible. Arrows indicate new bone. (a) Corticotomy and completion of distraction. (b) Two weeks after completion of distraction, the edges of the distraction gap are clearly visible, and bridging calluses can be seen near the lingual border. New bone becomes more uniform and mature in the distraction gap as the time after completion of distraction lengthens.

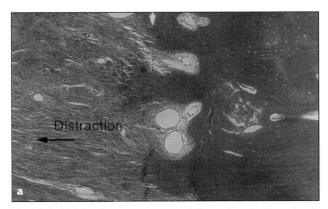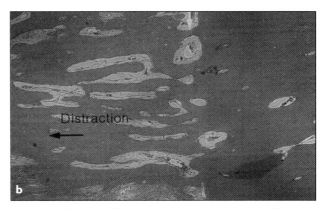

Fig 10-9 (a) Histologic appearance of distraction site 2 weeks after completion of distraction. Short, immature, woven bone is visible close to proximal edge. Blue arrows indicate the direction of distraction; yellow arrows indicate the edge of the area of distraction (hematoxylin-eosin stain; original magnification ×10). Longitudinal connective tissue is oriented in the same direction as the distraction. (b) Histologic appearance of distraction site 6 weeks after completion of distraction. Regenerated bone close to edges demonstrates more advanced calcification and the formation of networks of new bone.

crease during the waiting period, indicating the start of bone healing. As distraction began, the mandible was separated into proximal and distal segments. At the end of distraction, the lengthened area was found to be a clear radiolucent space (Fig 10-8). In the occlusal radiograph, the edges of the distraction gap were clearly observed 2 weeks after the completion of distraction, and parallel columns of bone extended from the cut edges toward a central radiolucent zone (Fig 10-8). By 4 weeks, bone was found bridging the gap, with the radiolucent zone diminishing (Fig 10-8). By 6 and 8 weeks, radiopacity of the gap became more advanced, indicating further maturation (Fig 10-8). Moreover, no bone resorption was observed around the titanium implants (Fig 10-8).

Histological sections showed connective tissue in the distraction gap 2 weeks after completion of distraction (Fig 10-9). Collagen fibers were rectilinear, stretched out, and oriented in the tension vector. The short, immature (woven) bone, oriented in the direction of the distraction, was shown to be close to the proximal edges of the corticotomy. At 4 weeks, regenerated bone close to the edges demonstrated more advanced calcification, and networks of immature bone were formed (Fig 10-9). The central radiolucent zone was composed of the woven bone and connective tissue. This finding seemed to re-

flect the characteristic structure shown radiographically. At 6 weeks, the distraction gap was filled with a network of newly formed bone. However, various stages of bone maturation and two types of ossification could be seen within the same specimen (Fig 10-9). The main histological feature was fairly mature bone that had a lamellar structure surrounding vascular canals. On the surface of the new bone, the arrangement of active osteoblasts was visible on a layer of lighter-stained primary bone. There were also some fibrocartilage islands in the central radiolucent area and near the proximal end. New bone had been formed in the matrix of hypertrophic chondrocytes. At 8 weeks, regenerated bone close to the proximal segments had acquired a mature lamellar structure.

Tooth development in lengthened mandible

In growing animals, would tooth buds in the distracted area develop normally? Little had been described about this question. We therefore performed an additional study to observe a developing tooth in the area of mandible lengthened by distraction osteogenesis. Canine mandibles in the primary dentition were lengthened and clinical, radiographic, and histological evaluations were performed (Fig 10-10).

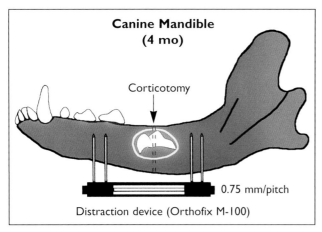

Fig 10-10 Schematic drawing of the corticotomy on a tooth bud.

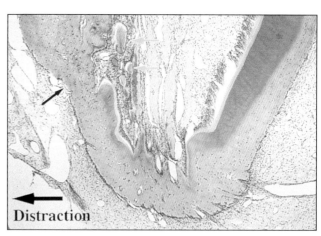

Fig 10-11 Histologic appearance of the molar growing in the distracted site of the mandible. Red arrow indicates a wavy cement line; yellow arrows indicate a typical denticle.

Fig 10-12 Longitudinal section of elongated mandible 6 weeks after completion of distraction. The inferior alveolar nerve *(arrows)* was elongated without interruption. RB, N, and B indicate regenerated bone, nerve, and blood vessel, respectively (azan stain; original magnification ×10).

The surgical procedure was almost the same as previously described. The tooth bud of a permanent first molar had been confirmed radiographically. A corticotomy was done on the buccal and lingual aspects with a water-cooled drill, and every effort was made to preserve the dental follicle. Eruption of the first molar in the distracted region was observed in all animals, at the same time as or earlier than the eruption of the contralateral tooth. The size, shape, and color of the crown showed no particular differences. On radiographic evaluation it was found that, as distraction began, the space between the wall of the follicle and the crown of the tooth bud had expanded, as did the width of the radiolucent line. Bone apposition and root formation continued in the furcational septum during distraction. Compared with the tooth bud developing on the contralateral side, initially the open end of the growing root became wider and showed a wavy appearance; then the apex closed (Fig 10-11). The formed root in the distraction site was shorter than that of the contralateral side. Although there was no particular change in the pulpal side, expansion and hyperemia were observed in the follicle.

The mandibular canal, with the surrounding bone tissue, was lengthened without a continuity defect. The inferior alveolar nerve demonstrated a normal appearance in the distraction site (Fig 10-12).

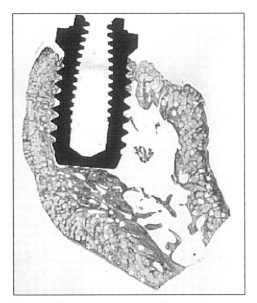

Fig 10-13 Implant-bone interface at the proximal implant. Direct bone contact with the implant surface can be seen (toluidine blue stain; original magnification ×10).

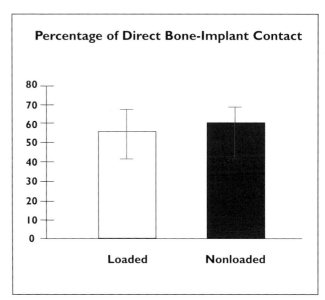

Fig 10-14 Percentages of bone-implant contact at nonloaded (control) and loaded implants.

Direct bone contact with the implant surface could be seen in a specimen obtained 8 weeks after completion of the distraction. There was no evidence of pseudoperiodontium (fibrous connective tissue) and no sign of inflammation at the bone-implant interface (Fig 10-13). Direct bone-implant contact was 61% on the mesial and 58% on the distal side of the anterior implant, and 60% on the mesial and 65% on the distal of the posterior implant. Bone contact was 62% in the nonloaded implant (Fig 10-14).

Maxillary Advancement Using Osseointegrated Implants

Advancement of the anterior maxilla is often required to correct skeletal deformity and malocclusion (Fig 10-15). Block and Brister[26] showed the possibility of maxillary advancement in the dog by distraction osteogenesis, using an intraoral device supported by the teeth.

In the study[27] described below, we examined maxillary advancement by distraction osteogenesis in dogs, using an intraoral device and osseointegrated implants. In this study, the healing process of tabular bone, which was distracted vertically, was clarified.

Experimental maxillary advancement in an animal

According to the experiment schedule shown in Fig 10-16, premolars and molars were extracted from the maxilla and, after 3 months, four osseointegrated titanium implants were placed in the alveolar ridge. The implants were cylindrical, threaded, 10 mm long, and 3.75 mm in diameter.

After 3 months, abutments (5.5 mm in length) were connected to the implants and the osteotomy was performed (Fig 10-17a). Vestibular incisions were made to expose the lateral maxillary walls and the piriform rim, and the mucosa was elevated

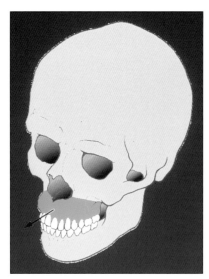

Fig 10-15 Schematic diagram of maxillary advancement.

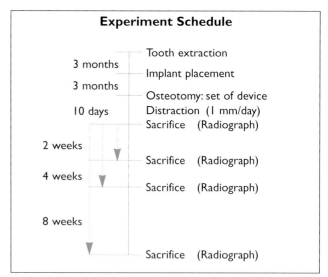

Fig 10-16 Experiment schedule of distraction osteogenesis in the maxilla.

to expose the bony nasal floor. Osteotomy was performed from the lateral maxilla to the piriform rim using a reciprocating saw and a fissure bur. The medial portion of the implants in the palate was separated in the same manner. When the osteotomy had been completed, the anterior bone segment could be mobilized manually. The mucosal incision was closed with 5-0 nylon sutures. Finally, the originally fabricated distraction device, consisting of an orthodontic rapid expansion screw, was connected to the abutments.

Ten days after the operation, distraction was performed at the rate of 1 mm per day for 10 consecutive days. After achieving elongation of 10 mm (Fig 10-17b), the device was used to stabilize the bone segments.

At 2, 4, and 8 weeks after fixation, morphological and radiographic observations were carried out simultaneously and the specimens, including the distraction gap, were harvested for histological examination. Each maxillary bone was removed, and each specimen was prepared in the usual manner and stained with hematoxylin-eosin. Tissues surrounding the implant were then observed under nondecalcified staining with toluidine blue stain.

Bone healing of maxilla after distraction

Morphological observations after distraction showed a definite anterior protrusion of the maxilla with no adverse soft tissue reaction 8 weeks after fixation. From the occlusal view, a definitive elongation of the premaxilla and a severe overjet were observed (Figs 10-18a and 10-18b). Upon gross examination of the removed maxilla, the distracted area was found to be filled with newly formed bone; fibrous tissue became indistinguishable as the stabilization period lengthened. Eight weeks after fixation, the matured bone that had formed in the distraction gap became hard to the touch.

Radiological observations showed a typical healing process. The farther the anterior maxillary segment advanced during distraction, the wider the radiolucent area created at the osteotomy site became. Calcification in the distraction gap increased so as to become symmetrical and uniform. After 2 weeks of fixation, the distraction gap showed rounding of the bony edges, and after 4 weeks new bone was found bridging the gap; by 8 weeks the border between original and regenerated bone was difficult to distinguish. Soft-ray radiographs of the removed

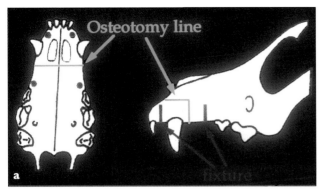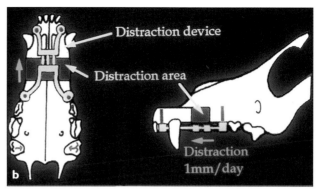

Fig 10-17 Diagram of surgical procedure for maxillary advancement and of distraction using osseointegrated implants as anchors.

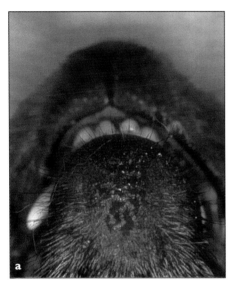

Fig 10-18 Inferior view before distraction and after completion of distraction, showing severe overjet.

maxillary specimen showed that as the stabilization period became longer more and more radiopaque bone filled the distracted area. All the anterior bone segments had advanced; the radiographs revealed increased radiodensity of the bone, making it indistinguishable from the original bony edges as the area filled with mature bone tissue (Fig 10-19).

Histological findings showed that the gap had filled with fibrous connective tissue within 2 weeks. The course of the fibers was in the same direction the bone was pulled. The development of newly formed bone, indicating lamellar structures along the fiber bundles from one part of the bone stump, was evident. Osteoblasts, osteoids, and pre-

calcification of newly formed bone were seen on the side of the marrow cavity, indicating the presence of active osteogenesis (Fig 10-20a).

During the fourth week after fixation, active outgrowth of newly formed bone was observed along the fiber length, developing toward the center portion. In the sixth week, the bone gap had completely filled with mature bone and was continuous with the matrix bone (Figs 10-20b and 10-20c). Observation of the implant-bone interface 6 weeks after fixation showed no fibrous connective tissue around the implant, which was surrounded by mature, newly formed bone having no inflammatory cellular infiltration (Fig 10-21).

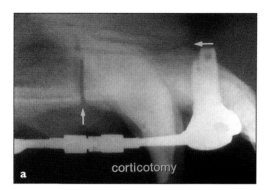

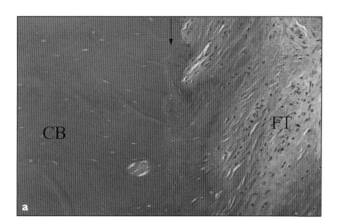

Fig 10-19 Radiographs of distracted maxilla. As the stabilization period increases, more radiopaque bone can be seen in the distracted area. (a) Corticotomies were made on the palate and on the frontal part of the maxilla (arrows). (b) Two weeks after completion of distraction. (c) Eight weeks after completion of distraction.

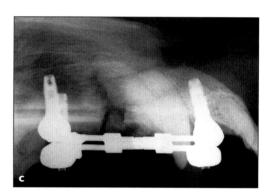

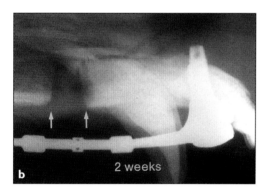

Fig 10-20 (a) Histologic appearance of the distraction site 2 weeks after completion of distraction. Connective tissue was seen in the distraction gap; collagen fiber (FT) was seen along the direction of distraction. CB indicates cortical bone; arrow indicates edge of distraction gap (hematoxylin-eosin stain; original magnification ×40 before 42.2% reduction). (b) Histological appearance of the distraction site 4 weeks after completion of distraction. Active outgrowth of newly formed bone was observed along the fiber. The emergence of cartilaginous tissue (CB) was observed in the middle portion of the bone gap (hematoxylin-eosin stain; original magnification ×40 before 42.2% reduction). (c) Histologic appearance of the distraction site 8 weeks after completion of distraction. The bone gap was completely filled with mature bone. NB indicates new bone (hematoxylin-eosin stain; original magnification ×40 before 42.2% reduction).

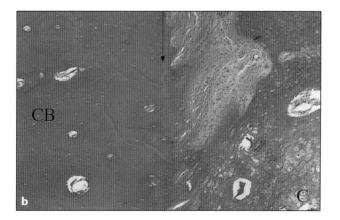

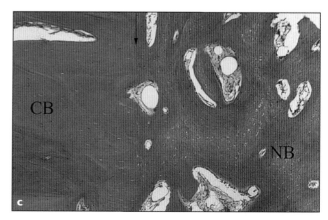

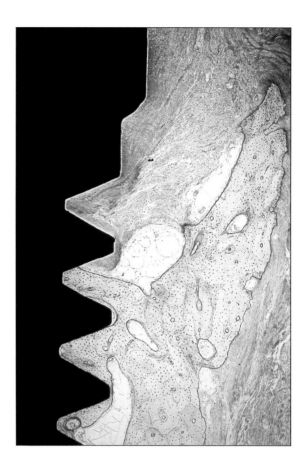

Fig 10-21 Implant-bone interface. The implant was surrounded by newly formed bone, and there was no evidence of fibrous connective tissue and no sign of inflammatory cell infiltration (toluidine blue stain; original magnification ×40).

Alveolar Ridge Augmentation Using Osseointegrated Implants

Alveolar ridge augmentation (ARA) is required for Class V and VI mandibles,[28] when treatment is planned for a conventional or implant-supported denture (Fig 10-22). Bone grafting,[29] guided bone regeneration[30] (GBR), and alloplastic materials[31] have been used for this purpose; each method has advantages and disadvantages. When using bone grafting, donor site injuries are unavoidable and some resorption of the grafted bone may occur. The GBR technique for ARA has been extensively documented[30]; however, because it is difficult to provide adequate space for regeneration and to obtain sufficient bone, this technique is useful only for limited defects of the alveolar ridge. Alloplastic materials are inherently unsuitable for implant placement.

Distraction osteogenesis has also been applied to the maxillofacial skeleton with good experimental and clinical results. However, studies of distraction osteogenesis of atrophic alveolar ridges are scarce. A suitable distraction device generally requires room to maneuver and bone volume for the connection to both the transport and base segments, but the anatomical characteristics of the atrophic ridge preclude circumferential devices. Hence, the purpose of the following study[32] was to examine the suitability of an implant device.

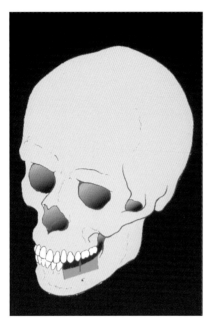

Fig 10-22 Schematic drawing of alveolar ridge augmentation.

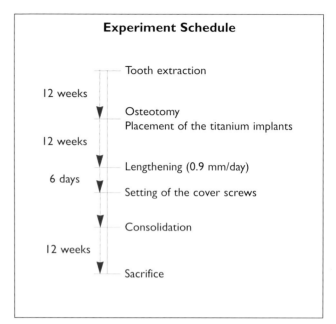

Fig 10-23 Schedule of the experiment.

Experimental alveolar distraction in an animal

According to the experiment schedule shown in Fig 10-23, the left mandibular premolars were extracted and alveoloplasty was performed to reduce alveolar height. After 12 weeks, following alveolar crest incisions, buccal mucoperiosteal flaps were elevated, extending from the distal of the canine to the mesial of the first molar. Vertical and horizontal alveolar osteotomies were carried out with a reciprocating saw, and a transport segment (5 × 30 mm) was constructed. At this time, the vertical osteotomy was kept within the buccal cortical bone, as it is difficult to place implants in an unstable transport segment if the osteotomy is complete. A guide drill was first used to mark the implant site. The sites were then sequentially enlarged with twist drills (2.0- and 3.0-mm diameters) and a pilot drill. Two endosteal titanium implants were placed 5 mm into the transport alveolar segment, leaving

5 mm exposed. The implants were cylindrical, threaded (0.6 mm in pitch), 10 mm long, and 3.75 mm in diameter. After confirming initial fixation of the implants, the vertical osteotomy was completed in the lingual cortical bone. Mobility of the transport segment was confirmed. The wound was sutured and the exposed parts of the implants were covered with the gingival flap, but the top 2 to 3 mm was left uncovered and exposed to the oral cavity to provide access during the distraction period. A circummandibular 3-0 silk suture was placed to help stabilize the transport segment. The crowns of the maxillary premolars were cut to reduce mechanical interference with the surgical sites from the opposing dentition (Fig 10-24a).

After 7 days, the circumferential fixation and sutures were removed and distraction was started. Bone lengthening was achieved at a rate of 0.9 mm/day by turning the implant slowly by hand 1.5 times. Before turning, the implants were brushed with a solution of 0.5% chlorhexidine gluconate to

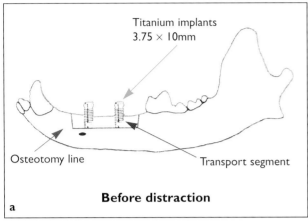

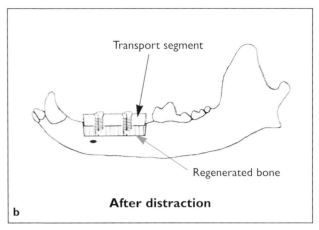

Fig 10-24 Schematic drawings before and after the procedure of distraction incorporating the use of implants.

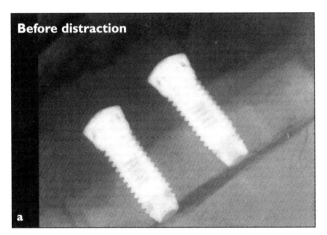

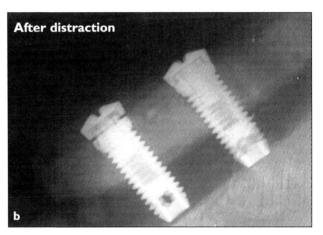

Fig 10-25 (a) Radiograph of the alveolar bone at the stage of corticotomy. (b) Radiograph of the alveolar bone at the completion of distraction.

prevent infection (Fig 10-24b). It took 6 days to complete distraction; lengthening of 5 mm was confirmed by radiographs (Figs 10-25a and 10-25b). After distraction, cover screws were inserted into the implants, which were then left as they were for consolidation and integration in the bone. The animals underwent radiographic examinations at 4, 8, 12, 24, and 50 weeks after distraction. For evaluation of the augmentation, the thickness of the transport segment was subtracted radiographically from the distance between the top of the transport segment and the inferior edge of the implants. Macroscopic gingival changes over the distraction area were also examined.

All the animals were sacrificed by an intravenous overdose of pentobarbital sodium 50 weeks after the surgery. The implants, together with the surrounding bone and soft tissues, were removed en bloc and examined radiographically to evaluate bone regeneration. The specimens were fixed in 10% phosphate-buffered formalin, dehydrated in alcohol, and embedded in acrylic resin. The implants were cut midaxially in the buccolingual plane into 150-μm-thick sections using an Exakt cutting and grinding system (Exakt Apparatebau). The specimens were stained with toluidine blue, and the sections were studied and photographed using a light microscope. Then the images of the

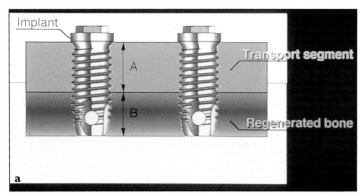
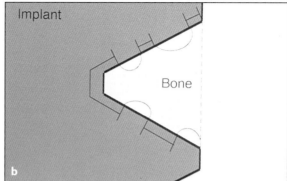

Fig 10-26 (a) Histomorphometric parameter interface between implant and bone. Bone area and bone-implant contact were measured separately in the transport segment (A) and regenerated bone (B). (b) In each thread of each implant the area occupied by mineralized bone and the amount of bone-metal contact were calculated and expressed as percent of total area and length of the thread.

sections were digitized on a Macintosh computer equipped with the NIH Image version 1.55 image-analysis program (Fig 10-26). In each thread of each implant, the size of the area occupied by mineralized bone and the amount of bone-metal contact were calculated and expressed as the percentage of total area and length of the thread. The following parameters were recorded for the buccal and lingual aspects of each implant:

- Bone-implant contact within transport segment
- Proportion of bone-implant contact within the 5-mm upper portion of the titanium implant
- Bone-implant contact within regenerated bone
- Proportion of bone-implant contact within the 5-mm lower portion of the titanium implant
- Bone area within transport segment
- Proportion of bone area in each thread of the 5-mm upper portion of the implant
- Bone area within regenerated bone
- Proportion of bone area in each thread of the 5-mm lower portion of the implant

Healing of alveolar bone after distraction

All animals tolerated the entire experiment well. During the distraction period no problems were encountered, either with the animals or with the implants. During the experiment period, all the ani-

mals were able to eat without difficulty. After the latency period, the mobility of the transport segment gradually decreased. The transport segment became elevated as the implants were turned. No evidence of infection or breakdown of the soft tissues was observed, except that, during the distraction period, partial soft tissue dehiscences were observed in two animals. After distraction was stopped for 3 days and the wounds treated with chlorhexidine, these wounds healed and distraction was resumed. As the alveolar bone lengthened, the lingual attached gingiva over the distraction site also lengthened and appeared normal. The buccally attached gingiva had moved upward together with the transport segment, whereas the buccal alveolar mucosa over the distraction site showed little change. The alveolar ridge appeared bonelike 4 weeks after distraction. All the cover screws became exposed to the oral cavity during the consolidation period. The vertical augmentation, on average, was 4.80 ± 0.19 mm after the completion of distraction.

The rise of the transport segment was documented radiographically. A radiolucency was still seen in the distraction site 4 weeks after distraction; a radiopacity had increased by degrees (Fig 10-27). The radiograph showed considerable density of distracted bone after 12 weeks, but there was no difference in bone density between 24 and 50 weeks. The anterior and posterior edges of the transport segments appeared to be smooth. Bone resorption was recognized in part of the transport segment in one

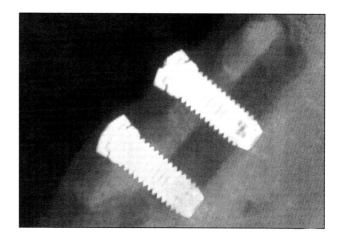

Fig 10-27 Radiopacity of the distraction site was increased and the edge of the transport segment appeared to be smooth 4 weeks after distraction.

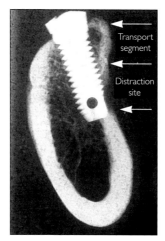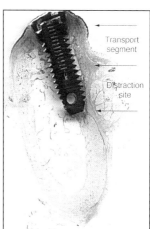

Fig 10-28 Cross-sectional radiograph *(left)* and histologic appearance *(right)* of a specimen 50 weeks after completion of distraction. The distraction site *(arrows)* appeared as smooth and continuous as cortical bone and almost as radiopaque as the base segment.

case. On cross sections, the distraction site appeared to be smooth with cortical bone of the same density as that of the base segment (Fig 10-28).

Fifty weeks after the operation, integration of the implants within the transport segment and the regenerated bone was observed. Histologically, the lengthened bone consisted of mature lamellar and cancellous bone. The thickness of the cortical bone in the distracted areas was slightly less than that of the cortical bone in the transport and base segments. Newly formed osteoid was observed in a large part of the regenerated bone and vertical orientation of the nutrient canals and cementing lines in a small part of the regenerated bone. No histo-

logic differences were found between the lengthened and normally attached gingiva, as shown in Fig 10-28. There was no absorption or inflammatory reaction in the boundary region between implant and bone (Fig 10-29). Histomorphometric analysis was performed according to the parameters shown in Fig 10-26. The mean values for the measured bone-implant contacts were 48.5 ± 4.2%, 47.2 ± 6.7%, and 47.8 ± 4.7% for transport segment, distraction region, and overall, respectively. The corresponding values for the bone area were 52.7 ± 5.1%, 48.6 ± 34.3%, and 50.6 ± 20.2%, respectively (Fig 10-30).

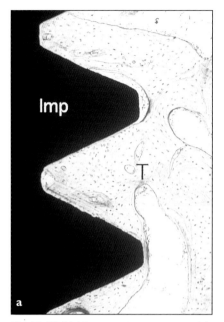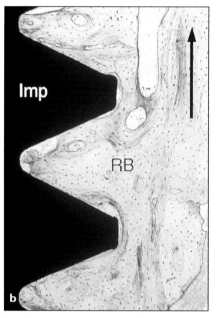

Fig 10-29 (a) Microscopic appearance of the interface between the implant and transport segment (T) demonstrating osseointegration (toluidine blue stain; original magnification ×15). (b) Microscopic appearance of the interface between the implant and regenerated bone (RB) in the distraction site, again showing osseointegration. The arrow indicates the direction of distraction (toluidine blue stain; original magnification ×15).

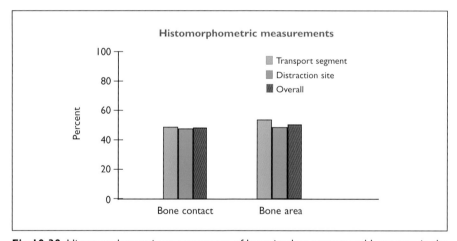

Fig 10-30 Histomorphometric measurements of bone-implant contact and bone area in the transport segment, the distraction site, and overall.

Discussion and Conclusion

Slow bone movement, resulting in bone production without the need for grafting, has been accomplished in long bones and in jaw bones.[2] Our previous work[25,27,33] and that of others on the mandible and maxilla indicate that these bones can be expanded in length and width using distraction osteogenesis principles. The soft tissues, as well, were found to stretch and cover the distracted region without evidence of breakdown. This may have occurred by hyperplasia of the gingival mucosal cells in a manner similar to that of soft tissue epidermal expansion by balloonlike devices.[34] We have now shown three skeletal movements using distraction osteogenesis—anterior maxillary advancement,[27] mandibular advancement,[25] and vertical augmentation of alveolar bone[32]—that were not limited by the soft tissues, as might have occurred with slow movements of the bones. In general, devices for distraction osteogenesis should transfer the distraction force directly to the bone and provide adequate rigidity for osseous consolidation to occur. Distraction devices that are solely toothborne have been found to produce increased linear displacement of the distraction gap at the level of the alveolus and decreased linear movement at the level of the inferior mandibular border, resulting in V-shaped regeneration. Additionally, endochondral ossification using solely toothborne devices has been reported, an indication of device instability resulting in too much movement during consolidation. The fact is that only 85% of bone expansion occurred versus 100% of device expansion. According to our pilot studies, osseointegrated titanium implants can transfer the continuous distraction force directly to the bone. Furthermore, after distraction and fixation, the abutments can be eliminated, and the implants can be used repeatedly if they remain subcutaneous.

The use of osseointegrated implants is also advantageous for correcting bone shape during the growth period. As evidenced by the gaps produced between the distracted bone fragments and the surrounding bone, it is clear that bundles of connective tissue fiber formed during the healing period are pulled in the direction and angle of the distraction, along which bone formation can be seen. In our series of experiments, cartilaginous cells appeared in the middle section of the bone gap; there were also sections indicating endochondral ossification. This is different from longitudinal distraction of long bone, with its abundant circulation. The appearance of cartilage is likely a result of limited circulatory conditions of the maxillofacial bone, with its small area of contact. Therefore, in distraction osteogenesis of tabular bone, fiber formation in the early stages and preservation of the periosteum as a circulatory route are important. Further, a sufficient healing period is needed before beginning distraction.

For morphological correction in the maxillofacial region, the key to success is the amount of three-dimensional (3-D) reconstruction in the shape of maxillofacial bone that can be accomplished. Therefore, due thought must be given to the 3-D orientation of gap movement for a given patient; at times it may be necessary to apply a shearing external force. The present results indicate that bone formation can occur even with vertical movement. Thin facial bone, misshapen by tumors or deformity, may be corrected three-dimensionally by distraction osteogenesis using osseointegrated implants as a fixed anchor.

As with most pilot studies, more questions were created than answered. The stability of the movement with regard to skeletal relapse was not evaluated nor were the limitations as to the extent of advancement and the rate of movement. However, these preliminary studies have shown the potential for applying this orthopedic technique to the maxillofacial bone using an intraoral distraction device and osseointegrated implants.

References

1. Codivilla A. On the means of lengthening, in the lower limbs, the muscles and tissues which are shortened through deformity. Am J Orthop Surg 1905;2:353–369.

2. Ilizarov GA. The principles of the Ilizarov method. Bull Hosp Jt Dis 1998;48:1.

3. Ilizarov GA. Transosseous Osteosynthesis. Berlin: Springer-Verlag, 1992.

4. Costantino PD, Friedman CD. Distraction osteogenesis: Applications for mandibular regrowth. Otolaryngol Clin North Am 1991;24:1433.

5. Snyder CC, Levine GA, Swanson HM, et al. Mandibular lengthening by gradual distraction. Plast Reconstr Surg 1973;5:506.

6. McCarthy JG, Schreiber J, Karp N, et al. Lengthening the human mandible by gradual distraction. Plast Reconstr Surg 1992;89:1–8.

7. Oda T, Sawaki Y, Fukuta K, Ueda M. Segmental mandibular reconstruction by distraction osteogenesis under skin flaps. Int J Oral Maxillofac Surg 1998;27:9–13.

8. Sawaki Y, Hagino H, Yamamoto H, Ueda M. Trifocal distraction osteogenesis for segmental mandibular defect: A technical innovation. J Craniomaxillofac Surg 1997;25: 310–315.

9. Costantino PD, Friedman CD, Shindo ML, et al. Experimental mandibular regrowth by distraction osteogenesis: Long-term results. Arch Otolaryngol Head Neck Surg 1993;119:511.

10. Higuchi KW, Slack JM. The use of titanium fixtures for intra-oral anchorage to facilitate orthodontic tooth movement. Int J Oral Maxillofac Implants 1991;6:338–344.

11. Paley D. Current techniques of limb lengthening. J Pediatr Orthop 1988;8:73–92.

12. De Bastiani G, Aldegheri R, Renzi-Brivio L, Trivella G. Limb lengthening by callus distraction (callotasis). J Pediatr Orthop 1987;7:129–134.

13. Bloom W, Fawcett DW. A Textbook of Histology, ed 10. Philadelphia: Saunders, 1975;244–287.

14. Brighton CT, Sugioka Y, Hunt RM. Cytoplasmic structures of epiphyseal plate chondrocytes: Quantitative evaluation using electron micrographs of rat costochondral junctions with special reference to the fate of hypertrophic cells. J Bone Joint Surg Am 1973;55-A:771–784.

15. Hatori M, Klatte KJ, Teixeira CC, Shapiro IM. End labeling studies of fragmented DNA in the avian growth plate: Evidence of apoptosis in terminally differentiated chondrocytes. J Bone Miner Res 1995;10:1960–1968.

16. Holtrop ME. The ultrastructure of the epiphyseal plate, II: The hypertrophic chondrocytes. Calcif Tissue Res 1972;9: 140–151.

17. Kojimoto H, Yasui N, Goto T, et al. Bone lengthening in rabbits by callus distraction: The role of periosteum. J Bone Joint Surg Br 1988;70-B:543–549.

18. Ilizarov GA. The tension-stress effect on the genesis and growth of tissues, I: The influence of stability of fixation and soft-tissue preservation. Clin Orthop 1989;238: 249–281.

19. Beresford WA. Chondroid Bone, Secondary Cartilage and Metaplasia, ed 1. Baltimore: Urban & Schwarzenberg, 1981.

20. Descalzi-Cancedda F, Gentili C, Manduca P, Cancedda R. Hypertrophic chondrocytes undergo further differentiation in culture. J Cell Biol 1992;117:427–435.

21. Yasui N, Sato M, Ochi T, et al. Three modes of ossification during distraction osteogenesis in the rat. J Bone Joint Surg Am 1997;79-B:5.

22. Michiele S, Miotti B. Lengthening of mandibular bone by gradual surgical-orthodontic distraction. J Oral Surg 1997;35:187–192.

23. Karaharju-Suvanto T, Karaharju EO, Ranta R. Mandibular distraction. An experimental study in sheep. J Craniomaxillofac Surg 1990;18:280–283.

24. Karp NS, Thorne CH, McCarthy JG, Sisson HA. Bone lengthening in the craniofacial skeleton. Ann Plast Surg 1990;24:231–237.

25. Sawaki Y, Ohkubo H, Yamamoto H, Ueda M. Mandibular lengthening by intraoral distraction using osseointegrated implants. Int J Oral Maxillofac Implants 1996;11: 186–193.

26. Block MS, Brister GD. Use of osteogenesis for maxillary advancement: Preliminary result. J Oral Maxillofac Surg 1994;52:282–286.

27. Yamamoto H, Sawaki Y, Ohkubo H, Ueda M. Maxillary advancement by distraction osteogenesis using osseointegrated implants. J Craniomaxillofac Surg 1997;25: 186–191.

28. Cawood JI, Howell RA. A classification of the edentulous jaws. Int J Oral Maxillofac Surg 1988;17:232–236.

29. Triplett RG, Schow SR. Autologous bone grafts and endosseous implants: Complementary techniques. J Oral Maxillofac Surg 1996;54:486–494.

30. Caplanis N, Sigurdsson TJ, Rohrer MD, Wikejo UME. Effect of allogeneic, freeze-dried, demineralized bone matrix on guided bone regeneration in supra-alveolar peri-implant defects in dogs. Int J Oral Maxillofac Implants 1997;12:634–642.

31. Sigurdsson TJ, Rohrer FUE, MD, Wikesjo UME. Bone morphogenetic protein-2 for peri-implant bone regeneration and osseointegration. Clin Oral Implants Res 1997;8:367–374.

32. Oda T, Ueda M. Alveolar ridge augmentation by distraction osteogenesis using titanium implants: An experimental study. Int J Oral Maxillofacial Surg 1999;28:151–156.

33. Block MS, Daire J, Stover J, et al. Changes in the inferior alveolar nerve following mandibular lengthening in the dog utilizing distraction osteogenesis. J Oral Maxillofac Surg 1993;51:652.

34. Squier CA. The stretching of mouse skin in vivo: Effect on epidermal proliferation and thickness. J Invest Dermatol 1980;74:68.

35. Stucki-McCormick SU. Skeletal and dental movements after anterior maxillary advancement using implant-supported distraction osteogenesis in dogs. J Oral Maxillofac Surg 1997;55:1439–1440.

36. Costantino PD, Shybut G, Friedman CD, et al. Segmental mandibular regeneration by distraction osteogenesis. An experimental study. Arch Otolaryngol Head Neck Surg 1990;116:535–545.

Index

V

VDO. *See* Vertical dimension of occlusion.
Vertical dimension of occlusion
    description of, 171
    malocclusions secondary to alterations of, 184, 184f
    in partially edentulous patients, 185

W

Wire angulation, for implant anchorage in partially edentulous patients, 48, 50f, 51